D0955433

The **WISE** Handbook

OF BASIC
HOME CARPENTRY

Carl W. Bertsch

1952

WM. H. WISE & CO., INC.

NEW YORK

Introduction

Repairing and replacing damaged woodwork in the home is thought of frequently, and just as frequently, only thought about. The offending molding, warped floor board, or whatever it may be, is examined with a shake of the head and a decision is made to get the carpenter in to fix it. Then the matter is put off until that inevitable moment arrives when there is no choice but to have something done about it immediately. By then the little thing has usually become a big and expensive one.

The same general procedure quite frequently occurs when some needed improvement such as removing an old or constructing a new structural unit or units is considered. All too often high labor costs make repair and new construction an impossibility. What to do? There is a simple answer to this economic riddle . . . do it yourself! Not only will you save a considerable amount of money, but perhaps of greater importance, you will enjoy that feeling of personal achievement, that indescribable pleasure of having created something worthwhile with your own hands.

It is possible that at this point you may say, "But — I'm helpless with tools, and I know less than nothing about the ins and outs of carpentry, of home construction. Why, when I hammer a perfectly straight nail it turns into a pretzel, and what I do with a saw isn't possible. The thing cuts curves when I want to go straight and straight when I want to curve—I need a steering wheel on the thing. Tools are just not for me."

Actually, you are quite wrong in assuming that tools are not for you. Tools are for anyone having the desire to learn how to use them, and learning is not a tedious, difficult art. It is fun. As in sports, there is always *one* right and a lot of wrong ways to use a tool, determined largely by the design of the tool itself. And the right way is the easiest every time. All good tools are precision made, masterpieces of scientific engineering. Every inch of them is planned for easy manipulation, and designed so that the tool itself will do its work with a minimum of human effort. All any tool asks of you is that you lend it human intelligence in guiding it on its mission. If you do that one simple thing, you will be amazed how the tool—if it is a good one—will cooperate beyond your wildest dreams.

It is the purpose of this book to give you the how and when of practically everything to do with hand tools, thereby opening the door to new pleasurable adventures in transforming pieces of raw wood into useful "live" things. It will make you acquainted with the materials tools were designed to work, and explain a variety of fasteners that join and articulate wood. Moreover, it will tell you about wood itself, its temperament, how to cope with it, and all about the modern fabricated wood and wood-pulp panels, many of them superior to nature's own product. You will learn easily how and why to make the tried-and-true wood joints —as the professional makes them.

If you do not have a tool box, cabinet or workbench—one of which you really should have—you are all set to try your hand at making these items so that your tools will be easy to find in their appointed places, and properly protected against damage. Remember that a good tool is a precision instrument and will last a lifetime if properly cared for. (I have some molding planes made of wood, with hand-wrought irons, that are well over a hundred years old. Except that they have none of the precision adjustments of the modern plane, they will do as fine a job as anything bought today.) Never toss a tool in a corner or among a collection of household items that will dull or nick its cutting edge or impair its future performance.

Having taken care of your tools, you will want to know all about how that house of yours is put together. Then you can diagnose its "ailment" and cure it. Chapter 7 of this volume will take you step by step and introduce you all the way round, suggesting what to do about that creaking or warped floor board and the many other minor and major ills peculiar to houses.

Finally, Chapter 8 will offer many suggestions for making structural changes both inside and outside your home to enhance its charm and efficiency through the medium of old and new techniques and materials. In addition, many ideas of your own that hitherto have been only fond dreams you will now be able to bring to reality. Nothing is difficult if you have the know-how, and this book will do its best through its text and several hundred illustrations to acquaint you with whatever you wish to know about home carpentry.

ACKOWLEDGEMENTS: We wish to express our thanks to the illustrators of this book: Carl T. Sigman, William J. Ward, Jr., Walter J. Karl, Carl R. Kinscherf, William A. Patrick, Fergus Retrum, and R. E. White.

CONTENTS

1. USE OF HAND TOOLS—*Continued*

2. USE OF FASTENERS.. 61

2. USE OF FASTENERS—*Continued*

3. LUMBER 80

4 PLYWOOD 88

5. WOOD JOINTS 93

7. HOW YOUR HOME IS BUILT — *Continued*

7. HOW YOUR HOME IS BUILT—*Continued*

7. HOW YOUR HOME IS BUILT—*Continued*

8. HOME IMPROVEMENTS 207

8. HOME IMPROVEMENTS—*Continued*

9. PAINTING AND FINISHING — *Continued*

BASIC HOME CARPENTRY

CHAPTER 1

USE OF HAND TOOLS

Do not be dismayed by the number of hand tools discussed. A few good basic tools will do a lot of diversified jobs, and if you already have such tools, they will probably be all you will need for average jobs around the home.

If you have a curved-claw hammer, a nail set, a cross-cut saw, a couple of chisels, several screwdrivers of various sizes, and a brace with an assortment of bits, you have the average collection found in most homes. These will serve for a start. However, just any hammer equipped with a head and a claw will not necessarily make its use a joy forever, but more about hammers later. Neither can you do good work with just any old saw with assorted teeth too frequently requiring major dental care. Most sawing around the house has to do with cutting off a piece of lumber to size; therefore the cross-cut saw. It will also function if you have a short piece of lumber to cut the long way, that is, rip it. But this could be one of your troubles.

The backbreaking, muscle-aching job of ripping a long piece of lumber with a cross-cut saw may have soured your outlook on tools in general. You need a rip saw to do the job of ripping a long piece or pieces of lumber. There is a whale of a difference be-tween the number and design of the teeth in rip and cross-cut saws, and for good reasons as will be explained in detail. You will also need a folding, six-foot rule to measure with, and a try-square or combination square with which to mark lumber squarely.

Today we usually buy our lumber kiln-dried and surfaced on all sides. Such is smooth and free from warp —if we personally select it. Therefore a smoothing tool — the plane—is not used quite as much around the home as it used to be. There was a time when a collection of planes, each for a particular purpose, was a must. A plane is still an essential tool, particularly so if you are confronted with the problem of truing a door or window sash, or fitting new ones in their frames. It will also save a lot of tedious labor with makeshifts when trimming the length or width of a board to exact dimensions; or reducing its thickness, and for beveling and tapering. With lumber costing what it does, many a piece that has warped because of improper storage can be salvaged by a bit of work on it with a plane.

As new woodworking problems come up you can acquire additional tools that do the specific job best, bearing in mind that the greater variety you can afford, the easier and quicker you will be able to do the job.

1

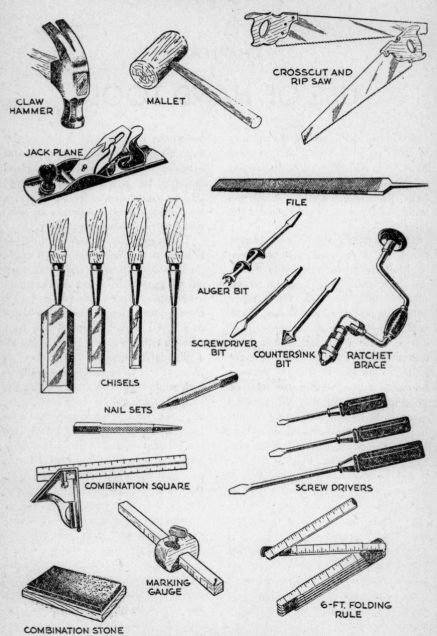

CLAW HAMMER

MALLET

CROSSCUT AND RIP SAW

JACK PLANE

FILE

CHISELS

AUGER BIT

SCREWDRIVER BIT

COUNTERSINK BIT

RATCHET BRACE

NAIL SETS

COMBINATION SQUARE

SCREW DRIVERS

MARKING GAUGE

6-FT. FOLDING RULE

COMBINATION STONE

Fig. 1. Suggested basic assortment of tools.

The following list is suggested for a basic tool assortment:

1 Curved-claw Carpenter's Hammer, 16-ounce weight
1 Wood Mallet
1 Rip Saw, 26″ long, 5½ points to the inch
1 Cross-cut Saw, 26″ long, 10 points to the inch
1 Jack Plane No. 5, 14″ long
4 Chisels, ¼″, ¾″, 1″, 2″
1 Flat, Double-cut Bastard File, 12″ long
1 Ratchet-type Brace
4 Auger Bits for the brace, ¼″, ½″, ¾″, 1″
1 Countersink Bit, rose type for the brace, ¾″ diameter
1 Screwdriver Bit for the brace
3 Screwdrivers, 4½″ x 3/16″, 6″ x ¼″, 8″ x 5/16″
2 Nail Sets, 1/16″ and ⅛″ points
1 Combination Square, 12″ blade
1 Folding-type Rule, 6 feet long
1 Carpenter's Marking Gauge
1 Oilstone, fine and coarse combination, 1″ x 2″ x 8″

Buy Good Tools

A word of caution when buying tools. Buy only top-quality, name-brand tools. Do not purchase alleged bargains. The difference in price between top quality and poor quality is slight, and a good tool will repay you many times over for its slightly higher cost. Not even an expert can do good work with a poor-quality tool. You have numerous brand names to choose from and your dealer will be happy to advise you on their respective merits.

THE HAMMER

You can pound a nail with a rock or anything as hard as the nail itself and the chances are you will be able to drive it—after a fashion. But to do the job easily without bending the nail and marring the surface being nailed, you need a forged, hardened steel hammer scientifically designed for driving and extracting nails. There is a wide variety of hammer shapes and sizes, each designed to do its particular job best. Hammers range from the large, heavy sledge to the small, light tack hammer.

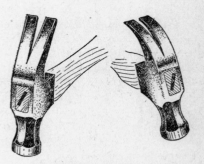

Fig. 2. Straight and curved claw hammers.

Nailing hammers come in two types: the curved and straight claw. A curved-claw carpenter's hammer has slightly better balance than a straight claw—also called a rip hammer—and will pull nails better than the latter. For all-round house carpentry a curved-claw is the best.

The straight claw is used extensively in rough building construction where the claw is frequently used by the expert to split a board and save

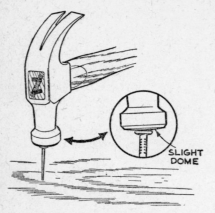

Fig. 3. Face of hammer is domed.

without success, it's not your fault for you probably have a poorly made hammer. A loose hammer head is dangerous to everything near it, and a wobbly one will not nail properly. To tighten the head, remove the wedge in the eye and replace it with a metal wedge stocked at hardware stores.

Hammer Weights

Hammers are sold in many weights ranging from 5 to 20 ounces. Choose the weight that feels most comfortable as you heft and try a few swings with it. Keep in mind that a hammer that is too light requires too much muscular effort, while one too heavy will tire you unnecessarily. If your budget permits, select two curved-claw hammers of different weights, the most popular being 10 to 12 and 16 to 18 ounces. One is for small nails and the other for the larger sizes. For house-framing work, carpenters usually prefer the 20 ounce weight. Rust corrodes steel, so keep your hammer free from dirt and rust—a drop of oil wiped over the head is a good idea.

time. Old style carpenter's hammers have a smooth-shank head tapering to a slightly less diameter at the cheek, and a flat face. A modern hammer head consists of a face, poll (varying in design), neck, cheek, adze eye and claw. The face is slightly domed so that even though the nail is not struck squarely the face will compensate for this to some degree with a fair chance of the nail remaining straight. A flat face will bend the nail if not struck squarely. Also the domed face permits the nail head to be driven flush without marring the surface. You may have such a hammer. Examine it carefully, however, and check the face. If it is chipped and battered from much use or abuse, it will probably bend more nails than drive them and should be discarded.

A good curved claw is designed with sharp edges tapering to a pointed V and will pull anything from the smallest brad to a spike. If you have ever tried to extract a thin nail

Fig. 4. Starting to drive in a nail.

If you have been experiencing nailing trouble, the chances are that you've been choking the handle of your hammer. Doing this throws the knuckles of your hand out of alignment with the face of the hammer, causing it to strike the nail head at an angle and bending it. It also requires all *your* effort with little help from the hammer head. To start a nail, grip the handle midway as if you were shaking hands with it with the thumb,

Fig. 6. Using piece of wood to pull a nail.

Fig. 5. Finishing the driving of a nail.

2nd, 3rd and 4th fingers gripping and the 1st finger slightly extended and around the handle. Tap the nail a few light blows, holding it with your free hand (Fig. 4). Then change the grip to about the end of the handle and finish driving it with *medium*-heavy blows (Fig. 5).

A nail driven hard breaks the fibers of the wood and loses some of its holding power. Lighter blows tend to bend the fibers aside and downward, and when pulling strain on the nail occurs, these fibers pull upward also, exerting considerable grip on the nail. Take a piece of scrap wood and prac-

tice driving a few nails of different sizes as suggested, and you will be amazed at the ease and accuracy with which you are able to nail. If the nail bends—it happens to the most expert—do not try to straighten it. Pull it out, but be sure to put a piece of wood (the longer the nail the thicker the wood) under the claw to prevent marring the surface and exerting undue strain on the neck of the handle. The nail pulls easier, too (Fig. 6).

Woods that have a tendency to split should be bored with a lead hole smaller than the nail to be driven.

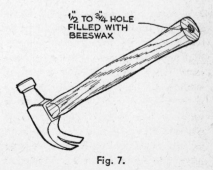

½" TO ¾" HOLE
FILLED WITH
BEESWAX

Fig. 7.

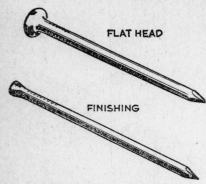

Fig. 8. Two basic types of nails.

Clipping the point of a nail will also tend to prevent its splitting the wood, the nail acting as a punch rather than a wedge. When nailing hard woods, a lot of bent nails and exasperation can be avoided by sticking the nail point in some beeswax or paraffin. Do not use soap, the caustic it contains may corrode the nail. Here is an old trick: bore a hole ½″ to ¾″ deep in the handle end of your hammer and fill the cavity with beeswax. Then you will always have a lubricant handy when you need it (Fig. 7).

There is a bewildering variety of nails, most of the varieties designed for specific purposes. Whatever the type, all have a head and a point of some sort. For the moment, the flat head and finishing nail, the two basic types (Fig. 8) will be considered. Flat-head nails are used for general work where the nail head is driven flush with the surface, there being no need to hide it. For finished work such as molding, floors, trim, and wherever the nail is to be hidden, the finishing nail, having a barrel-shaped head slightly larger in diameter than

the shank, is used. This nail head is driven a bit below the surface with a tool called a nail set (Fig. 9). The small hole is then covered with regular, water-mix wood putty or plastic wood.

Clinching

For added holding power where the nail point does not show, nails longer than the thickness of the wood are frequently used and the ends bent over on the blind side of the wood. This is called *clinching* (Fig. 10A). The common practice is to just hammer the nail over, flat with the surface, but a workmanlike and perfect clinch is made by using another larger nail laid flat against the point and then hammering the point over the nail, forming a staple which is driven flush into the wood (Fig. 10B, C, D). To clinch, use a metal plate between

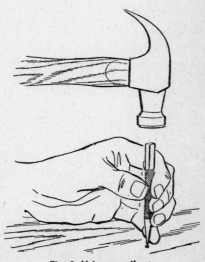

Fig. 9. Using a nail set.

the head and work surface, otherwise the head will be driven out.

Where two pieces of hard wood are to be nailed edge to edge, but not to another surface, the trick is to file the nail point on one side to a chisel edge (Fig. 10E). The nail will then, on entering, bend in the direction of the flat side of the point. Nails are manufactured this way for curve nailing.

Blind nailing is not recommended as it is a tricky technique dependent on the type of wood being nailed which, if brittle, does not work too well. Moreover, there is always a slight depression left which must be filled where the chisel enters the wood. However, here is how it is done: Use a razor-sharp ¼"-wide chisel and lift a shaving, being careful not to break it. Then drive a finishing nail in the opening, set it below the underside of the shaving, and apply glue to the underside. Clamp until the glue has dried and smooth with abrasive paper.

Toenailing

Toenailing is employed when the pieces to be nailed cannot be joined by straight nailing, such as when nailing the feet of studding and laying finished flooring. Toenailing exerts considerable drawing power to the part nailed and is frequently used for that purpose, like pulling siding into position. As a rule, toenailing is done from both sides and frequently on all sides of the piece (Fig. 11).

First place the piece on the line marked for its position, then drive the nail almost in. The piece will have moved somewhat from the line. Then

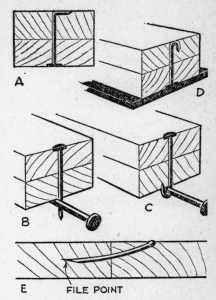

E   FILE POINT

Fig. 10. Three methods of clinching nails.

toenail the opposite side all the way in which forces the piece back on line again. Finish driving the first nail and toenail the remaining sides. This is the way studding feet are framed to soles and plates.

As mentioned earlier, extracting nails successfully depends on the condition of the hammer claw. A good claw will oftener than not extract even a headless nail by twisting the claw edge against the shank of the nail when pulling. When removing nails from framed wood, as for example, box-like assemblies, drive the joint apart slightly, placing a piece of wood between the hammer head and piece to prevent marring and splitting. Then tap the piece back again, using a piece of wood to pry against as before.

This usually leaves the nail heads protruding far enough to insert the claw, under which you have placed a piece of cardboard or anything thin.

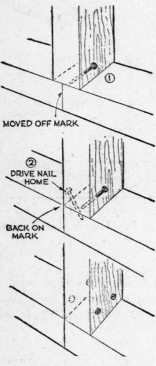

MOVED OFF MARK

② DRIVE NAIL HOME

BACK ON MARK

Fig. 11. Toenailing.

When the nail is sufficiently extracted, use a block of wood under the claw. Where this method cannot be employed, chisel away the wood around the nail head sufficiently to grip it with a pair of end-cutters. Then use the claw. When removing finishing nails from old lumber you wish to salvage, pull the nails through from the back if you do not want to disturb the filling and paint on the face side.

THE NAIL SET

A nail set is a hardened steel tool having a round or square head and a tapering cupped point, tempered. The shank is knurled for the fingers and the point is cupped so that it won't slip off the head of the nail. In use, it should be slightly smaller in diameter than the nail head. Nail sets are usually available in five point diameters: 1/32″ to 5/32″ and are not expensive. Lacking a nail set, substitutes of all sorts are used, such as a much larger nail with its point filed flat. However, substitutes have marred more wood surfaces by slipping off the nail than hammer heads, thus a few nail sets of different sizes are a must.

Fig. 12. Nail set.

With much use the cupped points become flattened. To restore them, place the nail-set point flat along its taper on some hard metal surface, and with a hammer gently tap the flattened edges all around. When setting a nail, recess it only deep enough for whatever filler you plan to use to take hold. Too shallow a set will result in the filler coming out when sanded.

THE MALLET

Mallets have various shapes depending on what profession uses them. They are primarily used for driving chisels. The carpenter's mallet is usually a large, double-face hammer made of hard, close-grained wood. There are mallets on the market made of rubber; leather; wood, leather faced; plastic; and wood, plastic-faced.

The common variety of wood mallet is fine and inexpensive. When using a chisel, *never* use a steel hammer head to drive it. That will destroy the end of the chisel handle and ruin the chisel's efficiency. Lacking a mallet, some workers use the cheek of the claw hammer, but this is obviously doing it the hard way and will, in a short time, also badly damage the handle. A mallet is one of the cheapest tools you can buy and it is poor economy not to get one. This is one instance when the very best is not vital, and you can readily make one from a 3"x3" or a 4"x4" block of maple or oak and a 1" hardwood-dowel handle if such materials are at hand.

THE HATCHET

The half-hatchet, so named because of the width of its blade, is in every carpenter's tool box, and in his hands becomes a tool with amazing possibilities. He can almost build a house with it, albeit roughly. Variations in its design are used for lathing and shingling by the experts. It should be made of forged, hardened steel with a nail-driving head and a slot on the inner edge of its blade for pulling nails. A good one has a razor-keen edge and will hold it. Such a hatchet, with practice, will quickly rough out a board requiring a narrow strip to be

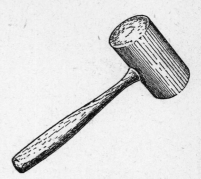

Fig. 13. Wooden mallet.

otherwise rip sawed, ready for planing. It is also a handy tool for rough-tapering lengths of board that must fit a particular space; for irregular shapes; pointing stakes; rough-rounding shelf ends, and many other jobs of speed roughing. It is not an essential tool for average home repair.

THE WRECKING BAR

Here's another special tool that most carpenters use on construction

Fig. 14. Hatchet.

Fig. 15. Wrecking bar.

and remodeling jobs. It is a hardy tool for rough work. A well designed one has a gooseneck equipped with a nail and spike puller at one end and a chisel point with a deep bevel at the other, both for prying lumber. Both ends are ground and heat treated, the bar being a forged piece of high-quality steel usually hexagonal in section. For remodeling, where studding and flooring must be removed, the tool is essential as it exerts terrific leverage with a minimum of effort. One ¾″x24″ long is inexpensive.

SAWS

Hand Saw

You probably use a hand saw of-tener than any other tool in wood-working and, because it is a much-used cutting tool, only the best is good enough. The reason for this is not apparent until one understands the precision engineering that goes into a fine saw.

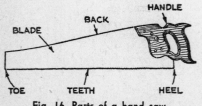

Fig. 16. Parts of a hand saw.

Two hand saws are essential to cut lumber easily and accurately: the rip saw and the cross-cut saw. The design of the teeth of the rip and cross-cut are entirely different because the rip saw is designed to cut with the grain of the wood, while the cross-cut saws straight or diagonally across the grain (Fig. 17).

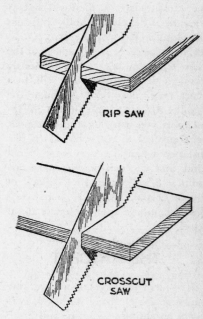

RIP SAW

CROSSCUT SAW

Fig. 17. Rip saw and crosscut saw.

Rip-saw teeth are ground straight across like vertical chisels, each tooth chipping out a small portion of the wood from the kerf (kerf is the width of the cut in wood made by the set of the teeth, meaning their spread, one bent to the right, one to the left alternately, for both rip and cross-cut—and all types of saws) (Fig. 18). Without set, the saw would bind and

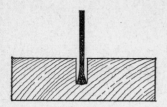

Fig. 18. Rip saw teeth cutting a board.

lock tightly in the wood. This happens at times when ripping green (unseasoned) and wet lumber with a saw set for dry lumber. If the set is unequal along the blade, the saw will not cut accurately.

Top-quality rip and cross-cut saws are taper ground from the cutting edge to the back edge, the back edge being thinner than the cutting edge. They also taper from point to butt on the back edge. This gives added clearance to the saw and requires less set to the teeth, therefore a cleaner cut. The wider the set the rougher the cut will be. In addition, a good rip saw has finer teeth at the point of the blade to make the starting cut easier —an engineering refinement not found in all saws. The angles of rip-saw teeth differ from those of a cross-cut, their front angle being 8 degrees and their back 52 degrees. Cross-cut saw teeth have a front angle of 15 degrees and a 45-degree back angle (Fig. 19).

Points

Both rip and cross-cut saws are made in a variety of lengths and number of teeth to the inch, called points. They are also made in "regular" and "lightweight pattern," both "straight" and "skew-back." The lightweight pattern is a more pointed saw than the regular, having less weight, and a skew-back has a slightly concave back. There is no difference in performance in any of these four types, it being merely a matter of personal choice. The length and points of a saw, however, are important. Not only the set, but also the number of points per inch contribute to fine or rough sawing. The more teeth per inch the finer the cut, but the sawing will take longer with more effort.

The length of a saw determines the ease and speed of cutting. A short saw will require more strokes to cut a given length or width of lumber than a long saw. The tendency of the beginner in woodworking is to choose a

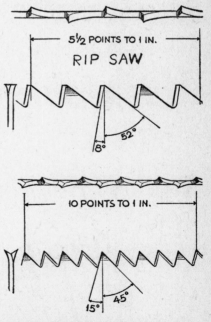

Fig. 19. Angles of rip and crosscut saws.

Fig. 20. Proper angle for rip sawing.

short saw because it "feels" better in his or her hands. There is nothing wrong with this choice if a longer saw seems unwieldy; it just means more shoulder and elbow work when saw-

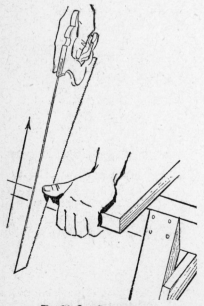

Fig. 21. Starting a saw cut.

ing. If you plan to do much ripping of long pieces of lumber, however, the 26″ rip saw with 5½ points per inch is recommended. The length of a saw is measured from point to butt along the cutting edge. Rip and cross-cut saws are usually made 20″, 22″, 24″ and 26″ long, with rip teeth 5, 5½, 6 and 7 points to the inch.

When ripping a long piece of lumber, support it on two saw horses in such a position as to permit *long, easy* strokes (Fig. 20). Grip the handle of the saw with the thumb overlapping the second finger, the forefinger extended along the side of the handle. Do not take a "death" grip. All you want to do is hold and guide the saw, not force it; let the saw do the work. Start the cut with the fine teeth at its point, using a short *upward* stroke, the thumb of your free hand along the side of the blade as a "guide pin" (Fig. 21).

When ripping along a scribed line, cut on the waste side of the line, do not try to halve it. Having started the cut, use long, easy strokes the length of the blade, sawing at an approximate angle of 60 degrees between the cutting edge and lumber face (Fig. 22).

An amazing number of "rippers" use short strokes, employing only the middle portion of the saw teeth. Since only this small portion gets all the wear, the saw dulls quickly and requires "jointing" much sooner than necessary (jointing is filing all the teeth down to an even length), in this case quite a chore as a depression is made for some distance in the cutting edge. Some beginners fight the saw as if it were a balky mule, the saw winning every time—and a bent saw cuts *curves*. If you saw unhurriedly, body relaxed, you can do an amazing amount of ripping without becoming fatigued, once your muscles have been introduced to this form of exercise.

As you rip, the board will have a tendency to close the kerf at the starting point, so insert a narrow wedge of wood or anything that will keep the kerf open. If you should happen to wander from the straight line, a twist of the blade will get you back on, and if you are not sawing squarely, bend the blade sidewise to get square again. A fine saw with perfect set and sharp teeth will almost saw squarely of its own accord, provided you do not force it. Short pieces of lumber, not long enough for saw horses, should be clamped in a bench vise in such a position as to maintain the 60-degree angle.

Cross-cut saws are sold with a choice of 7, 8, 9, 10, and 11 points per inch. If only an occasional piece of wide lumber is to be cut, a 22″, 10-point saw is easier to handle, but the 26″ saw works best when cutting panels of plywood and other large-dimension wall board. The teeth of a cross-cut saw are alternately ground double-edged with a bevel of about 24 degrees. The action of the teeth is similar to that of a lot of small knife blades severing the fibers of the wood. These teeth are also set alternately, one to the right, one to the left for clearance.

The method of using a cross-cut saw is the same as the rip saw, except

Fig. 22. Use long, easy rip saw strokes.

for the cutting angle. This should approximate 45 degrees to get the maximum sheering action (Fig. 23). To cross-cut correctly, keep the shoulder, arm and hand roughly in line with the saw blade and cutting line. Start the cut with a few, short, upward strokes until a slight groove is

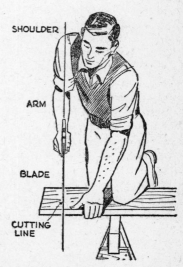

Fig. 23. Hold cross-cut saw in line with arm and shoulder.

WOOD
BLOCK

Fig. 24. Use wood block as a guide.

formed; then cut with a full stroke. If you are having trouble cutting squarely, either ripping or cross cutting, a square placed along the side of the blade will guide you—but keep the square blade away from the teeth, or use a square piece of wood and hold it against the saw (Fig. 24).

On nearing the end of a cut, always support the waste piece by reaching over the saw blade with your free hand and holding the piece to prevent it from splintering the underside of the cut. If it's a long waste piece, support it adequately with a saw horse. Never twist off waste with the saw blade.

It seems unnecessary to warn against cutting old lumber with hidden nails, but it's surprising how often this is done with the disastrous result of breaking off teeth and ruining the saw or, at best, mangling them so that a resharpening job costs almost as much as a new saw. Often when saw-

ing fatty (resinous) lumber, the saw blades becomes coated with resin. Remove this with turpentine, wipe the blade clean, dry with a clean cloth, and apply a few drops of light machine oil, spreading it over the blade with a cloth.

Before putting your saws away, always wipe them clean and apply oil to prevent rust pits. Moreover, always store your saws with the teeth well protected from damaging objects such as metal and masonry, and in such a manner as to prevent personal injury through accidental contact.

Compass-Keyhole Saw

Compass and keyhole saws are designed for cutting curved shapes, circular openings, disks, starting a saw cut from a hole bored in wood, and where the hand saw cannot start a cut—a problem quite frequently encountered in remodeling. Compass saws are made 10″, 12″, 14″ and 16″

HOLD HERE

Fig. 25. Support waste piece at end of cut

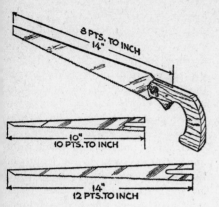

Fig. 26. Nest of compass saw blades.

long, usually with 8 points per inch. They taper to a sharp point and are narrow in width.

Keyhole saws are much the same, but much narrower and usually come 10" and 12" long, 10 points per inch. Good compass and keyhole saws are taper ground the same as hand saws, and tempered to withstand the strain of curve sawing. When using a compass or keyhole saw, use it vertically, gripping it in the same manner as a hand saw.

In the basic tool list the compass and keyhole saw are not included only because they are tools for special purposes. However, a well equipped tool box contains one of these saws against the time when its use will be necessary.

Nests of these saws are obtainable and are a worthwhile investment. The nest consists of a handle designed to receive three different blades: a compass blade 14" long, 8 points per inch; a tempered blade 14" long, 12 points per inch (for cutting lead pipe, thin metal, and wood in which nails are imbedded), and a keyhole blade 10" long, 10 points per inch for very sharp curves (Fig. 26). It takes but a moment to change the blades and the nest has the advantage of being three tools in one, taking up less storage space in a tool box or cabinet.

Back Saw

This saw is designed to do fine joinery and cabinet work. It has a heavy, reinforced back which stiffens the saw blade (of heavier gauge and with finer teeth and less set than the hand saw). Smooth, accurate sawing is the purpose of this tool, and when

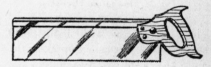

Fig. 27. Back saw.

cutting miters, tenons, dovetails, rabbets, dadoes and other forms of wood joints, and moldings, it is an invaluable adjunct to woodworking. Get one if you are planning to do much shallow, precision sawing. Back saws are sold in a variety of lengths, usually from 8" to 16", 8 to 16 points per inch. The depth of the blade under the back varies with its length, about 2¼" to 4". The most popular back saw is 12" long, 3" deep, 14 points per inch.

When using a back saw, start the cut with a short, *backward* stroke, elevating the handle a trifle, then as you saw, gradually lower the handle so the blade is parallel to the surface

START WITH ELEVATED HANDLE
AND LOWER GRADUALLY

SHORT BACKWARD

Fig. 28. How to use back saw.

(Fig. 28). Saw with light, level strokes, using the same grip as for the hand saw. Long grooves, dadoes and rabbets can easily be cut by clamping a wood straight-edge to the surface as a guide for the saw, with another strip clamped to the saw blade for a depth gauge. Without a gauge, watch the depth at both ends of the cut, the natural tendency being to cut deeper with the butt-end of the saw.

Miter Box

Companion to the back saw is the Miter Box. This device is used for cross-cutting narrow lumber and molding squarely, or diagonally at a 45-degree angle. A miter box can be quickly made from three pieces of board 1" x 4" (¾" x 3½", dressed), about 18" long. Hardwood is preferable to soft wood, as the box will last

longer, but softwood will do (Fig. 29). Nail two pieces, for sides, securely to the base with 4d (1½") flat-head nails. Using a combination square, carefully mark a line across the top edges of the sides 6" from one end, continuing this line down one inner and one outer side, so you can see the line to cut.

This line must be an exact right angle (90 degrees) to the length of the box on both sides, and at right angles, vertically, to the base. Then, with your square, mark a 45-degree-angle line, about 6" away from the first one, across the top edges and down the sides as before. Reverse the 45-degree angle and do the same thing in the other direction, forming an X.

With the back saw—or lacking this, a cross-cut saw — carefully saw along the guide lines, straight across and diagonally, to the base of the box. The slots thus formed are the guides for the saw blade when using the miter box. Accuracy of your future miter-box sawing will depend on your accuracy in making the guide cuts.

In practice, be sure the line to be cut lines up with the guide slots in the box, then hold the piece against the back and proceed with the cut as suggested, whether you use a back or cross-cut saw. If you plan to use the miter-box on a workbench, nail a ¾"x¾" strip on the underside of the base, flush with one side (Fig. 30). This strip engages the front edge of the workbench and prevents the box from sliding—important when doing accurate sawing.

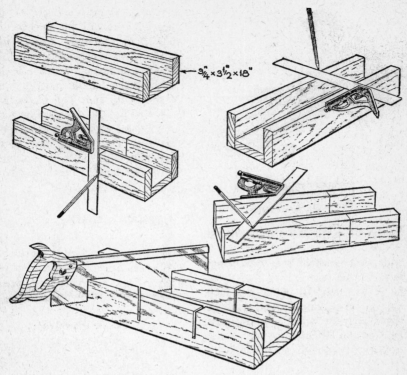

Fig. 29. Steps in constructing a miter box.

With use, this type of miter box becomes inaccurate due to the widening of the slots and a groove deepening in the base from sawing. When this happens, throw it away and make another. If you use a back saw without a miter box, and when crosscutting for a dado and rabbet, use a bench hook or several of them to support the work (Fig. 31). Commercial miter boxes are precision made with metal guides for the saw, adjustable both to accommodate different depths of saw blades, and to a number of cutting angles. A good one is expensive.

Coping Saw

This saw is designed for cutting intricate curved shapes in narrow lumber; contours, when one piece of molding is butt-joined to another; or the end of a piece of lumber when it has to fit against an existing irregular-shaped piece. The coping saw consists of a steel frame, rectangular in section, or a heavy-gauge steel-wire frame. Frames are usually about 5″ deep from tooth edge to the inside of the back, but some, known as fret saws, are deeper for wider materials.

Detachable blades are usually ⅛″ wide with pins at each end, or 1/16″

¾"x¾"x18" STRIP

Fig. 30. Attach strip to bottom of miter box.

wide, and about 6" long with looped ends for the wire frame. Both types have set teeth, 16 points per inch, designed for wood only, and combination blades for wood, plastics, brass, copper and aluminum, bone, composition board and other hard mate-

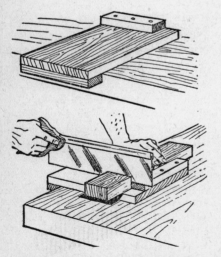

Fig. 31. A bench hook and how to use it.

rials. The standard coping saw is more versatile and will cut thicker materials than the wire frame, being designed to receive the saw blade between stretchers which are tightened by the handle having threads at the blade end. The blade, when stretched tightly, can then be turned for material wider than the depth of the saw. The coping saw is used vertically, with the teeth slanting toward the handle for a downward stroke. Use a long stroke.

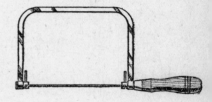

Fig. 32. Coping saw.

A Coping-Saw Saddle is generally used to support scroll work and short pieces of lumber such as shelf brackets (Fig. 33). To make a saddle, three pieces of wood are required: a piece ¾"x5½" or 7½"x12", a table ¾"x6"x5½" or 7½" wide, and a small bracket ¾"x1½"x1½". Nail the table securely to the end of the other board with 4d flat-head nails, bracing it with the bracket glued to both pieces with household cement. Then cut a V-notch 3" wide and 3½" deep in the table edge. When using the saddle, clamp it in a bench vise and shift the work held on the slotted table to accommodate the curves of the design. Change the angle of the blade when making sharp turns to avoid the possibility of breaking the blade.

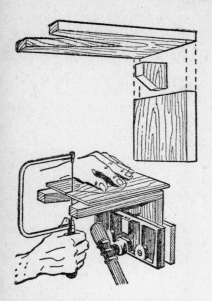

Fig. 33. Coping saw saddle.

PLANES

Planes are basically smoothing tools, and come in many types and sizes, each designed for its particular job. Besides smoothing planes there are also shaping planes that groove, bead, dado and rabbet. You can even buy a combination plane that is sold with over 50 different types of cutters for making molding shapes (besides tongue and groove) and to plow, dado, rabbet, bead and do about everything that can be done in wood. The latter is a masterpiece of engineering but, needless to say, not for everyone's purse.

Basically, a plane is nothing more than a chisel fixed securely in a metal frame equipped with adjusting devices. There are two basic types of smoothing plane: the Bench and the Block (Fig. 34). The bench plane is used for smoothing the face and edge of lumber with the grain, and the block is designed for smoothing end grain, that is, the ends of boards. Bench planes are identified by their four names: Smooth, Jack, Fore, and Jointer, terms somewhat confusing to the uninitiated. The Smooth plane is short, and its blade (called an Iron or Cutter) is finely set for smoothing and finishing. Smooth planes are 7", 8", 9" and 10" long with cutters from 1⅝" to 2⅜" wide. Jack planers are 11½", 14" and 15" long, with cutters from 1¾" to 2⅜". The latter are intended for truing the edges of boards after ripping.

On good authority, Jack is short for "Jackass," quite descriptive of a plane designed for the roughest kind of work if need be. The Fore plane is 18" long, with a 2⅜" cutter used for finishing large surfaces. The Jointer is sold 22" and 24" long with cutters 2⅜" and 2⅝" wide, and is used for the same purpose as the Fore. The angle of the bevel of bench-plane cut-

Fig. 34. Jack and block planes.

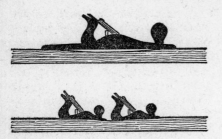

Fig. 35. Top jack plane shown bridging high spots. Bottom, short plane riding the waves.

ters is from 25 to 30 degrees, while that of the regular block plane is about 20 degrees. Bench planes are also furnished with smooth and corrugated bottoms, some craftsmen being of the opinion that corrugated bottoms slide easier.

For all-round use, if the budget permits only one plane, it is best to get a Jack No. 5 (14″ long). The reason for this length is that a short plane will ride the "hills" and "valleys" in a board, and if too short will plane the valleys deeper, while a long

plane bridges the valleys, shaving off the hills (Fig. 35). This plane can be used for smoothing the end of a board but it is a bit awkward in length. When thinking about getting another plane, perhaps the Smooth No. 4 (9″ long, 2″ cutter) would be a good choice for finishing the work of the Jack. Some craftsmen, with this combination of planes, grind the Jack cutter curved which transforms it into a Scrub plane, designed to remove a considerable amount of wood quickly on edges too narrow for practical ripping, and to level surfaces quite rough or uneven. For general planing, however, leave the Jack cutter as it is.

Before trying out a bench plane, first acquaint yourself with its construction and adjustments (Fig. 36). Everything except the frame (bottom) of any type plane is demountable, requiring only a screwdriver to disassemble it if necessary. Bench planes have a front hand Knob and a Handle at the back; a Plane Iron

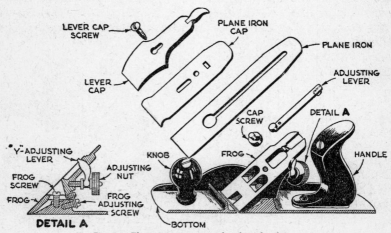

DETAIL A

Fig. 36. The various parts of a bench plane.

(cutter) and a Plane-Iron Cap, its sharp edge held tightly against and slightly back of the cutter's edge. The cap iron acts as a shaving deflector and prevents the wood from splitting

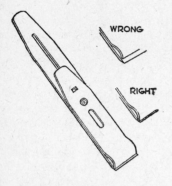

Fig. 37. How to adjust cap iron.

ahead of the cutter. Assembled, the irons become a Double Plane Iron, secured by a Cap Screw. This assembly is held in place by a Lever Cap which fits over the irons and secures the assembly to a Frog by means of a Lever-Cap Screw. The frog in turn is so fastened with screws to the "toe" and "heel" supports of the bottom of the plane that it is rigid and free from vibration.

To regulate the "mouth" (the slot where the iron's cutting edge projects from the bottom) of the plane, remove the lever cap and irons, loosen the two screws which secure the frog, and turn the center adjusting screw as required. Then tighten the frog screws and replace the irons and cap lever. Double plane irons are adjustable for depth of cut, controlled by a finger Adjusting Screw which raises or lowers the cutter. The iron's cutting edge can also be aligned squarely with the bottom by a Lateral Adjusting Lever which is part of the frog (Fig. 37). For hard word, set the cap iron just back of the cutter edge and farther back for soft wood—about the thickness of a dime.

Always make certain that the cutter corners are evenly placed in the mouth, that is, that one corner does not project more than the other, otherwise you will ruin the piece you are planing. To check alignment of the blade, turn the bottom up, toe facing you, and sight along the length of the plane. Let the edge of the iron protrude a hairbreadth which you adjust with the adjusting screw. If the iron edge is out of alignment, adjust this with the adjusting lever.

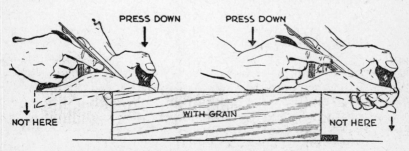

Fig. 38. Push the plane with the grain and press it firmly against the wood.

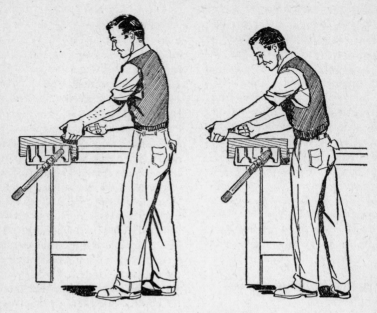

Fig. 39. The proper method of holding and using a plane.

Using a Plane

Using a plane is not difficult, requiring only a little practice and correct procedure. The smoothing plane is always pushed with the grain, that is, in the uphill direction of the fibers (Fig. 38). If the plane bucks, you are planing in the wrong direction, or the cutter is out too far. At such times when a board has grain running in opposite directions, change the plane's direction with the grain.

With the board to be planed firmly secured either in a bench vise or on the bench or other surface, face the direction of planing, with the left foot out a trifle (right if you are left-handed). (See Fig. 39.) Hold the knob with the left hand and the handle with the right (reversed if you're left-handed), and press down on the knob as you start the stroke. Then gradually ease up on the knob pressure and apply it to the handle at the end of your stroke, leaning forward with your body as you push the plane. End the stroke with your weight carried easily on the left (or right) foot. Never let the plane drop at the end of the stroke as this would round the edge of the board, and never drag the plane backward on the surface; lift it clear for the next forward stroke. When squaring an edge, always keep the plane bottom at a right angle to the vertical face of the board, no matter how much bevel or center peak the edge may have. Plane the high edge in this manner until the edge is square. To do this easily, hold the knob with the crotch of the thumb, your fingers supporting the bottom of the plane (Fig. 40). Test for squareness frequently with a square.

When planing the end of a board, never carry your stroke to the edge end. This invariably splinters off the corner. To avoid this, either bevel the corner (if it is waste to be removed), or plane from both directions to the center (Fig. 41). You can also tightly clamp a scrap piece of lumber to one edge end in a vise, the face of the scrap piece flush with the piece to be planed. However, good general practice calls for planing from each edge end.

Block Plane

The block plane is a very handy tool, designed for planing board ends, and can also be used for many other jobs where a short plane works better than a long one. It is sold in a number of sizes from about 3½" to 7" long, with cutters 1" to about 1¾" wide. It is a single-iron plane, and most have an adjustable throat which permits the mouth to be quickly opened or closed for coarse or fine work. It is fully adjustable for depth of cut and

Fig. 40. How to hold plane steady.

alignment of cutter but, unlike the bench planes, it is designed for use with one hand. Block planes come in "regular" and "low angle," the latter having a cutter bevel of about 12 degrees, making it easier to plane across the grain of hard woods. Both types consist of a Bottom, Iron, Lever Cap, Lever-Cap Screw and Adjusting

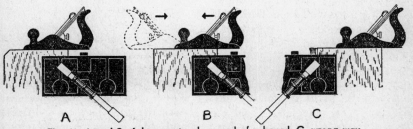

Fig. 41. A and B, right ways to plane end of a board. C, wrong way.

Screw, and some have a Knuckle-Joint Lever Cap which snaps into position and holds the cutter firmly. The plane is equipped with a finger rest at its toe, and the lever cap is designed to fit the palm of your hand. If you intend getting a block plane, the 6″, 1⅝″ cutter "regular" is excellent for all-round block planing.

To adjust the plane iron for thickness of shaving (depth of cut), sight along the plane bottom and turn the adjusting screw right or left; to adjust the iron laterally, loosen the lever-cap screw, sight along the bottom, press the plane iron to the right or left, and tighten the cap screw. The technique of using a block plane is the same as that for the bench plane. There are many types of special planes designed for various woodworking professions, but for general use around the home, two types only need be discussed—the Rabbet and Dado planes.

Rabbet and Dado Planes

When making a rabbet, a saw, preferably the back saw, and a chisel are used—lacking a rabbet plane. However, the rabbet plane does the job much easier and quicker, particularly so if the board is a long one. A rabbet plane has a single iron which is adjustable for depth of cut and alignment. It is fitted with a spur flush with the side and projecting slightly below the bottom, designed to cut the rabbet shoulder while the cutter shaves down the bottom of the rabbet. There is also an adjustable, removable depth gauge attached to the side.

Some rabbet planes are also equipped with an adjustable guiding fence usable on either side, and an extra seat at the nose for the plane cutter to get into corners. The latter plane is about 8¼″ long, 1½″ cutter and as it costs very little more than a plane not equipped with a fence and extra iron seat, it is wise to pay the difference. These planes will also cut multiple shoulders (one at a time) on the edge of a board by adjusting the fence and depth gauge. If you have much rabbeting to do, investing in a fully equipped rabbet plane will repay you in time and labor saved. In use, the rabbet plane cuts best with the grain, but it's awkward to change this plane to humor the grain. The best plan, when this occurs, is to take as deep a cut as works well to rough out the rabbet and finish with light cuts.

Dado planes are also time and labor-saving tools. They are equipped with two spurs for clean side cuts, and a depth gauge. However, the single-width cutting plane is somewhat impractical as several of them are needed for different width dadoes.

The Combination Plane is much more versatile (Fig. 42), furnished

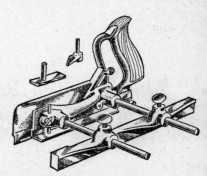

Fig. 42. Combination plane.

with over 15 cutters of different widths and shapes to cut dadoes, grooves, beading and match cutting (forming the male for tongue and groove edges). The cutter sizes run for the Plow: ⅛″ and 3/16″; Plow and Dado: ¼″ to ⅞″; Beading: ⅛″ to ½″ and a Match Cutter: 1⅛″. The cost is less than three ordinary dado planes and it will do many jobs not possible with other planes. This plane is also a single iron type, fully adjustable, equipped with two spurs, depth gauge and fence, match board beading gauge and lever adjustment.

Fig. 43. Spoke shave.

The Spoke Shave is also a plane of special design. It is invaluable for planing convex and concave edges, having an adjustable iron and raised handles extending from each side of the bottom. They are made with straight and convex bottoms (for use on concave and curved edges with small sweeps). The normal method of using a spoke shave is to push it in the direction of the grain, but it can also be used to advantage by drawing it toward you when grain changes. Besides planing curved edges, it can be used for beveling and rounding sharp edges. It is an inexpensive tool and a handy one to have in your tool box.

The Router Plane is another special tool, designed for surfacing the bottom of grooves and other depres-

sions parallel to the surface of the work. In addition, it will quickly chip out in successive stages and then smooth a dado, the sides of which have been sawed to depth. The router plane has an open throat about 7½″ long with a cutter post, an adjustable depth-gauge shoe and a removable fence on the underside so designed to follow straight, concave or convex surfaces. It is equipped with two knobs, one on each side of the cutter. The cutters are furnished in three sizes: ¼″, ½″ and a V or smoothing cutter. They have vertical shanks, the cutting end bent at right angles and parallel to the surface. These are held to the cutter post with a clamp and thumb screw, and are notched 1/16″ apart for easier depth adjustments.

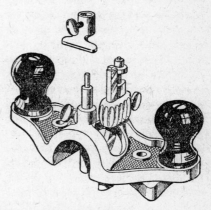

Fig. 44. Router plane.

The cutters can be used in the regular way on the front of the post or on its back for close work. In use, the plane is pushed and, for smoothing large sunken areas in wood, is a great time saver.

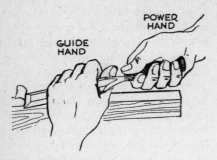

GUIDE HAND

POWER HAND

Fig. 45. How to hold a chisel.

CHISELS

The chisel is probably the third ranking essential tool in woodworking. Without it most woodworking problems having to do with joining would be almost impossible. You can get by without a plane by using laborious makeshifts, but wherever wood is joined to another piece of wood, other than the common butt joint; where hinges and other devices are to be recessed; locks mortised; stopped dadoes and rabbets and other problems are to be solved, the chisel must be used. Woodworking chisels are basically of two types: the carpenter's-cabinetmaker's, and the wood-carver's chisel, the latter having an almost endless variety of shapes, each for a special purpose. Carpenter's chisels can be roughly divided into three categories: Butt, Pocket and Firmer; with blades 3¼", 4½" and 6" long, respectively. The Butt comes in blade widths from ⅛" to 2", and the Pocket and Firmer blades range from ¼" to 2", all sized in 8ths to 1", 4ths to 2". The Butt chisel is easier to control because it's short, while the

longer chisels can be used with less angle because of their blade lengths.

Most carpenter's chisels have sockets in which the handle of hardwood, capped by leather washers, fits. There are also heavy-duty chisels with shanks and plastic handles of one piece in the Butt and Pocket sizes. Top-quality chisels have a beveled cutting edge and beveled sides, the blade ground the same width and tempered its entire length so that successive grinding, sharpening and honing will always produce the same width cut.

There are a number of ways of holding a chisel, depending on what you intend doing with it. When using the chisel, the hands are oftener employed to drive it than the mallet which is usually used to drive the chisel blade across grain; when cutting a mortise which has been previously bored out with an auger bit; when roughing out where a large amount of material has to be removed, and in hard wood. Using a

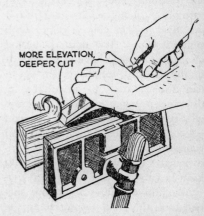

MORE ELEVATION, DEEPER CUT

Fig. 46. To cut deeper, lift handle.

mallet to drive a chisel edge with the grain quite frequently splits the wood due to the force of the blows.

The left hand guides the chisel edge by pressing firmly on the blade and the wood being worked. The right hand supplies the power (Fig. 45). Use a slicing cut whenever possible, rather than a straight pushing stroke. The former makes it easier and imparts to the edge a knife-like action resulting in a cleaner cut. To cut horizontally with the grain, hold the chisel slightly to one side and push away from you, bevel down for roughing cuts, bevel up for paring cuts. With the bevel up, hold the chisel as parallel as possible to the surface, holding down the chisel with all the fingers of the left hand—the more elevation the deeper the cut— and cut with the grain as in planing, otherwise you will split the wood (Fig. 46).

To cut horizontally across the grain, guide the chisel edge with the thumb on top and the first two fingers under the blade, pressed together. This acts as a brake to the edge, permitting delicate cuts to be made. To prevent splintering the corners, cut toward the center each way, removing the middle portion last (Fig. 47). When chiseling any wide surfaces, cut with the bevel down so that the handle clears the surface and the blade does not dig in as you push it forward.

If you are rounding a corner, use short, slanting cuts across the edge and tangent to the curve guide line. When using the chisel vertically across grain, the bevel should face

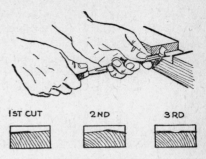

1ST CUT   2ND   3RD

Fig. 47. Chiseling out small joints.

out, the edge cutting with the grain in a slicing motion. Corners on boards, cut vertically, should be started from the edge of the board, working toward the end so the waste will split away from the scribed line— otherwise you will split the wood and ruin the work. When you are cleaning the corners of a tenon, dado or rabbet, grasp the chisel near the cutting edge with the handle tilted to one side so that you are working with the corner of the blade. Draw the blade toward you, holding the work with your left hand. To cut concave

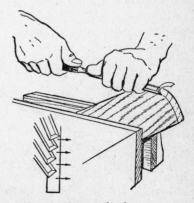

Fig. 48. How to chisel a curve.

corners, the bevel should be against the surface, and as you press down on the chisel, pull the handle slightly toward you, producing a sweeping curve cut. Again, always cut with the grain from the edge toward the end. Fig. 48.

Practice these basic cuts on a piece of scrap wood and in no time you will have the knack of handling a chisel for every type of problem. Just remember that it is better to take numerous small cuts rather than a couple of large ones, if you are doing a precision job. Also bear in mind that the chisel is in many respects somewhat of a knife, and at other times does the work of a plane where a plane cannot reach. As with all cutting tools, the edge must be razor sharp, and if it is kept in this condition, the pleasure of seeing it respond to your slightest touch will be ample reward for the time taken to keep it in condition.

Gouges

Gouges are chisels also, but with rounded cutting edges which make a concave cut. They are known as Firmer and Paring gouges, and range

FLAT   MEDIUM   REGULAR

Fig. 50. Cutting edges of three gouges.

in blade widths from ⅛″ to 2″ (Fig. 49). Firmer gouges are sold with the bevel on the inside or outside, and with tang or socket shanks, while the Paring gouge has its bevel on the inside and is furnished with a tang handle, straight or offset. Both types come in flat, medium and regular sweeps with parallel sides, allowing them to be ground, sharpened and honed for a considerable distance back from their original length (Fig. 50). Although, strictly speaking, not a wood-carver's tool, they can be classified as such, being used for irregular grooving and where a groove width is small and cannot be handled in any other manner. They are usually manipulated with the hands. A few of these, such as the ⅛″, ¼″ and ½″ widths, are handy to have when needed for cabinet making and repair jobs, but they are not essential for average home carpentry.

When storing edged tools, or even laying them down, never let their cutting edges contact metal or other hard objects which, more likely than not, will nick or at best dull sharp edges. A moment's carelessness may cost you hours of needless grinding, sharpening and honing.

THE POCKETKNIFE

One of the most versatile of small tools is the lowly pocketknife of whittling fame. You have undoubtedly

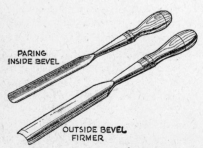

PARING
INSIDE BEVEL

OUTSIDE BEVEL
FIRMER

Fig. 49. Two types of gouges.

seen amazing carving feats accomplished with only a pocketknife which required extraordinary skill. However, the use of a pocketknife for home carpentry does not require a lot of practice in its use. For *precision* marking of lumber, the pocketknife is invaluable as it scribes a hair line which a pencil or other device will not do. It is also the best of small chisels for delicate work difficult to reach otherwise, and for many other cutting uses that will occur to you. A good knife is not cheap, but it is worth many times its cost in service rendered. Do not purchase a fancy, multi-blade job; buy a two-blade knife with one blade 2″ to 2½″ long, shaped like a hunting knife, the other about 1½″ to 2″ long of orthodox pattern. Keep it razor keen, and always cut away from yourself to avoid serious injury. To use a knife as a chisel, guide the blade with the first two fingers of your left hand along the flat or back edge, pushing the blade with the right hand in a slicing motion whenever possible.

WOODWORKING ABRASIVES

Sandpaper—misnamed as it contains no sand and never did—is an essential tool in woodworking. Without sandpaper you just could not finish a piece of wood "glass" smooth, nor would you be able to give wood a smooth protective coating of lacquer, varnish, stain or paint.

Sandpaper was first made by crushing glass and sprinkling it on gummed paper. It was called glass paper, and

Fig. 51. A two-bladed pocketknife.

worked after a fashion. Then crushed flint replaced glass and, because it looked like white sand, it was dubbed sandpaper and the name has been used ever since—but not by manufacturers of abrasive papers.

Flint paper is still used in tremendous quantities as it works well enough and is slightly cheaper than the modern abrasives, ranked according to their degree of hardness as follows: Silicon Carbide; Aluminum Oxide; Emery; Garnet, and Flint. Flint is effective when gummy surfaces such as paint, varnish and highly resinous wood require discarding the abrasive frequently due to clogging. It does not last as long as other, harder abrasives but, when breaking down from use, it breaks into sharp fragments and continues to cut. Silicon carbide is used chiefly for plastics, stone, glass, leather or soft metals like brass, copper and aluminum. Aluminum oxide is hard and tough enough to stand up at extremely high, power sanding-belt speeds, and its hardness is capable of penetrating any type of wood or metal.

Garnet Paper

For all-round woodworking, garnet paper (the crystals are actually garnet, the semi-precious stone) is best, being ideal for hand sanding as well as for all types of normal power sanding. It outlasts flint considerably, negating the difference in cost, cuts sharper and longer.

ABRASIVE GRADING CHART

	Garnet	Flint
Very Fine		7/0
	280 — 8/0	6/0
	240 — 7/0	5/0
	220 — 6/0	4/0
Fine		3/0
	180 — 5/0	
	150 — 4/0	
		2/0
	120 — 3/0	
		0
	100 — 2/0	
Medium		½
	80 — 0	
		1
	60 — ½	
	50 — 1	1½
Coarse		2
	40 — 1½	
		2½
	36 — 2	
	30 — 2½	3
Very Coarse	24 — 3	3½
	20 — 3½	

Abrasive papers, other than flint, are graded by numbers, meaning the number of holes in one linear inch of the screen through which the abrasive particles have been sifted. Garnet paper is so marked, besides the old "0" marking, thus: 2/0–100. Garnet comes in Cabinet Paper in the coarser grits, and Finishing Paper in the finer grits, the latter being much more flexible and capable of being bent around round surfaces without cracking. A supply of 1, ½ and 0 should take care of most of your rougher sanding, and 3/0, 5/0 and 7/ should be adequate for finishing. In the flint papers a good selection would be: 3, 2, 1, 0, 2/0 and 4/0. Abrasive sheets measure 9″x11″.

Hand Sanding

There are two basic methods of using abrasive papers when hand sanding: with and without a sanding block that is either square-surfaced or irregular shaped for special uses. A block of wood of suitable size is best for all flat-surface sanding, as it gives a square and hard foundation to the paper. Unless one is very careful, using the hands alone on flat-surface sanding will result in uneven small or large depressions. A block works best for all-round sanding if a ¼″-thick felt pad is glued to the surface. This padding helps the smoothing action and

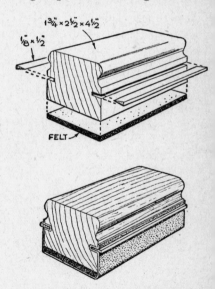

Fig. 52. How to make a sanding block.

prolongs the life of the paper. However, when sanding fir-plywood surfaces, a block without the pad works best, as the hard and soft grain of fir plywood is evenly smoothed with a hard-surfaced block.

Make a number of sanding blocks, some with and some without felt bottoms. A block 1¾″ thick, 2½″ wide and 4½″ long is a convenient size to fit the hands and enables you to cut sheets economically: 6 pieces, 4½″x 3⅜″. To make a good sanding block, cut a groove on each side, the length of the block, about ⅛″ wide and ½″ deep with your back saw or, if you do not have one, your rip saw. Then bevel two pieces of ¼″x½″x4″ wood with your plane, for wedges. Round all edges of the block on the top surface. To attach the abrasive paper, bend it around the bottom edges and into the slots. Insert the wedges and tap them tightly. (Fig. 52.) The removable wedges enable you to quickly change the paper and prevent the abrasive from roughing the skin of your hand.

There are inexpensive commercial sanding blocks of metal, some using a continuous roll of abrasive cloth in a number of grits. The latter are somewhat narrower than the homemade block described, and the rolls of abrasive run proportionately higher in cost than sheets.

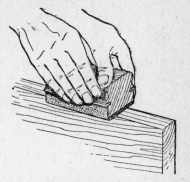

Fig. 54. Use both hands to square an edge.

Sand with Grain

Always sand a wood surface in the direction of the grain (Fig. 53). Across-the-grain sanding invariably results in scored surfaces, sometimes impossible to remove. Apply even pressure at the front and back of the block and use long strokes to insure even sanding. On edge sanding, where a square edge is desired, use both hands to support the block and keep it square (Fig. 54). Short, narrow pieces of lumber whose ends are to be sanded, are best upended on abrasive paper placed on the bench, the piece pushed forward and backward instead of the abrasive. Be careful when doing this not to rock the piece as this results in tapered or rounded corners.

Large holes bored in wood that require sanding are best done with a dowel slightly less in diameter than the hole, with the abrasive paper wrapped around the dowel. Round edges and pieces like dowels and "rounds" are sanded with the hands shaped around the surfaces. Molding shapes are sanded with the hands for

WITH GRAIN

Fig. 53. Sandpaper in direction of the grain.

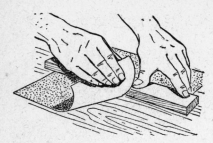

Fig. 55. Proper way to tear sandpaper.

convex and concave faces, and with a block for their square faces. Abrasive paper will last longer and cut sharper if clogged material is removed with a stiff wire brush.

Never cut abrasive papers with a cutting tool if you respect its edge—it will dull quickly. Use either a cheap knife-blade whose edge would not stay sharp in any event, or a pair of scissors you do not care about. You can also tear the paper by placing it along the sharp edge of some flat surface or use a sharp-edged piece of wood as a straightedge (Fig. 55).

When smoothing a surface, start with a coarse grit—if the surface is very rough—and progressively use finer grits, never jumping more than two grades at a time. For surfaces that are to be painted, finish with garnet 5/0 or 7/0; flint 4/0. Some excessively fiberous woods — bass wood is one — just will not sand smoothly. When this occurs, apply a thin coat of white shellac reduced with wood alcohol, after a final sanding; let dry for about three hours and then sand off the fibers raised by the shellac with a very fine grit. This procedure is also used when preparing wood surfaces for painting.

FILES

Files are fast cutting tools used chiefly to shape and sharpen metal, and to shape wood. Some are designed for woodworking only and are known as wood Rasps. The wood rasp is not recommended because its coarse teeth chew the wood surface about as much as it reduces dimensions. Much added work is needed after a rasping job to get the wood surface reasonably smooth for sanding.

Files are classified according to their shape and cut. Shapes of files are designed as Flat, Hand, Round, Half-Round, Square, Three Square (triangular), Knife and Mill, along with numerous other forms, such as Regular Taper, Slim Taper, etc., each for a specific purpose (Fig. 56). Files have three kinds of cut, meaning the character of the teeth: Single Cut, Double Cut and Rasp Cut. The degree of coarseness and fineness is defined also by three styles: Bastard (coarse), Second Cut (medium), and Smooth Cut (fine). The length is measured from point to heel, excluding the tang.

Single-cut files have one unbroken course of teeth or chisel cuts across their surfaces parallel to each other, but at an oblique angle to the length of the files. The single cut is used on Mill and Taper files and on special types of some saw files. The double-cut file has two courses of teeth or chisel cuts crossing each other, one course being finer than the other. This cut is used on all machinist's files, such as the Flat, Hand, Square, Round, Half-Round and Knife.

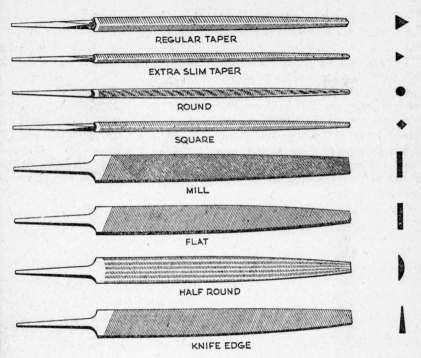

Fig. 56. Various types of files.

The Rasp cut differs from both single and double cut. The teeth are not in parallel rows across the file, but each tooth is punched in separately by a single-pointed tool. If you plan to sharpen your own saws, you will require Extra Slim Taper, Three-Square files of the following lengths, depending on the points per inch on your saws:

5, 6 points cross-cut saw....... }	—7″ file
5, 5½, 6 points rip saw......... }	
7, 8, 9 points cross-cut saw..... }	—6″ file
7 points rip saw............... }	
9, 10 points cross-cut saw.......	5½″ file
10, 11, 12 points cross-cut saw....	4½″ file

A Mill file, smooth cut, 8″ long is needed to sharpen a cabinet scraper, and an auger-bit file for auger bits.

Four very useful files for woodworking are the Flat, double-cut bastard; the Round, double-cut bastard; the Square, double-cut bastard and the Half-Round, double-cut bastard—all 12″ long. The flat file will shape hard and soft woods, bevel, round edges and corners, and do many other shaping jobs speedily without tearing the fibers. The round file is invaluable for enlarging holes bored in wood; the square file for squaring round holes and other square-hole projects. The half-round file serves a double purpose with its flat and half-round surfaces and is very useful for enlarging shallow curves and concave edges.

All files should be used with handles: No. 1 for files 3″ to 6″; No. 2 for 6″ to 10″; No. 3 for 10″ to 12″. To attach handles, do not drive the file from its point and do not hit it with anything — push the handle on and, holding the file point up, tap the butt end of the handle on the bench to drive the tang into place. Files, because of their temper, are very brittle and liable to break if struck with a hard object, or dropped on a hard surface.

Fig. 58. Push forward only with a file.

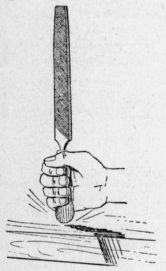

Fig. 57. Tap butt of file handle.

Using a File

To use a file, grasp the handle with the right hand and the point with the left, and push forward without undue pressure, but keep the file cutting. When filing hard metals, use only a forward stroke, lifting the file clear of the work for a return stroke (Fig. 58).

Dragging it back will dull and wear down the backs of the teeth. Wood, and soft metals like lead, aluminum, copper and brass do not require this technique. Work the file forward and backward on these materials as the backward stroke cleans the teeth somewhat. When the teeth become clogged, a stiff wire brush, or better still, a File Card will clear them.

A file card is made for cleaning files and is inexpensive. The card contains short, stiff tempered wires so spaced as to get in between the courses of teeth. Do this often, particularly so when filing wood, otherwise the teeth will become so clogged

Fig. 59. A file card.

that they drag instead of cut, dulling the teeth. If the card does not remove all clogging, a large needle run along the courses will do it. Then use a stiff brush to finish cleaning.

LONG SWEEP

Fig. 60. Draw file sidewise in long stroke.

Draw filing is the reverse of normal filing. You draw the file *sidewise*, right and left along the face of the work (Fig. 60). This stroke is used mostly on metals, like the preliminary step in sharpening a cabinet scraper, and on wood when shaping a concave edge.

Besides the files mentioned for woodworking—they can be used also on metal—files of medium and smooth cuts for metal can be purchased as the need for them arises.

CABINET SCRAPER AND BURNISHER

For finishing the work of the plane —there are always plane-iron marks

no matter how smoothly it shaves— the cabinet scraper is used. It is also employed where a plane cannot be used readily, like finishing hardwood floors. For cabinet work and on veneers, it is the only tool you can use for smoothing cuts.

The cabinet scraper is made in a number of shapes for cabinet work, but the usual form is a small piece of highly-tempered saw steel (about 1/32″ thick) in sizes from 2″x4″ to 4″x6″. All sides are square with true edges. It is a mistaken idea that scrapers are supposed to remove only dust-like particles. If correctly sharpened and properly used, the scraper will actually plane—remove a shaving.

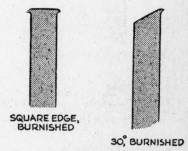

SQUARE EDGE, BURNISHED

30° BURNISHED

Fig. 61. Two types of scraper edges.

Cutting edges on scrapers are of two types: edges ground and honed square, resulting in sharp corners to the edges, all of which can be used, and the other type which has its edge ground to a 30-degree bevel, the beveled edge turned over slightly with a tool called a Burnisher. This latter type cuts much faster than the square edge, but it is a bit trickier to sharpen (Fig. 61).

There are different types of holders made for scrapers, one being similar in appearance to the spoke shave, and another having a handle attached to the scraper clamp. For heavy work, such as scraping a floor, the handle type is used. For average work the scraper works just as well when held in the hands, better perhaps, there being more control in finger pressure (Fig. 62).

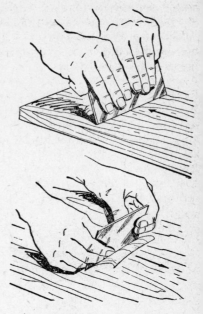

Fig. 63. Using a scraper.

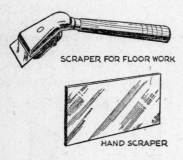

SCRAPER FOR FLOOR WORK

HAND SCRAPER

Fig. 62. Two types of scraper.

Using a Scraper

To use a scraper successfully it must be sharp with true edges, otherwise it will do more damage than good. Grasp the scraper with both hands with the first two or three fingers of each hand pressing against the blade about ½″ from the scraping edge, thumbs bracing the back. Tilt the scraper slightly in whatever direction you are working; toward you if you are pulling, and away from you if you are pushing (Fig. 63). With pressure applied evenly (heavy or light), pull or push the tool—that is all there is to using a scraper. The method of using this tool requires that it be sharpened frequently to per-

form properly, so keep your mill file handy and your burnisher also if you are using a scraper with turned-over edges. With the latter type a number of resharpenings can be done only with the burnisher.

BORING

Wherever a screw is to be driven, two holes *should* be bored, and when a dowel is used for joining two pieces of wood two holes *must* be bored— making boring tools essential. Holes in wood are "bored" while holes in metal are "drilled." There is no good reason why these terms meaning the same thing should be used in describing hole-making operations. However, since they are used universally for wood and metal, you may as well know the technical terms.

There are three basic types of boring devices used to hold tools that bore holes in wood: The Brace for Auger and Twist Bits; the Hand Drill for Twist Drills; and the Automatic Push Drill for drill points especially designed to fit the drill. There are also variations of the push drill that take standard bits and twist drills. The automatic push drill permits one-hand operation, while the brace, hand drill and other types of push drills require both hands.

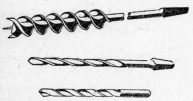

Fig. 64. Auger bit, twist bit, twist drill.

Auger Bits

Auger bits (Fig. 64) come in sizes from ¼″ to 1″ graduated in 16ths. Their sizes are stamped on the bit as the numerator of the fraction: 8 stands for 8/16″ or ½″ diameter of the hole bored. Twist bits for wood (Fig. 64) come in sizes from 1/16″ to 1″ graduated in 32nds, and are marked similarly to the auger bit: 8 stands for 8/32″ or ¼″ diameter hole. Bit Stock Drills are for metal or wood and are marked like the twist bits, 1/16″ to 1¼″.

There is a Forstner Bit which has no feed screw that is used to bore wood part way when the screw of the auger bit would come through the

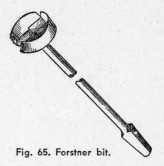

Fig. 65. Forstner bit.

wood; for end-grain boring, thin wood, or near an end where the auger bit might split the wood. Its sizes are marked like the auger bit, in 16ths. For holes larger than 1″ in wood, there is the Expansive Bit which

Fig. 66. Expansive bit.

comes in two sizes: for holes from ½″ to 1½″ and for holes from ⅞″ to 3″. These two sizes have adjustable cutters for any diameter within their limits.

Hand-drill twist drills are straight shanked for use in metal or wood (Fig. 64c). Their sizes are designated in fractions of an inch from 1/64″ to ¼″ (limit of chuck capacity of a hand drill) and up. Straight-shank twist drills are also made in Wire Gauge sizes from Nos. 1 to 80. These can be bought singly or in sets from 1 to 60 with a holder to contain them. The automatic-push-drill point is for wood and plaster. It comes in sets of 8, from 1/16″ to 11/64″; a set is housed in the handle of the drill when bought. These drill points are short, limited to about 1¼″-depth holes, and

Fig. 67. Push-drill and point.

are designed to bore with a continuous reciprocal motion (Fig. 67). In practice, you push the drill, which at the end of its stroke returns by spring action to its original position, the drill point boring with both motions.

THE BRACE

The Brace goes back in history to the days when it was first made of wood. The modern brace is scientifically engineered to do a number of jobs other than just bore in wood. When buying a brace, get one with a "ratchet." An 8" or 10" "sweep" (diameter of swing) ratchet brace is good for all-round work. The ratchet attachment transforms the brace into an improved screw-driving tool for large screws requiring considerable hand power to drive, and when a number of screws are to be driven.

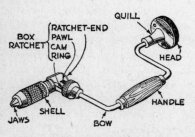

Fig. 68. Various parts of a brace.

The ratchet works three ways: driving to the right, inoperative to the left; center neutral, operative right and left; extracting to the left, inoperative to the right. A good brace has a chuck (jaw assembly to hold bit shanks) which will firmly grip all tapered-hank bits and also small and medium-size straight-shank drills. A ratchet brace in the medium-price class is fine (Fig. 68). The ratchet brace is comprised of Jaws enclosed in a Shell; adjustable Ratchet; Bow; Handle; Quill; Head (either bronze bearing or ball bearing).

Two hands are usually required to operate a brace, but when boring horizontally, you can rest the head of the brace against your stomach or chest if necessary. To insert a bit, turn the shell to the left until the jaws are wide open and be careful to center the shank of the bit in the V-jaws. Turn the shell to the right tightly. Set the ratchet to 'neutral" when boring, countersinking, reaming and starting a screw. To bore vertically, hold the brace and bit perpendicular to the surface, left hand cupped over the head.

There are a number of ways to bore straight: by sighting frequently; by comparing the bit to some near straight object; setting a square near the bit, and by clamping, when feasible, a square piece of wood along the bit. If you are going off the straight, you can adjust the bit at the start of the hole.

When using an auger bit to bore through a board, never bore all the way through from one direction (Fig. 69). This splinters the edges of the

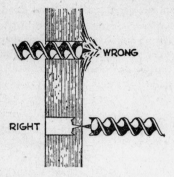

Fig. 69. Using an auger bit.

quill. Use a brace and bit for holes larger than ¼" and a hand drill for holes ¼" and smaller.

Frequently you will want to bore one or a series of holes of certain depth only partially through a piece of wood, either with an auger bit or a Forstner bit. To do this accurately, a depth gauge is necessary. You can buy such a gauge, or you can easily make one from a block of hard or soft wood. For the auger bit, bore a hole with the bit you intend to use in a short length of ¾"x2" wood. (See Fig. 71.) Cut this off with your back saw or cross-cut saw so that you have a

hole as the bit emerges. Bore until the point just shows, then, with the hole as a guide, finish boring from the other side. When using an expansive bit, clamp a piece of waste wood against the piece to be bored and bore all the way through. This also applies

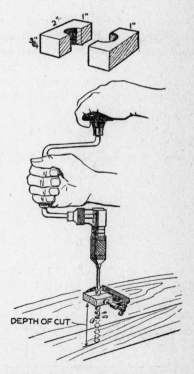

Fig. 70.

to boring with twist bits and drills in wood. To bore horizontally, hold the brace cupped in the left hand against your stomach when possible, with the thumb and forefinger around the

Fig. 71. Easily made depth gauge.

block 2″x2″ with the hole centered. Then saw the block in half across the center of the hole. To use, clamp the halves of the block on the bit with a small C-clamp, the depth of the hole to be bored. For the Forstner bit, bore a hole the diameter of the straight shank, and proceed as with the auger-bit gauge. Make a gauge for each of your bits against the time when you will need them, and mark each pair with the size bit to be used.

COUNTERSINK BIT

A Countersink Bit is used to ream a conical hole of shallow depth in an existing hole bored for a flat-head screw so that it may be driven flush with or below the surface. Hand-operated countersinks for wood and metal are usually of the "rose" type (Fig. 72). They have courses of cutting edges tapering to a point of the

same angle as that of the head of a flat-head wood screw. Flat-head screws should always be driven either flush, or a bit below the surface (when the heads are to be covered with putty, wood putty or plastic wood).

Fig. 73. Reamer bit.

A Reamer Bit is of longer taper than the countersink and is used to taper existing holes for tight fits of tapered handles and such. Two sizes are good to have when the need for them arises: one that reams from ⅛″ to ½″, and the other from ¼″ to ⅞″ holes.

Fig. 74. Screwdriver bit.

The Screwdriver Bit is nothing more than a short screwdriver blade with a tapered shank to fit the brace. Three sizes should be included in your brace accessories: ¼″, 5/16″ and ⅜″ widths. The ease with which the brace and screwdriver bit will drive screws into any kind of wood makes it worthwhile getting a selection and they are inexpensive.

A Hand Drill is powered by a hand wheel geared to the drive shaft, to which is attached a chuck for twist drills. The drill is steadied by the left

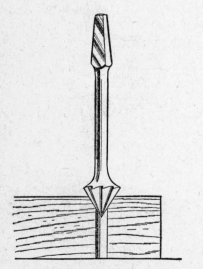

Fig. 72. Rose countersink bit.

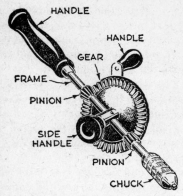

HANDLE
HANDLE
GEAR
FRAME
PINION
SIDE
HANDLE
PINION
CHUCK

Fig. 75. Various parts of hand drill.

crank with the right hand while holding the shell tight with the left. You can make depth gauges for use with the hand drill, too, as follows: Cut a small block of wood the depth you intend to bore; bore through it with the drill you intend to use and slip the block on the drill so that it rests against the chuck, leaving exposed only that part of the drill to be used (Fig. 76).

hand on either of the two handles, while the right hand turns the crank attached to the drive wheel (Fig. 75). To insert a drill, open the chuck only slightly more than the diameter of the drill. With the drill centered, tighten the chuck by pushing forward on the

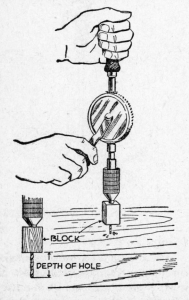

BLOCK
DEPTH OF HOLE

Fig. 76. Depth gauge for hand drill.

SCREWDRIVERS

The screwdriver is certainly a well known tool and it hardly seems necessary to mention its purpose, but the truth is that an amazing number of users of screwdrivers are unaware of their proper use. The users may have been mislead by the claims of manufacturers who, in their enthusiasm over their fine products, state that their handles are virtually breakproof; that their steel defies bending stresses, and on and on. Yet no manufacturer would dream of suggesting that his screwdriver be used as a substitute for a crowbar, a cold chisel, a nail extractor, or a can opener! Nevertheless, a surprising number of owners of screwdrivers employ them for everything but driving screws — with the result that when needed for their original purpose, their tips are so badly chewed up that that is about all they will do to the wood surface and screw head.

A good screwdriver is a well-engineered tool. It is forged from special analysis alloy steel best suited for driving screws, with a flat, slightly tapered tip in most sizes, ground flat

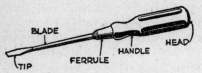

Fig. 77. Parts of a screwdriver.

and true. Handles are of various compositions and wood. Regardless of how tough these handles may be, do not hit them with a hammer. A good screwdriver is not particularly cheap, so why ruin it unnecessarily?

Look at your collection of screwdrivers and examine their tips (Fig. 77). If they have rounded corners, twisted or damaged edges, they will do more damage to the wood surface or/and screw slot than they are

worth. Take your mill file and file the faces of the tip edges *square* and *true* — and keep them that way. Then use each screwdriver only for the size screw slot it fits properly.

The width of the tip edge should not be wider than the slot of the screw head, otherwise, when driving it flush, the tip will damage the wood. It should not be too small as this results in scarring the slot. If the corners are rounded and the edge beveled, it will slip out, scarring the slot and damaging the wood. If the tip-edge does not fit snugly in the slot full depth, it will also scar the slot and wood.

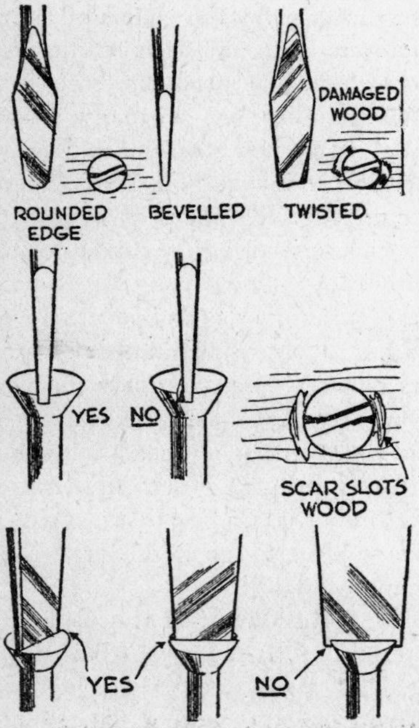

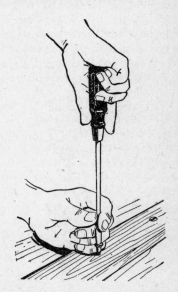

Fig. 79. Proper way to drive in a screw.

Fig. 78. Good and bad screwdrivers.

Using a Screwdriver

When using a screwdriver, choose the longest one convenient for the work. More power can be applied to a long blade than to a short one, with less chance of the tip slipping out (Fig. 79). Grasp the handle firmly in the palm of the right hand, the thumb and forefinger holding it near the ferrule. With the left hand, steady the tip and keep it pressing in the slot while renewing your grip on the handle. Keep the screwdriver vertical, or horizontal, with the screw — slanting it will result in the tip slipping out and marring both slot and work. The following table shows what width tip to use for a particular size flat, oval and round-head, slotted wood screw.

Screw Size	Blade-tip width
0	1/8", 9/64"
1	9/64"
2	5/32"
3, 4	3/16"
5	7/32"
6, 7	1/4"
8, 9, 10, 11	5/16"
11, 12, 14	3/8"
14, 16, 20	7/16"
20, 24	1/2"

There is also a patented screw head which is recessed and partially cross-slotted, known as the Phillips screw which requires a screwdriver tip designed to fit the recess (Fig. 80).

Screwdrivers are also made with ratchets built in the ferrule, doing away with grip changing. Some of these types have interchangeable tips, housed in the handles. Then there is

Fig. 80. Phillips screwdriver.

Fig. 81. Spiral ratchet screwdriver.

the Spiral Ratchet screwdriver with removable tips, ideal for production work where innumerable screws must be driven quickly (Fig. 81). This driver works like the automatic push drill in principle, the main difference being the cross-spiral driving shaft, and the ratchet which permits positive motion three ways. The driver comes in medium, heavy and light-duty design, and can also be used as a drill with the same drill points used in the automatic push drill.

SHARPENING CUTTING TOOLS

Good craftsmanship is dependent on tools being in perfect condition. This is doubly true of tools with cutting edges. A dull tool just cannot be made to do good work, and the wear and tear on temper and nerves caused by using a dull tool is most certainly not worth the small loss of time required to bring it to a keen edge. With the exception of saw sharpening, little or no skill is necessary to keep tools sharp — only a bit of care and know-how. 'Touching up' crosscut and rip-saw teeth when they become *slightly* dull is not difficult, and well worth doing frequently to save the chore of jointing, reshaping, resetting and resharpening — or paying to have it done.

To sharpen the teeth of saws you need a Saw Clamp or Vise with an eccentric lever which opens and closes the jaws with one motion. The clamp is not too expensive and, being designed for saw filing only, is much

Fig. 82. Saw clamp.

superior to other makeshift methods of clamping the saw blade. The top of the clamp should be about level with your elbows for an efficient working position. Use a file for the points-per-inch of your saw.

Filing Cross-Cut-Saw Teeth

First Position: Place the point of the saw in the clamp with the *handle to your right*. The bottom of the gullets (space between teeth) should be ⅛″ above the jaws of the clamp (Fig. 83). If more of the blade projects, the file will chatter and dull quickly. A trick used in filing a saw properly is to pass your file *lightly* over the tops of the teeth the length of the saw to form a *very small* flat top on each tooth. The purpose of this is to guide you in filing the teeth so that you can see which tooth you have just sharp-

ened. With the point of the saw blade clamped in the vise, handle to your right, stand to the *left* of the point (Fig. 84). Pick out the first tooth that is set *toward* you. Place the file directly across the blade, then swing the file handle toward the *left* to the correct angle. Hold the file level at this angle; do not allow the file to tip upward or downward. Make certain the file sets well down into the gullet — let it find its own bearing against the teeth it touches. It will help you to get the right angle for filing if you will study the teeth near the handle-end of the saw which are usually untouched after leaving the factory. The file should cut only on the push stroke and file the tooth to the left and the tooth to the right at the same time. File until you cut away *one-half* of the flat tops you made on the teeth as a guide (Fig. 85). Then *lift* the file from the gullet, *skipping* the next gullet to the right, and place the file in the following gullet. File as before, same angle, sharpening two teeth at one time. Continue this procedure, filing every second gullet until you have reached the handle-end of the saw, moving the blade, of course, along the vise as you reach the end of the jaws.

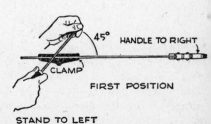

45° HANDLE TO RIGHT

CLAMP

FIRST POSITION

STAND TO LEFT

Fig. 83. Sharpening a cross-cut saw.

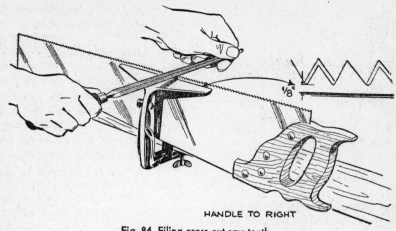

HANDLE TO RIGHT

Fig. 84. Filing cross-cut saw teeth.

Second Position: Turn the saw around in the clamp, *handle to the left,* and stand to the *right* of the point (Fig. 86). Place the file in the gullet to the *right* of the first tooth set *toward* you. This is the first gullet you skipped when you filed the other side of the saw. Turn the file handle to the *right* to the correct angle and file until you cut away the other half of the flat top made on the teeth as

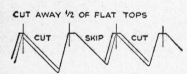

Fig. 85. Cut away half of the flat tops.

a guide, now a sharp point. Continue filing every second gullet until you reach the handle. The gullets must all be of even depth and the teeth shaped alike, otherwise the saw will not perform properly. Teeth of uneven size will jump or bind in the

kerf, causing in many cases the blade to kink throwing it out of true.

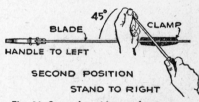

Fig. 86. Second position to sharpen saw.

Filing Rip-Saw Teeth

The method of filing rip-saw teeth is the same as that for cross-cut saws — *with one exception:* You file straight across the teeth, not at an angle as with the cross-cut saw (Fig. 87). Also, the file should be placed in the gullet so as to keep the angle on the front of each tooth 8 degrees, at its back 52 degrees. Otherwise, proceed exactly as with the cross-cut teeth: every other tooth filed with the saw handle first to the right of you, then the blade turned around and every

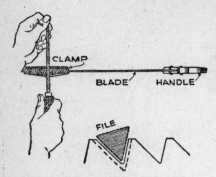

Fig. 87. Sharpening rip saw teeth.

other tooth filed with the handle to your left. Do not be tempted to file all the teeth without turning the blade around. This lazy practice is one of the things that makes a saw run to one side. Always turn both rip and cross-cut saws after reaching the handle-end.

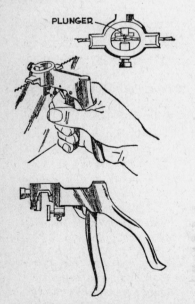

Fig. 88. Resetting teeth with saw set.

After numerous sharpenings, the set of the teeth lessens, causing the saw to bind. They must be reset *before* another sharpening (Fig. 88). Resetting teeth calls for a Saw Set which is a plier-like tool having two plungers: one to hold the saw set securely in position against the saw blade, and the other to set the teeth. The saw set is adjustable for amount of set, automatically setting each tooth at the same angle. The part of the tooth set should not be more than *one-half* the tooth from the point, each tooth set alternately, one to the right, one to the left (Fig. 89). The idea is to make the teeth cut a kerf *slightly* wider than the thickness of the saw blade at the teeth. If more than half the tooth is set, it is likely to crimp or crack the blade — or break off the teeth.

Top-quality saws, as mentioned before, are taper ground from the tooth edge to the back, wider at the tooth edge than at the back edge. They are also taper ground on the back edge from point to heel. Therefore, such a saw requires comparatively little set, producing a cleaner and narrower cut. Care must be taken that the set is regular. It must be the same width on both sides of the blade, otherwise the saw will run out of line and the cut will be "snaky."

Fig. 89. Proper kerf for saw teeth.

Jointing a Saw

Jointing a saw means to file down all the teeth to the same height, to be done only when the saw teeth are of uneven depth or badly shaped. To joint a saw, place the saw in the clamp, handle to the right. Lay your Mill file lengthwise on the teeth and lightly pass it back and forth the length of the blade until the file touches the *top of every tooth*. If the teeth are very uneven, it's best not to make all the teeth the same height the first time they are jointed, otherwise you may lose some of the gullets. In this case, joint only the highest teeth first, then shape the teeth that have been jointed. Then joint the teeth a second time, passing the file along the tops of all the teeth until it touches every tooth. Do not allow the file to tip to one side or the other — keep it flat — otherwise you will make rounded points.

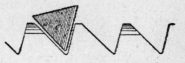

Fig. 91. Shaping saw teeth.

teeth, disregard bevel for the crosscut saw which you take care of when sharpening (Fig. 91). Place the file (three-square) well down in the gullet and file *straight across* the saw at *right angles* to the length of the blade. If the teeth are of unequal size, press the file against the teeth having the widest tops, until you reach the center of the flat top made by jointing. Then move the file to the *next* gullet and file until the rest of the top disappears, bringing the tooth to a point. Continue this procedure to the handle-end. The saw is now ready to be set, after which it is sharpened.

SHARPENING PLANE IRONS AND CHISELS

A plane iron and chisel must be kept razor keen to do good work, and to keep these edges in condition, you need an Oilstone. You will also need a hand-operated, or power grinding wheel for the time when you will have to regrind edges due to repeated oilstoning, or because you have been careless and nicked the blade. There are many types of oilstones, some of natural stone, others artificial, produced in electric furnaces at terrifically high temperatures. The man-made crystals resulting are harder than any of Nature's handiwork except the pure diamond. Good natural oilstones

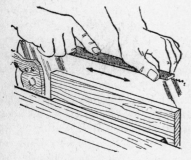

Fig. 90. Jointing a saw.

Shaping Teeth should be done only after jointing. All teeth must be filed to the correct shape, the gullets of equal depth. The fronts and backs of the teeth must have the proper angle, and be uniform in size. To shape

HAND
GRINDING
WHEEL

Fig. 92.

are quite expensive and are not uniform in quality of hardness, while artificial stones are harder, wear longer and are uniform.

Two important types of artificial oilstones are chemically known as Aluminum Oxide and Silicon Carbide. The best known form of Aluminum Oxide is Alundum abrasive which is a reproduction of the natural mineral Corundum. This electric - furnace product, when made into an oilstone, will sharpen any steel quickly, no matter how hard the steel may be, yet it is not hard enough to cause tools to groove or wear down the stone unevenly when properly used. The stone is factory oil-filled, reducing its tendency to "glaze" and does away with the otherwise necessity of oil soaking for days. All you need to do when using the stone is to apply a light coating of oil.

Silicon Carbide

Silicon Carbide produces another artificial stone much in favor in home workshops. This stone cuts speedily

with less pressure than the Alundum product. It is oil-saturated at the factory, ready for immediate use as is, but a light application of oil each time it is used will produce easier and smoother cutting. A combination stone, one side "coarse," the other side "fine" will take care of all your oilstone sharpening. The coarse side restores dull edges quickly, while the fine side produces a finished edge.

When using an oilstone, or grinder, where the *tool* is moved, the rule is to sharpen with the edge working *against* the stone. The reason for this is that it produces less "wire" edge

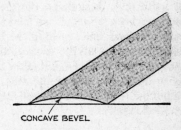

CONCAVE BEVEL

Fig. 93. Concave bevel produced by grinder.

All cutting edges of tools that have been ground on a grinder — and all are originally, even a pocketknife — have a slightly concave bevel (hollow ground) similar to an old-fashioned razor, due to the curvature of the grinding wheels (Fig. 93). This is as it should be for it produces the best and lasting cutting edge. The grinder produces the bevel, but it takes the *flat* surface of an oilstone to produce the keen, lasting edge.

Most cutting tools have chisel-like edges and are, with slight variations, all sharpened in the same manner.

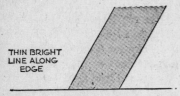

THIN BRIGHT LINE ALONG EDGE

Fig. 94. Sharpen till thin line disappears.

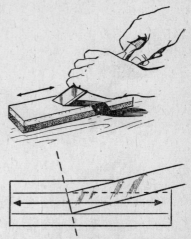

Fig. 96. Move chisel forward and backward.

Tools of this nature show their dullness in the form of a thin, bright line along the edge (Fig. 94). Until the bevel-edge has become so obtuse (from oilstoning) as to need the grinding wheel, this dullness is best removed on the oilstone. The test for sharpness is the disappearance of the thin, bright line.

First see that the oilstone lies perfectly level to insure a true edge. Apply a few drops of light oil to the stone and grasp the plane iron or chisel with the left hand gripped over the blade and near its cutting edge, the right gripped around the end

(Fig. 95). Hold the hands low to make the tool correspond to the bevel made by the grinder. With each sharpening it is necessary to hold the hands a trifle higher until, finally, the bevel becomes too obtuse and must be reground.

Move the blade forward and backward in a straight line along the entire length of the stone, with the

Fig. 95. Sharpening a chisel.

Fig. 97. Hold chisel firmly.

Fig. 98. How to remove burr or wire edge.

strokes, remove any burr or wire edge. Use the grip illustrated in Fig. 98 when gradual elevation of the blade is necessary for each repeated sharpening. A piece of razor strop about 8″ long glued to a *flat* ¾″-thick piece of wood, strop-width and 8″ long, is a handy supplement to the oilstone for stropping a razor-edge on your tools. To strop the sharpened blade, use the same general method of oilstoning, except that you move the blade *backward* only (Fig. 99).

blade-end slightly to the left, producing an oblique-straight motion. Bear down with both hands (Fig. 96). Swing the right arm from the shoulder, bending it only at the elbow and holding the wrist *rigid*. Any twisted or turned position of this wrist is sure to give a certain amount of roll or twist to the blade, changing the true sharpening angle (Fig. 97). In rubbing over the stone, move the hands *horizontally*, parallel with the stone. *Do not use a circular motion* when returning with a backward stroke, or a *rotary motion* which constantly changes the angle at which the tool is held and prevents the edge from being true. Think of your hands as a sort of vise guiding the blade without variation forward and backward, and turn the oilstone around now and then to prevent it from wearing down unevenly.

When, after wiping the tool clean, you find the thin line of dullness has disappeared, turn the blade over, keeping it *perfectly flat* on the stone and, with one or two *light* sidewise

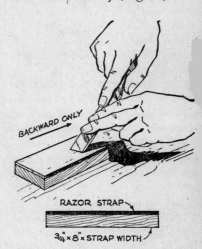

Fig. 99. Strop chisel backward only.

Gouges with Bevels

To sharpen gouges with outside bevel, an added technique is required. Bevels on gouges must follow evenly the curve of the tool. For this reason it is necessary to give the bevel a rocking motion from side to side as it passes back and forth over the stone in the same manner as flatedged tools (Fig. 100). To remove the wire-edge on the inside of an out-

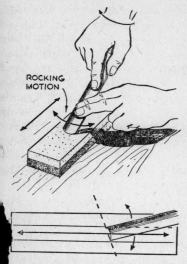

Fig. 100. Rock gouge while pulling back.

els are sharpened by holding them firmly against the bench while an oilstone slip of the correct shape is rubbed against the bevel. The slip for inside bevels is a wedge-shaped, concave-convex, fine grit stone.

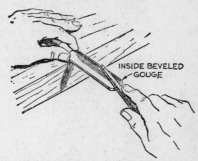

Fig. 102. Sharpening inside beveled gouge.

le-bevel gouge, you will need an stone "slip" which is a short piece "fine" stone, narrow and wedgeped with rounded edges. Hold the uge firmly against the bench and *ntly* rub the inside groove edge th the slip a few times, making cer- n to hold the slip flat against the oove to avoid turning the edge ig. 101). Gouges with inside bev-

Pocketknives

Pocketknives should be sharpened on the fine side of the stone only. Hold the blade with its back tilted slightly upward; place it obliquely across the face of the stone and smartly rub straight back and forth a few times. Then turn the blade over and repeat, using the same number of strokes (Fig. 103). Do this until

Fig. 101. Rub gently with oilstone slip.

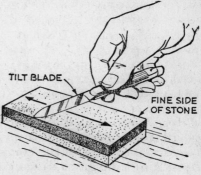

Fig. 103. Sharpening a pocketknife.

the blade is sharp, which you can
judge by the disappearance of the
thin, bright line. Remove any wire-
edge by stropping the blade on the
leather stropper.

To sharpen scissors, apply the
blade so that the bevel lies accurately
on the face of the stone, with the
blade crossing the stone at right
angles. Then draw the blade smartly
across the stone from heel to point.
Do not run the blade back and forth
— start each stroke at the heel.

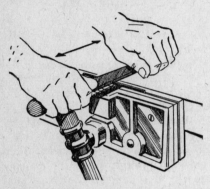

Fig. 104. Sharpening a scraper with a file.

When the square edges of a cabinet
scraper become dull, clamp it in a
vise with the edge about ⅛" above the
vise jaws (Fig. 104). Draw-file the
edge by placing the Mill file across
the scraper at right angles to its
length, and square with the edge face
— perfectly flat. Now move the file
left and right the length of the edge
a few times, and then check the edge
by holding it against a hard, flat surface toward a strong light. No light
should be visible under the edge. If
light shows, there is a depression in
the edge. Continue filing until the de-

Fig. 105. Sharpening scraper on a stone

pression disappears. Hollows in scrapers produce scratches on work (F
105).

Now lay the scraper flat on y
oilstone and move the scraper left a
right the length of the stone until t
edge corner is sharp. Turn the scrap
over and do the same thing with t
other edge corner.

Burnisher

To put a fast-cutting edge on
scraper, you need a Burnisher. Thi
a round tapered, or oval-shaped pie
of highly polished steel sufficien
hard to turn the edge of cabine
scrapers, and is about 4½" long wi

Fig. 106. Burnisher.

a wood handle. First file a bevel
about 30 degrees, similar to that
a chisel. Put a keen edge on the bev
on the oil stone, turn the scraper ov
flat, and remove any wire-edge. The
clamp the scraper in a vise and ru
the burnisher over the keen edge wit

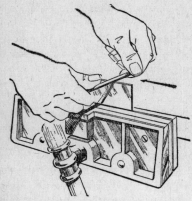

Fig. 107. Burnishing a scraper.

care. Touching up the scoring nibs and cutting lips now and then is all that is required to keep the bit in

Fig. 109. Auger-bit file.

good working order. An auger-bit file is used for this purpose. The file is usually double-bladed, the blades tapering to a blunt point somewhat like a screwdriver, designed for the close quarters of an auger bit. The scoring nibs are sharpened only from

few firm strokes toward you, using both hands on the burnisher (Fig. 107). Tilt the burnisher initially at an angle of about 15 degrees and finally at about an 8-degree angle.

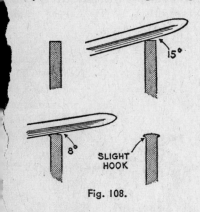

Fig. 108.

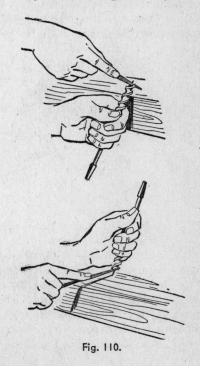

Fig. 110.

The burnisher first presses the edge outward, then tips it over slightly and finally bends it down to give it a slight hook. Several burnishings can be done to resharpen the scraper before it again needs the oilstone or file.

Auger bits seldom need sharpening if used only occasionally and with the inside to maintain their original dimension, otherwise the nibs would become smaller than the body of the bit. File the cutting lips on the side toward the shank to avoid losing clearance on the bottom. For a perfectly smooth edge, use an auger-bit oilstone slip, medium grit.

Like any good tool, an oilstone can be ruined by mistreatment and lack of care. Preserve the original life and sharpness of the grit by keeping the stone *clean* and *moist*. Always apply a few drops of light oil, Pike Oil preferably, on the stone. Pike Oil is free from acid, is non-gumming and non-drying. Your hardware store should stock it. In an emergency, lacking Pike Oil, kerosene will do. The idea of oil is to float the particles of steel that are cut away from the tool, thus preventing them from filling in be-

tween the crystals and causing the stone to "glaze."

After using the stone, always remove the dirty oil with a piece of cotton waste or a clean cloth, otherwise the oil will dry in with the steel particles, glazing the stone. Apply a few drops of oil to the stone and replace its cover so there is less tendency for the stone to dry out, which hardens it. Keep the surface of the stone flat and even—it will not sharpen edges accurately otherwise. To insure a flat, even stone, always use the entire length and turn it around frequently.

GRINDING WHEELS

When tool edges must be ground, as explained previously, the grinding wheel is a must. The power grinder

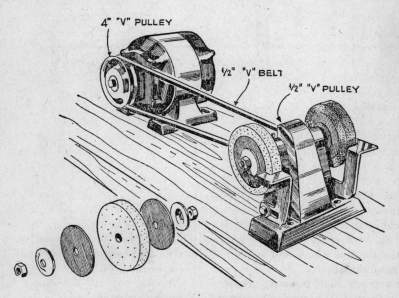

Fig. III. A power grinder and motor.

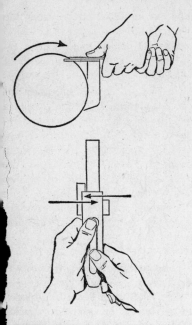

Fig. 112. Proper way to use grinder.

, of course, ideal because it allows
e free use of both hands while the
ctric motor does the work. If you
ve a ¼-horsepower motor around
e house, you can buy a 4″ grinding-
olishing head for less than a good
and-powered grinder. The head
omes equipped with a fine and
nedium-grit Aluminum Oxide wheel,
″ in diameter; an adjustable tool rest
or each wheel; a 2″ V-belt pulley for
:ither a ⅜″ or ½″ V-belt. A 4″ V-pully
)n the motor shaft of a 1750 R.P.M.
(revolutions per minute) motor
vould produce a wheel speed of 3,500
R.P.M., well under the safety speed
)f the abrasive wheel, and ample for
all grinding jobs.

Extremely light powered grinders
vith fractional horsepower motors

direct connected are not too efficient,
lacking the power for continuous operation. The advantage of a grinding
head, such as described, is that it can
also be used with cloth wheels and
wire-brush wheels for polishing and
"scratch brushing." Care must be exercised when using a high-speed
power grinder; your eyes are best protected with goggles.

When grinding any edge, pass the
edge at the correct angle left and
right across the face of the wheel,
dipping the edge in water constantly
so as not to draw its temper—an easy
thing to do with power grinders (Fig.
112). Passing the tool edge across the
face of the wheel keeps the wheel
from wearing unevenly and insures an
even bevel on the tool.

Abrasive wheels can be "dressed"
to any shape with a dressing tool
made of hardened, milled steel cutters attached to a handle. When connecting your motor to the grinding
head, be certain to place it so the
wheel revolves *toward* you.

SQUARES

To mark a line for cutting squarely
across a piece of lumber, you need a
square. There are four basic types of
squares: the Carpenter's Steel Square;
the Try Square; the Combination
Square; the T-Bevel. Where much
house framing is to be done: stair layout, roof-rafter layout and other projects with multi-angles, the carpenter's
steel rafter-framing square is an invaluable tool.

On the body of the square (the
long leg) is engraved a Rafter and

Framing Table, used to determine the length of common valley, hip and jack rafters and the angle at which they must be cut to fit at the ridge and plate. There is also the Essex Table which shows board measure in feet and 12ths of feet of boards 1″ thick of usual lengths and widths. On the tongue (short leg) you will find an Octagon Scale which is used to lay out a figure with eight sides on a square piece of wood. In addition, there is a Brace Table which shows the length of common braces. The faces of the square are graduated in 1/16″ and ⅛″, while the back faces are graduated in 1/16″, 1/10″ and 1/12″. Almost any angle can be plotted by using the body and tongue in combination. The standard square has a body length 24″x2″ and a tongue length 16″x1½″.

Fig. 113. Try square.

Try Square

The Try Square is perhaps the most universally used square, but is being replaced more and more by the Combination Square which has many advantages over the try square. A try square has a steel blade graduated in ⅛″ and a handle (short leg) of iron, or wood, brass faced. Both blade and handle come in various lengths, a good combination being a 12″ blade with an 8″ handle.

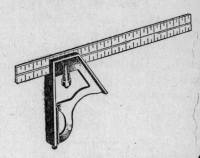

Fig. 114. Combination square.

Combination Square

The Combination Square has a removable steel blade graduated in 1/32″, 1/16″ and 1/8″. The blade is either slotted, or grooved its entire length so that the handle (short leg) can be moved along the blade, or removed. One or two level glasses are built into the handle, making a small level out of the handle. The handle also has a 45-degree angle on its inner corner, transforming the square into a Miter square. A steel scriber (for marking) is included in the handle. This square can be used as a try square, marking gauge, depth gauge, and a miter square, and its blade can be removed and used as a straight edge—five tools in one! If you are planning on getting only one square (which normally should be enough) by all means buy the Combination Square, 12″ blade, 4½″ handle.

There are combination squares equipped with a reversible Protractor Head, and Center Head. The protractor head is adjustable to any degree through 180 degrees of the circle (half circle), while the center head accurately locates the center of any round disk or rod. For an all-purpose square, the combination with protractor and center head is well worth its additional cost—if much angle plotting of odd-degree corners and edges is planned. These accessories are removable for ordinary square uses.

Fig. 116. Folding rule.

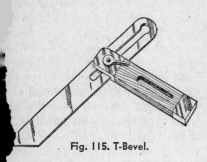

Fig. 115. T-Bevel.

The T-Bevel is a tool having a blade and a handle adjustable to any degree angle for marking lumber. The blade is slotted half its length in which slides the handle which can be locked in any position. For duplicating angles on lumber, for testing angles and for many other uses where an adjustable square can be used to advantage, the T-Bevel is a necessary tool for your tool box. A 12″ blade and 7½″ wood handle is about the largest made and a size which is convenient for any job requiring its use.

RULES

A good, accurate rule is essential for precision measurement of wood to be cut and fitted. There are many cheap rules on the market, but pass

them by and get a name-brand rule— there are a number to choose from— all precision made. The six-foot folding rule is the most common for all-round use. A good one will have inches and fractions graduated in 1/16ths engraved on both faces on the inner and outer edges—a distinct advantage over rules with graduations on only one edge. A good rule will also have joints so constructed that the "stretch" in this type of rule is virtually eliminated. When you select a folding rule, get one with a 6″ sliding extension built into one end. This type folding rule has square ends which, in conjunction with the sliding feature, makes possible measuring inside dimensions accurately, not possible with the ordinary folding rule.

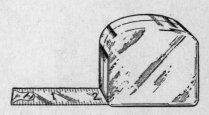

Fig. 117. Flexible steel pull-push rule.

There are also semi-flexible steel pull-push rules which slide back into their cases, one such is designed for outside, and inside measurements by adding 2″ (dimension of case) to the reading on the rule (Fig. 117). The latter rule is invaluable for measuring the circumference of round objects, for total angular measurements, and straight measuring. These rules come in 6, 8 and 10-foot lengths and their blades are replaceable.

MARKING GAUGE

The Marking Gauge is used to easily mark a parallel line for cutting, either across a board or for ripping the length of a board. It is particularly useful for marking long pieces. There are two types of marking gauges: one with a single beam containing a scriber point, and the other with two beams, each with a point, useful for marking a mortise. However, the conventional single-beam gauge is adequate for all marking purposes (Fig. 118). Made of hardwood, the gauge

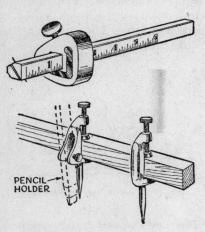

PENCIL
HOLDER

Fig. 118. Marking gauges.

consists of a beam, usually graduated in 1/16″, with a sharpened point at one end, and a sliding head which is locked by a thumbscrew.

To use, adjust the head the distance from the point that corresponds to the distance from the edge of the board you intend to cut. It is better practice not to use the inch scale as any variation in point sharpening will result in scale inaccuracy. A chisel edge to the point will produce a knifelike marking line with less tendency to gouge the wood or follow the grain. Grasp the head with the fingers your hand, thumb braced against t beam. Tilt the gauge slightly forward and with pressure applied downward and against the edge of the board push the gauge forward. If you decide to pull the gauge toward you tilt it slightly toward you, the ide being to cause the point to cut rath than scrape.

DOWELING JIG AND CENTERS

Accurately establishing the center of dowels in matching pieces of wood is not difficult but requires consider

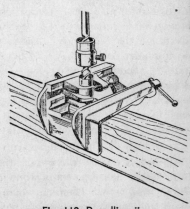

Fig. 119. Dowelling jig.

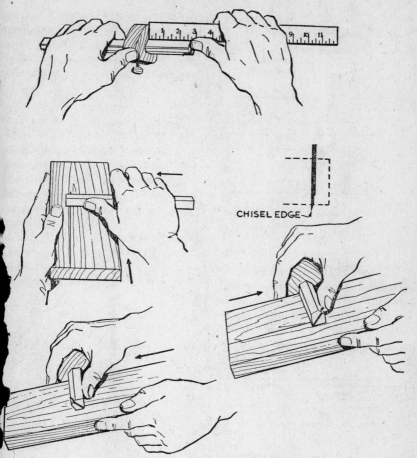

CHISEL EDGE

Fig. 120. Proper way to use a marking gauge.

le care. Centers can be established
ithout the aid of a doweling jig, but
e jig makes doweling error-proof.
nce set, it will match the holes for
owels in edges or ends of wood to be
ined. It is also an aid when boring
les for mortises. The jig comes with
bit guides of various diameters, in-
ring straight boring, and is adjust-
le for centering holes in thick stock.
depth gauge is also included.

Dowel Centers are short metal
dowels of varying diameters with
shoulders, with a point at their ends.
They are also intended to accurately
locate dowel holes. In practice, bore a
dowel hole in one piece of wood, insert the dowel center in this hole, and
butt the other piece of wood to be
doweled against the dowel center.
The point marks the center for the
matching hole.

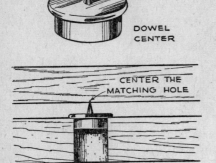

DOWEL
CENTER

CENTER THE
MATCHING HOLE

DOWEL
HOLE

Fig. 121. Dowel center.

CARPENTER'S LEVEL

In home repair and construction, "verticals" and "horizontals" must be true. The tool to determine this requirement is called a Level, consisting of a length of seasoned wood into

Fig. 122. Carpenter's level.

which is built one or more curved glass tubes containing liquid which forms a bubble. When this bubble is centered on the glass tube, the piece being tested is "level" horizontally, or "plumb" vertically, depending on the position of the level. As this, by its very nature, is a precision tool, a good one is imperative. There are many

types and lengths of levels for various purposes, but for general woodworking around the home, the 24" wood level with a glass for horizontal leveling, and a glass for vertical plumbing is adequate.

PLUMB BOB AND LINE

The plumb bob and line is a device for specialized techniques in determining corners of structures about be erected and other pre-structural projects. For average home use it

VERTICAL LINE

Fig. 123. Plumb bob and line.

not essential. It is a metal weight with a pointed end, the opposite end having a length of cord attached to it. When suspended and at rest, free from contact with anything, the line mathematically vertical, or plumb.

CHAPTER 2

USE OF FASTENERS

NAILS

Whoever first thought of the nail as a fastener of wood was a genius, because his idea has stood the test of more than 3,000 years! Mention in the Bible of David's use of nails is probably the first official recording of man's recourse to this ingenious metal device. Today there are more than 1,000 varieties and sizes of nails, both old and new forms developed for specific purposes. There are even certain types of lath nails that are sterilized by considerate manufacturers so that you can hold a mouthful while lathing without running the risk of infection. (Using the mouth as a receptacle for nails is not recommended, since the stomach has not as yet learned to digest nails.)

Nail sizes are designated in terms of "Penny" (d), a term which originated in England way back, and its original meaning is debated — some holding that it meant so many English pennies per 100 nails; others maintaining it signified 1,000 nails weighed 10 pounds—"pun"—"penny"; and still others, that the English measure of 1,000 nails to the "pennyweight" is the answer. Incidentally, the hand-forged nail of antiquity, now machine cut, still holds better than the "wire" nail because its tapered, four-corner shanks tend to cut rather

than spread wood as does the smooth, round wire nail.

Kinds of Nails

Nails are made of round steel, stainless steel, aluminum, copper and brass wire, also steel cut having four corners. Fig. 1 gives you some idea of the variety of head, shank and point design of the modern nail. But unless you have a particular project (roofing, lathing, etc.) requiring a particular nail, you need not be too upset by the bewildering variety. Four types will about take care of most woodworking problems around the home: Common, Box, Finishing and Casing. A mention, however, of the qualities of special-type nails is in order.

A nail, whatever its type, should be at least 3 times longer than the thickness of the wood into which it is driven. A "regular" diamond point (the most common form of four-cornered point on nails) works fine in all but hard wood—which it is liable to split unless a lead hole of slightly smaller diameter than the nail is bored. A blunt diamond point is best for hardwood, such as flooring—or a steel-cut flooring nail. The long diamond point is a "speed" nail to drive. Smooth, round tapered points are best for nailing fabrics, the points spreading rather than cutting the fibers.

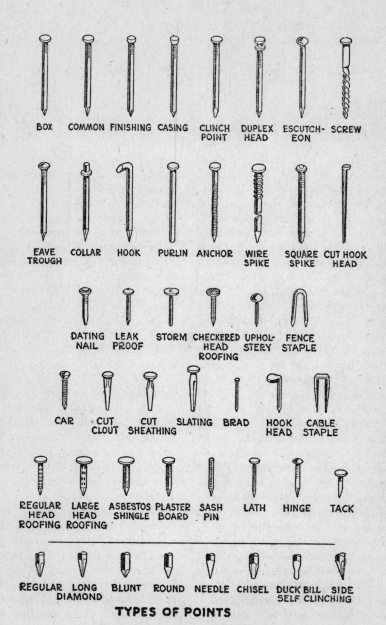

TYPES OF POINTS

Fig. 1. Various types of nails and types of points.

Chisel points are usually found on "spikes" for hardwood. Length of wire spikes start at 10d and run to 12″, their thickness being greater than wire nails of comparative lengths. They are used for heavy timbers, girders and the like. The following chart shows sizes and approximate number of nails per pound of the most commonly used nails.

WIRE NAILS AND SPIKES

	Bright Common			Finishing		Casing Box		Spikes	
Size	Gauge	Length Inches	No. per lb.	Ga.	No. per lb.	Ga.	No. per lb.	Ga.	No. per lb.
2d	15	1	876	16½	1351	15½	1010		
3d	14	1¼	568	15½	807	14½	635		
4d	12½	1½	316	15	584	14	473		
5d	12½	1¾	271	15	500	14	406		
6d	11½	2	174	13	309	12½	236		
7d	11½	2¼	161	13	238	12½	210		
8d	10¼	2½	106	12½	189	11½	108		
10d	9	3	69	11½	121	10½	94	6	41
12d	9	3¼	63	11½	113	10½	87	6	38
16d	8	3½	49	11	90	10	71	5	30
20d	6	4	31	10	62	9	52	4	23
30d	5	4½	24			9	46	3	17
40d	4	5	18			8	35	2	13
50d	3	5½	14					1	10
60d	2	6	11					1	9
		7						5⁄16 ″	7
		8						3⁄8 ″	4
		9						3⁄8 ″	3½
		10						3⁄8 ″	3
		12						3⁄8 ″	2½

Common flat-head nails of larger sizes are used chiefly on home-construction framing, although they are being replaced these days by box nails which are slightly thinner and can be driven in easier. Finishing nails are used when the nail head is to be set and covered. Casing nails are frequently used for "blind nailing" of flooring, their tapered heads fitting snugly into the base of the tongue of the board — a good "squeak" preventer. There is an expanding, self-clinching nail designed for use where asbestos or shingle siding is applied over fiber-board outdoor sheathing, doing away with the necessity of first nailing furring strips (wood nailing strips) on the sheathing—ordinary nails will not hold in fiber-board sheathing alone.

Corrugated Nail

The Corrugated Fastener is a form of nail, being a piece of corrugated steel in widths of ¼″, ⅜″, ½″ and ⅝″, one end chisel-edge pointed. It is driven between two joints, straddling them. It holds joints together well enough but allows some lateral mo-

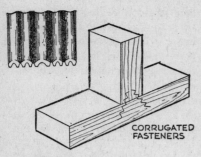

Fig. 2. Corrugated fasteners.

tion. It is used chiefly for repairing furniture when the parts cannot be readily taken apart to reglue, and for reinforcing weakened joints. It is not the best method of securing joints.

Clamp Nail

The Clamp Nail is a miter-joint nail requiring two saw kerfs 5/16″ deep on the face of each joint. The nail is driven wide end first into the kerf of the assembled joints, eliminating the need for glue or toe nailing. The nail comes ⅝″ wide and ½″, ¾″, 1″, 1¼″, 1½″ and 2″ long. The clamp nail is used more in production work than for an occasional miter joint which is still made in one of a number of orthodox methods. If you plan to use this nail, it is better practice to use two shorter ones, one from each side, instead of one long nail.

Copper, brass, aluminum, stainless steel, zinc-coated and cement-coated nails are used mostly outdoors where weather would rust the common steel nail, and cause rust stains to mar surfaces. Aluminum and stainless-steel nails are becoming more and more popular for exposed-to-weather nails.

They're made in sizes from 2d to 16d, but are not stocked at all hardware stores. For methods of nailing, refer to chapter 1.

SCREWS

The wood screw is a decided improvement over the nail as it will draw pieces of wood tightly together and, properly driven, will not loosen its grip. It also has the advantage of being removable when necessary without damage to the wood. For solid, permanent framing of wood members or other materials to wood such as cabinets, furniture, book shelves and the like, the screw should be used in preference to the nail. The added time required to prepare wood surfaces for screwing, in many instances, repays in quality results.

Fig. 3. Four types of screws.

Wood screws are made of steel bright finished; zinc, cadmium and chrome plated; blued steel; stainless steel; aluminum; and brass. These come slotted in Flat Head, Oval Head and Round Head design. There is also the Phillips screw, partially cross-slotted and recessed, with the same types of heads, requiring a special screwdriver. The flat head is measured from head-edge to point; oval head from bevel-edge to point; round head from shoulder to point.

Good practice, when driving screws, demands that you bore a hole

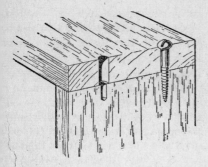

Fig. 4. Bore holes for screw body.

splitting. In hardwood, a screw can easily be twisted off attempting to drive it without lead holes. Remember it is the thread of a screw which holds, not the unthreaded portion.

Flat head and oval-head screws are either countersunk flush with the surface, below the surface, or the body hole is counterbored for the screw head to seat considerably below the surface (Fig. 5). Counterboring means boring a hole larger than the diameter of the screw head, just large enough to permit the widest part of the screwdriver blade to turn. This is done so that the screw slides into the wood for a given distance. Counterboring is usually done when a thick piece of wood is framed to another piece and, for practical purposes, the screw is only as long as or of shorter length than the thick piece.

the diameter of the body of the screw through the wood to be held by the screw, and a smaller lead hole in the piece anchoring the screw (Fig. 4). The smaller hole should have a diameter less than that of the threads, and a depth ½ to ⅝ the length of the threads anchored. The diameter of this hole depends on the wood. Hardwoods like maple and oak require a larger hole than softwoods, but no exact information is possible as the textures of woods differ. In end grain the hole should be smaller than in straight grain. The idea of boring holes for screws is accuracy of placement, ease of driving, and to prevent

Fig. 6. Counterbore before drilling.

If you intend counterboring with an auger bit, first bore the larger hole and then the body hole, otherwise the bit feed-screw has nothing to take hold of (Fig. 6). Where counterboring must be done on a surface which shows, good practice is to fit a wood plug, of the kind bored, and of shallow depth, glued in the hole flush with the surface. To do this, the

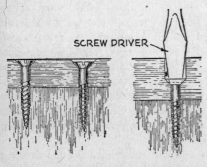

SCREW DRIVER

Fig. 5. Various levels of counterboring.

plug should extend *slightly* beyond the surface. When the glue has thoroughly dried, chisel off the projection flush. Round-head screws are not countersunk, but often counterbored. They are used when fastening metal, too thin to receive a flat head flush, to wood; also as pivots for wood to wood, or metal to wood.

When flat-head screws are to be hidden, they are countersunk slightly deeper than flush (Fig. 5), just enough for the covering material to take hold. Plastic wood is the usual covering for screw heads in wood and, as it is mostly an adhesive, it holds well. It shrinks, however, requiring the building of a slight mound above the wood surface which, when dry, is sanded flush. Water-mix wood putty is an excellent filler for countersunk screws and set nails, and wherever a depression or damaged corner needs filling. It comes in dry-powder form to which you mix enough water to make a stiff paste of the quantity you intend to use. Dampen the wood first, then apply the putty with a spatula or putty knife and let it dry about 15 to 20 minutes. It can then be sanded smooth, filed or carved, and has a finer texture than plastic wood. It will readily take any finish—stain, varnish or paint. Most paint stores carry it. Use the chart to guide you in selecting the right screw size for your particular project. The body diameters given are drill sizes which approximate the diameter of the screw for a loose fit.

SCREW SIZES AND APPROX. BODY DIAMETERS (FOR BORING)
Flat Head, Oval Head, Round Head

Nominal Size	0	1	2	3	4	5	6	7	8	9	10	12	14	16	18	20	24
Approx. Dia. Inches	1/16	5/64	3/32	3/32	7/64	1/8	9/64	5/32	11/64	11/64	3/16	7/32	15/64	9/32	19/64	21/64	3/8
Length in Inches																	
1/4	X	X	X	X	X												
3/8	X	X	X	X	X	X	X	X	X	X							
1/2			X	X	X	X	X	X	X	X	X	X					
5/8		X	X	X	X	X	X	X	X	X	X	X	X				
3/4			X	X	X	X	X	X	X	X	X	X	X	X			
7/8				X	X	X	X	X	X	X	X	X	X	X			
1				X	X	X	X	X	X	X	X	X	X	X	X	X	
1 1/4					X	X	X	X	X	X	X	X	X	X	X	X	X
1 1/2					X	X	X	X	X	X	X	X	X	X	X	X	X
1 3/4						X	X	X	X	X	X	X	X	X	X	X	X
2						X	X	X	X	X	X	X	X	X	X	X	X
2 1/4						X	X	X	X	X	X	X	X	X	X	X	X
2 1/2						X	X	X	X	X	X	X	X	X	X	X	X
2 3/4							X	X	X	X	X	X	X	X	X	X	X
3							X	X	X	X	X	X	X	X	X	X	X
3 1/2									X	X	X	X	X	X	X	X	X
4									X	X	X	X	X	X	X	X	X
4 1/2													X	X	X	X	X
5														X	X	X	X
6													X	X	X	X	X

Lag Screws

Lag Screws are much heavier and longer than slot-head wood screws and have coarser threads with bolt heads, either square or hexagon shaped. The square-head lag screw is most common and has a gimlet point. These screws are used to fasten timbers when spikes are not strong enough and ordinary screws would too short and light for the job.

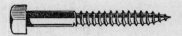

Fig. 7. Lag screw.

They are mostly used to frame timbers to existing masonry. Having a bolt head, a wrench is necessary to drive them. The accompanying chart gives the sizes of the most commonly used lag screws:

LAG SCREW SIZES

Diameter Inches	¼	⅜	½	⅝	¾	Thread Length Inches
Length Inches						
1½	X	X				1½
2	X	X				1½
2½	X	X				2
3	X	X	X	X		2¼
3½	X	X	X	X		2½
4	X	X	X	X	X	3
4½	X		X	X	X	3½
5	X	X	X	X	X	4
5½		X	X	X	X	4
6		X	X	X	X	4½
7		X	X	X	X	5
8		X	X	X	X	6

Also 9″, 10″, 12″ long and ⅞″ and 1″ diameter

Expansion Anchors

Expansion Anchors are used in combination with lag screws and bolts, when the screw or bolt is to hold in existing masonry, such as, stone, brick, cement or concrete. The expansion anchor is a thick metal shell with outer gripping ridges and inner threads which, when driven into a pre-bored hole, expands as the screw is driven into the anchor, causing the shell to wedge tightly against the masonry. Anchors come in sizes to fit the diameter of the screw or bolt.

A Star Drill is used to drill the hole to receive the anchor. This drill is

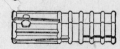

Fig. 8. Expansion anchor.

more like a special cold chisel than a drill, having a blunt point made of two crossed chisel edges, wider at the

Fig. 9. Star drill.

point and tapering to the diameter of the shank. The shank is long and usually octagonal in section. The drill is made of hardened steel and, like the cold chisel, is driven with a hammer. After each hammer blow, the drill is rotated. Here are the drill sizes for the outside diameters of expansion anchors: ¼″ dia. screw—½″; ⅜″ dia. screw—⅝″; ½″ dia. screw—¾″.

BOLTS

Bolts are basically of three types: Machine Bolts; Stove Bolts; Carriage Bolts, each with a distinct characteristic. All are tightened with nuts, either square or hexagonal.

Machine Bolts are precision ground, having cut threads, square or hexagonal heads. Threads usually run only part way. This bolt is used chiefly for fastening metal to metal where close tolerances are required.

Stove bolts are less precise and have either flat or round, slotted heads, with threads the length of the bolt. They are used for metal to metal, metal to wood, and wood to wood.

Carriage Bolts have round, domed, slotless heads with square shanks of shallow depth. The threads run only

part way, from 2 to 4 times the thickness of the bolt, depending on its length. This bolt is used chiefly for wood to wood, the square shank preventing the bolt from turning as it's tightened. It can also be used for metal to wood, the head on the wood side. When boring holes for carriage bolts, bore for a tight fit of the body of the bolt, and counterbore to depth for the bolt head to fit flush with or below the surface. Then drive the bolt with a hammer. With this method the square shank fits tight, having corners wider than the body of the bolt.

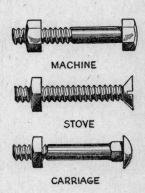

MACHINE

STOVE

CARRIAGE

Fig. 10. Three basic types of bolts.

Machine bolts have diameters from ¼″ to 3″, and can be had in any length desired. Stove-bolt diameters are from ⅛″ to ⅜″, and from ½″ to about 6″ long. Carriage bolts start at ¼″ diameter and go to 1″ diameter; from ¾″ to about 20″ long.

Toggle Bolts

Toggle Bolts have split wings in place of nuts. The wing is actuated

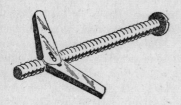

Fig. 11. Toggle bolt.

by a spring which, when pushed through material with open space behind it, opens the wings. The toggle bolt is used to attach material requiring a bolt in hollow walls, such as stud partitions, when it is impossible to use the usual bolt and nut. Three popular sizes are: ⅛" dia. x 3"; 3/16" dia. x 4"; ¼" dia. x 4". Holes for toggle bolts must be drilled of a diameter to pass the wings in folded position. Needless to say, if at some future time the bolt is removed, the wing is lost and another wing will be required.

GLUES

Glues play an important role in woodworking where permanency is essential, and many projects would be impossible to achieve were it not for glue of some kind. Modern chemistry has made tremendous strides in developing synthetic glues far superior to the old fish, animal and vegetable glues. And the double-boiler "glue pot," a necessary adjunct to every woodworking bench not so long ago, is now gradually disappearing and fast becoming but a memory of precise techniques of melting, and warming surfaces to be glued. While fish and hide glues are extremely

strong, they have the disadvantage of being highly moisture absorbent, react unfavorably to temperature changes, and fungi, and require special preparation of material, and speed for good glued joints.

Synthetic Glues

There are many synthetic glues on the market for every type of gluing job, but for practical purposes they can be divided into six classes: Resorcinol Resin Glue; Powdered Urea Resin Glue; Powdered Casein Glue; Rubber - base Glue; Thermoplastic Cements; Cellulose Cements.

Resorcinol Resin Glue is perhaps the most amazing of all the modern synthetic glues. It comes in two units: one a dark wine-colored, syrupy liquid, and the other a light-colored powder which is the catalyst, that is, the chemical agent which, when added to the liquid in a quantity needed at the moment, transforms it into probably the strongest glue yet devised for wood. Once set—and the higher the temperature the quicker it will set—nothing affects its adhesive power. It is absolutely waterproof, not affected by temperature changes or fungi, and can be used on *loose* or tight joints. It has but one disadvantage when applied to light-colored woods—it stains. However, if the excess is *immediately* wiped off with *cold* water, staining can be avoided to a large extent. If you want a wood joint to outlast the wood itself (boats have been built with it without any other fastening device!), use resorcinol resin glue. The directions on the containers are very easy to follow.

Urea Resin Glue comes in powdered form to which cold water is added for whatever quantity is needed for the immediate job. It is highly water *resistant* and stain free, but requires tight clamping of a *close-fitting* wood joint. It is an extremely strong glue for veneering, making inlaid pictures and all-round woodworking.

Casein Glue also comes in powder form and is mixed with cold water. This glue will join loose or tight-fitting joints of wood — also *oily woods* — is stain free but not highly water resistant. It is very strong and popular around home workshops.

Rubber-base Glue comes in a creamy paste and will glue metal to wood; metal to metal; glass to metal; glass to wood; cloth to cloth; cloth to wood; end-grain wood to wood. It will hold practically anything, but is not as strong on wood to wood as other glues formulated for wood.

transparent joint. It will separate when considerable heat is applied.

Cellulose Cement is a clear, syrupy adhesive which dries very quickly — too quickly for large areas. It makes a strong joint and will adhere to almost anything. It is usually sold in tube form and is excellent for household mending jobs, toys, and model projects.

CLAMPS

All glued joints whatever the glue should be and, with some glues, must be clamped until the glue has dried. A variety of clamps exist for this and other purposes, designed to do a particular job best. Clamps are known as C-Clamps; Hand Screws; Bar Clamps — all actuated by a threaded screw or screws capable of tremendous pressure. Whatever type clamp you use on a glued joint, use only enough pressure to hold the joint *tightly,* and no more.

Fig. 12. C-clamp.

Thermoplastic Cement (*polyvinyl*) is a clear, syrupy liquid with strong adhesive powers. It is fine for veneer work, furniture repair, toys and odd jobs around the house, and makes a

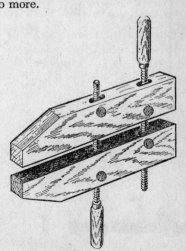

Fig. 13. Hand screw clamp.

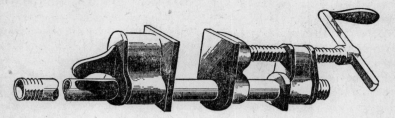

Fig. 14. Bar clamp.

C-Clamps are made of metal and come in many sizes. They are limited in thickness of material they will clamp, but are used oftener than other types.

Hand Screws are perhaps the oldest form of gluing clamp, having been in use since wood has been used for furniture. The hand screw has hardwood jaws actuated by two screws from opposite directions, and is fully adjustable for any type of gluing job within the limits of the length of the screws; the jaws can be offset, tapered, or set parallel.

The Bar Clamp consists of two metal jaws, one of which has a screw or is actuated by a screw, while the other jaw is fixed at the end of the bar. It is used to hold glued joints of wide dimensions, such as a table top made up of individual boards, etc.

The most popular clamp of this type has for its bar a ¾″ threaded, standard pipe which you buy separately — as short or long as you please. This assembly costs about half the price of the bar type which comes as a unit and is limited to length— about 3 to 6 feet. There is, however, a short-bar clamp which is inexpensive and will clamp up to 6″ material. This clamps weighs less than a C-clamp of the same capacity, and is quicker acting, having tooth edges on the bar for fast adjustment of one jaw. A few C-clamps and short bar clamps should be part of the equipment of every home workshop, the longer variety of bar clamp being

BRAIDED
CLOTHESLINE

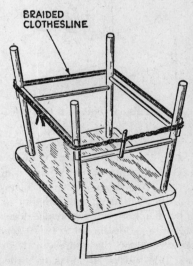

Fig. 16. Clothesline used as clamp.

Fig. 15. Short bar clamp.

necessary only if you plan to do wide jobs of gluing.

When a problem of this sort arises and you do not have a long bar clamp, you can rig a substitute by using light, braided clothesline over protecting blocks of wood, and tightening the line by twisting it with a short piece of dowel, anchoring the dowel so it cannot untwist. This method of clamping is necessary at times even though you have long bar clamps: when gluing material not possible to hold any other way, such as, chair assemblies, oval, circular and polygonal-shaped assemblies. You can also hold glued joints together, lacking the necessary clamps, by using a combination of wood wedges on the workbench (Fig. 17).

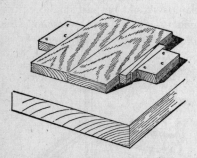

Fig. 17. Wooden wedges used as a clamp.

With all metal-jaw clamps, always protect the wood surfaces with thin pieces of scrap wood. When using clamps, remember that one clamp *may* be all that is required; but oftener than not two or more are necessary — the idea being to exert *even* pressure along the entire glued surface. This can often be accomplished with three clamps over a *straight* strip

of wood placed, if possible, edgewise. If you are using hand screws on parallel surfaces, see that the jaws are also

Fig. 18. Even pressure is desirable.

parallel, otherwise they act as essentric wedges when tightened, causing the joints to shift out of alignment.

MISCELLANEOUS FASTENERS

There are all sorts of metal fasteners used to frame and strengthen two or more pieces of wood; or to hold temporarily one piece against another, such as catches of various kinds; or to articulate wood, like a wide variety of hinges made for every conceivable purpose.

Permanent strengthening fasteners are basically of five kinds: Flat Corner Plates; Mending Plates; T-Plates; Inside Corner Irons; Steel Brackets. All but the steel brackets are recessed flush with the surface (for a workmanlike job), or attached to the surface with screws. All have predrilled,

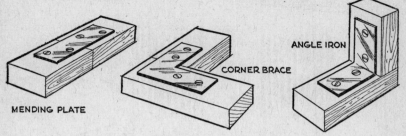

Fig. 19. Three types of braces.

countersunk holes for flat-head wood screws to seat flush.

Flat Corner Plates or Corner Braces are L-shaped for butt, lapped or mitered corners, and are made in a variety of leg lengths, thicknesses and widths proportionate to their size.

Mending Plates are flat, straight pieces of various lengths for strengthening running butt or lapped joints.

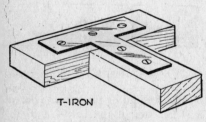

T-IRON

Fig. 20. T-Plate.

T-Plates are flat, T-shaped plates of various leg lengths for strengthening T-shaped joints.

Inside Corner Irons are narrow-width angle irons of various leg lengths used to reinforce pieces of wood at right angles to each other, on the inside faces, such as, cabinets, shelves, et cetera. Quite frequently wood joints and corners, although well glued and screwed, are not strong enough and require these additional methods of reinforcing — at-

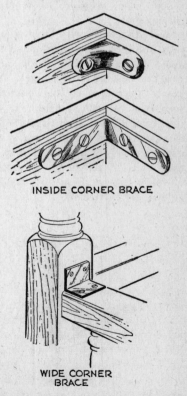

INSIDE CORNER BRACE

WIDE CORNER BRACE

Fig. 21. Other types of angle irons.

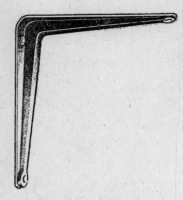

Fig. 22. Steel bracket.

tached, when possible, where they will not show.

Steel Brackets with reinforcing webs are used to support shelving under unusually heavy loads, and come in a number of leg lengths. The pressed steel bracket has no crosspiece to hamper stored materials.

Adjustable Steel Shelf Brackets for bookshelves and the like, are short brackets which fit in sockets in steel straps running the height of bookshelves or cabinet. Four brackets are required for each shelf.

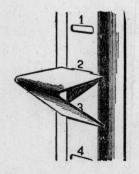

Fig. 23. Adjustable steel shelf bracket.

CATCHES

Catches are basically of six types: Hook-and-Eye; Sliding Bolt; Bayonet-type Friction; Friction; Snap; Bullet. The Hook-and-Eye and Sliding Bolt can be used for any door

Fig. 24. Hook-and-eye catch.

from cabinet to barn, depending on its size. Friction-type Catches are used to hold cabinet doors by friction alone, requiring only a pull on the door to open it. The Bullet Catch is a friction type which is used chiefly on furniture doors, being practically in-

Fig. 25. Sliding bolt catch.

visible. It requires a hole being bored, the diameter of the barrel, into the jamb of the door. The "bullet," actuated by a coil spring, projects slightly beyond the jamb and engages a "strike" recessed in the edge of the door.

Bayonet-type Friction Catches hold better than the bullet type and are quite frequently used on larger cabinet, light wardrobe, and kitchen-cabinet doors. Other types of friction catches are used for the same purpose (Fig. 26).

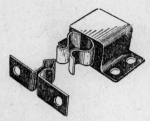

Fig. 26. Bayonet-type friction catch.

Snap Catches are usually used to hold one door of a two-door cabinet, requiring finger pressure to release it. The other door is usually secured by a Cupboard Turn which snaps shut when closed, but requires finger turning to open it (Fig. 28).

Fig. 27. Snap catch.

There are also hidden types of catches which are quite involved in their construction. They operate by pressing, or sharply striking the door at their location, causing the catch to release. These "secret" catches operate only for those in the "know," the door having no visible means of

Fig. 28. Cupboard turn.

being secured. One disadvantage to these trick catches is that if they should decide not to work, you open the door with a wrecking tool!

HINGES

There are all kinds of hinges made for all purposes, but basically they fall into three types, whatever their form: Strap Hinge; Butt Hinge; Knife Hinge. Originally hinges were of the strap variety only, masterpieces of

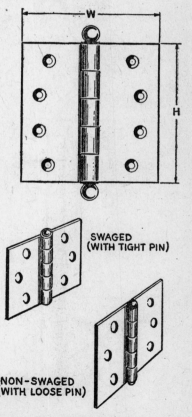

SWAGED (WITH TIGHT PIN)

NON-SWAGED (WITH LOOSE PIN)

Fig. 29. Butt hinge.

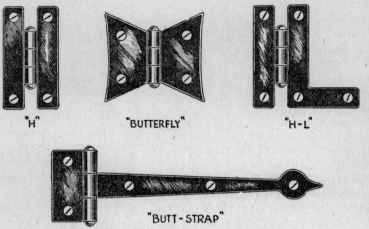

"H"   "BUTTERFLY"   "H-L"

"BUTT-STRAP"

Fig. 30. Four ornamental strap hinges.

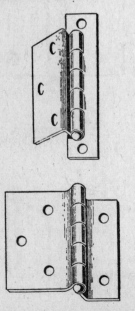

Fig. 31. Two types of cabinet hinges.

the blacksmith's art. They were forged into intricately designed scrolls, serving the purpose of swing- ing the door while being beautifull? ornamental and reinforcing the wood Cathedral and palace doors of Europ? are beautiful examples of the medi? eval strap hinge at its finest. Toda? ornamental hinges are rarely used ex? cept when simulating period furnitur? and architectural styles. Among th? period strap hinges most frequentl? used, are the 18th century America? "H," "Butterfly," "H-L" and orna? mental "Butt-Strap" (Fig. 30).

The Butt Hinge is probably use? oftener than any other type, all th? way from large doors between room? to small cabinet doors. There are tw? types of butt hinge: swaged and non? swaged, with pins loose, tight, an? half-tight. The swaged hinge permit? the leaves to almost touch whe? closed, while the non-swaged typ? produces a space between the leave? the diameter of the knuckles. Loos? and half-tight pins permit the doo? to be removed without removing th?

hinge — not possible with the tight pin. Cabinet and smaller doors are usually swung on tight-pin hinges, as they are seldom if ever removed. Narrow cabinet butt hinges are made to fit the lesser thicknesses of cabinet doors.

A butt-hinge width is measured with the leaves open, including the knuckle; its length is the length of the leaves. There are a number of ways to attach a butt hinge: recessed flush; recessed half the thickness of the leaves deeper than flush; attached without recessing, or only one leaf recessed. A hinge leaf that shows

should be recessed flush for a neat appearance, unless it's ornamental in design. Recessing half the thickness of the leaves deeper than flush is done where a hinged edge must fit tightly and squarely against the other piece to support it, like a folding table leg on a wall drop-leaf table when down.

Fig. 33. Continuous or piano hinge.

This can also be accomplished by recessing one leaf twice the thickness and the other leaf recessed flush.

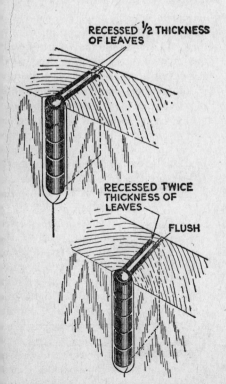

RECESSED ½ THICKNESS OF LEAVES

RECESSED TWICE THICKNESS OF LEAVES

FLUSH

Fig. 32. Methods of installing butt hinges.

CONCEALED

Fig. 34. Invisible cabinet hinge.

With either method, notches the length of the knuckle and clearing it in depth must be cut in the hinged pieces.

Cabinet hinges are also made in semi-concealed design for overlapping and flush doors, and full-surface types for flush and overlapping doors. These hinges have leaves of unequal width, one of which is offset. There are also Table Hinges with unequal-width leaves, and Chest Hinges with one leaf offset.

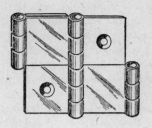

Fig. 36. Double-acting butt hinge.

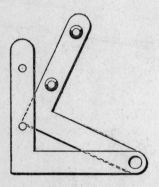

Fig. 35. Knife cabinet hinge.

When a door must fit with no possibility of sagging, there is the continuous or piano hinge which comes in long lengths and sizes for anything from a cigarette case to a ten-foot door. This type can be cut to exact lengths (Fig. 33).

Then there's the Invisible Cabinet Hinge which is of the knife type. This hinge must be recessed or mortised flush with the edge of the door and jamb, and operates by a series of flat metal, pivoted plates. Minimum thicknesses of doors for the several sizes are: 9/16″, ⅝″ and ¾″. There is also a Knife Cabinet Hinge used extensively on radio and TV cabinets, which is made of two flat metal strips

offset and pivoted, with a stop to prevent the doors from swinging back too far. Unlike other hinges, this one is recessed flush on the top and bottom edge of the door.

Screens for rooms are usually equipped with double-acting butt hinges which permit the screen sections to be swung right or left, or folded flat. And the kitchen swinging door has double-acting butt hinges with built-in springs to return it to normal position. A compara-

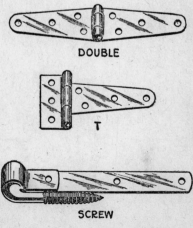

DOUBLE

T

SCREW

Fig. 37. Three types of strap hinges.

tively new, light butt hinge has appeared on the market which requires no mortising. One leaf is cut out in such a manner that the other leaf fits into it when the door is closed.

Strap Hinges are used mostly on frame buildings where doors are heavier. They are made in three types: Double Strap; T-Strap and Screw Strap. The Screw Strap has a long leaf looped at the end which fits over an L-shaped lag screw with a shoulder to support the strap.

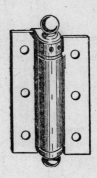

Fig. 38. Offset hinge.

CHAPTER 3

LUMBER

Wood as Nature produces it is a complex cellular structure with characteristics as varied as the kind of tree. These characteristics are not alike even in the same wood group, each tree being a decided individualist. Wood can, however, be classified into two groups: Soft and Hard, seasoned and unseasoned.

Lumber must be seasoned to be of any practical use in construction. This means it must be partially dried out to prevent excessive shrinkage, checking and splitting. There was a time when all lumber was seasoned naturally, requiring at least a year with each piece turned every few days. The result was a superior product with considerable elasticity not equalled by today's kiln-drying. Kiln-drying is an oven-heat process which cuts down the seasoning time to days instead of years, the result being satisfactory enough for all practical purposes, although it leaves the wood somewhat brittle, due to too fast drying. You cannot bend a piece of kiln-dried lumber the way you can bend a naturally seasoned piece.

Native Softwoods

Some of the most commonly used native softwoods are:

Basswood: Light, straight-grained and of fine texture. It is easy to work, suitable for both turning and carving, and is used mostly for picture frames, molding, furniture and toys.

Cedar: Light, fine textured with a beautiful grain. Works easily and takes a fine finish. It is used for mothproof chests and closets; toys; furniture; shingles; exterior trim; sheathing and siding.

Cypress: Easy to work and has a rich, reddish-brown color. It is highly weather resistant, and is used for interior and exterior trim; inside and outside flooring; shingles; sheathing and siding.

Fir: Stiff and strong and even textured. It has an orange-brown color and is used mostly for porch flooring; framing; roof boards; sub-flooring and sheathing.

Poplar: Light and very soft. It is easy to work but not too durable or subject to rough handling. Used for interior trim; shelving and laths.

Gum: Heavy and strong and fine textured. It is usually cross-grained and twists and warps easily when exposed to weather. It is used extensively for cheaper furniture and interior trim.

Redwood: Light and fairly strong and takes a fine finish. It is very durable and is used for cabinet work and exterior trim; porch flooring; shelving; shingles and siding.

White Pine: Very light and soft and varies greatly in quality. It is very easy to work and is used for cabinets; interior trim; paneling; laths; sash; shelving; siding and sheathing.

White Spruce: Light, stiff and fairly strong and can be used for the same purposes as White Pine.

Hardwoods

The most commonly used hardwoods are:

Maple: Heavy, strong and very hard. It has a fine texture, wavy grained. It is fine for carving, turning and scroll work. It takes a beautiful finish and is widely used for furniture; finished flooring; and occasionally shelving.

Oak: Very heavy, hard, strong and durable. It has a strong tendency to check (grain opening at board ends). It is used extensively for furniture; carving; exterior and interior trim; finished flooring; shelving; steps; and de luxe house framing.

Birch: Heavy, tough, close-grained and very durable. It is frequently stained to imitate black walnut and mahogany, and is used extensively for furniture. Other uses are interior trim and shelving.

Walnut: Hard, heavy and strong with a smooth grain which works well and takes a fine polish. It is used largely for fine furniture and cabinet work; also for interior trim and occasionally shelving.

Mahogany: Light to dark reddish-brown and fine-grained. It works easily with or against the grain, and takes one of the finest finishes. It is used for fine furniture and boats.

Yellow Pine: Varies considerably. It is light, medium hard with a smooth but pronounced grain. It works easily and is quite durable. It is used mostly for porch flooring; framing; interior trim; roof boards and sub-flooring.

The suggested uses for both soft and hardwoods mentioned are for first choice only, many of them being used as second and third choice for almost every project. Almost every species of wood grows in a number of varieties. For example Pine has a number of relatives: Northern White; Western White; Sugar; Ponderosa; Southern Yellow, each having its own characteristics. A fine softwood for all-round purposes in the home is Western White Pine in its several grades.

SAWING LOGS

Logs are sawed into lumber either by plain sawing or quarter sawing (Fig. 1), the latter method being used on some hardwoods, chiefly oak, producing a distinctive grain which identifies this type of sawing. It is superior to plain sawed, but quite expensive as it is a wasteful method resulting in relatively narrow widths. The log is first cut into quarters and then sawed into boards by different methods of arrangement. At one time it was extensively used for fine furniture and finished flooring.

Plain sawing produces lumber of two types of grain, depending on what portion of the annular rings (yearly growth rings) is sawed: Flat Grain and Edge Grain. There is also the Heartwood (center rings and best) and the Sapwood (outer rings).

QUARTER SAWING

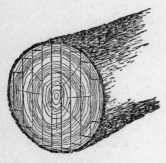

PLAIN SAWING

Fig. 1.

The best grade shingle, for instance, is edge-grain sawed—it having little or no warping tendencies. It also costs more since fewer pieces can be sawed out of a log. Flooring of hard and semi-hard woods comes in both flat grain and edge grain.

GRADES OF LUMBER

After the log has been sawed into planks it is graded for imperfections in the wood. The best grade is called by the "trade" Select which, in turn, is divided into four qualifications: A, B, C and D. "A-Select" is by no means flawless, but practically so, as no piece of lumber, however perfect, can be termed absolutely flawless. The four select grades are top-quality lumber, the C and D grades having only minor imperfections which paint usually covers.

Lumber is further graded from this point and is termed Common which is qualified by numbers: 1 to 5. Common Nos. 1 to 3 are used for rough carpentry, such as house framing which includes roof boarding and sheathing. Nos. 4 and 5 can also be used, but there is considerable waste in cutting out bad imperfections. These terms may be confusing at first, but when ordering lumber from a yard, the language of the lumber industry must be used if you wish to be understood.

Machining Lumber

Lumber as it comes from the mill saw is extremely rough and unusable for most woodworking projects. The mill, therefore, "machines" it—planes it smooth on one or two sides and edges. This planing is abbreviated to S1S; S2S; S1E; S2E; S4S. S1S means "Surfaced 1 Side;" S1E, "Surfaced 1 Edge;" S4S, "Surfaced 4 Sides." For lumber you plan to use around the home, get either A-Select S4S, or No. 1 Common S4S.

Lumber when sawed green is approximately in even inches, called Nominal Size. However, when kiln-dried and surfaced smooth, it is considerably less than the nominal dimensions. A nominal 2"x4" stud actually measures 1⅝"x3½" although it is called a 2x4, and so on—the size you pay for by the "Board Foot."

Board Foot

A Board Foot is a piece 1" or less thick, 12" wide, 12" long—a square foot. All lumber except moldings, splines and screening strips is sold by the foot (board foot—square foot) on the basis of it being 1" or less thick, nominal size. If no thickness is mentioned, it is assumed to be 1" or less. Therefore, a 1"x12"x12"; a 2"x6"x12"; a 3"x4"x12" are all 1 foot, board measure, or 1 square foot. Again, rather confusing, but necessary to understand when ordering from a lumber yard. One final example: a 2"x4" 12' length of studding would be sold as 8 *board feet:*

2" x 4"=8"=⅔ feet x 12 feet=8 feet

Moldings, screening strips and splines are sold by the linear foot. Softwood lumber is sold in lengths of 2-foot multiples (actual size). Hardwood usually comes in random lengths. You can usually save money by ordering "shorts" which most lumber yards have in short odd lengths. The following are other terms used in the lumber industry which will clarify the table of sizes:

Yard Lumber: Less than 6" thick.

Structural Timbers: 6" or more thick and wide.

Strips: Less than 2" thick and less than 8" wide.

Boards: Less than 2" thick, but 8" or more wide.

Dimension Lumber: 2" but less than 7" thick—any width.

Planks: 2" but less than 4" thick, 8" or more wide.

Scantlings: 4" but less than 6" thick, less than 8" wide.

Heavy Joists: 4" but less than 6" thick, 8" or more wide.

STANDARD SIZES OF YARD LUMBER
Thicknesses apply to all widths and widths to all thicknesses

Product	Nominal Thickness Inches	Nominal Width Inches	Actual Thickness Inches	Actual Width Inches
Finish	1 1¼ 1½ 1¾ 2 2½ 3	3 4 5 6 7 8 9 10 11 12	5/16 7/16 9/16 11/16 25/32 1 1/16 1 5/16 1 7/16 1 5/8 2 1/8 2 5/8	2 5/8 3½ 4½ 5½ 6½ 7¼ 8¼ 9¼ 10¼ 11¼
Common Boards and Strips	1 1¼ 1½	3 4 5 6 7 8 9 10 11 12	25/32 1 1/16 1 5/16	2 5/8 3 5/8 4 5/8 5 5/8 6 5/8 7½ 8½ 9½ 10½ 11½

STANDARD SIZES OF YARD LUMBER (Cont'd)
Thicknesses apply to all widths and widths to all thicknesses

Product	Nominal Thickness Inches	Nominal Width Inches	Actual Thickness Inches	Actual Width Inches
Dimension.	2	2	$1\frac{5}{8}$	$1\frac{5}{8}$
	$2\frac{1}{2}$	4	$2\frac{1}{8}$	$3\frac{5}{8}$
	3	6	$2\frac{5}{8}$	$5\frac{5}{8}$
	4	8	$3\frac{5}{8}$	$7\frac{1}{2}$
	5	10	$4\frac{5}{8}$	$9\frac{1}{2}$

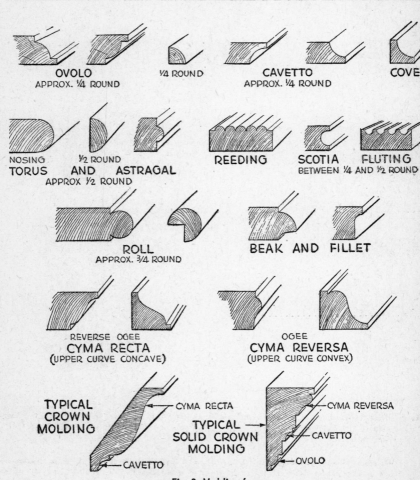

Fig. 2. Molding forms.

MACHINED LUMBER

Shiplap, Dressed and Matched (D & M—Tongued and Grooved)
Thicknesses apply to all widths and widths to all thicknesses, except as modified by footnote

Product	Nominal Thickness Inches	Nominal Width Inches	Actual Thickness Inches	Actual Face Width Inches
Bevel Siding...................		4 5 6	$\frac{7}{16}$ x $\frac{3}{16}$ $\frac{5}{8}$ x $\frac{3}{16}$	$3\frac{1}{2}$ $4\frac{1}{2}$ $5\frac{1}{2}$
Wide Bevel Siding.............		8 10 12	$\frac{7}{16}$ x $\frac{3}{16}$ $\frac{9}{16}$ x $\frac{3}{16}$ $\frac{11}{16}$ x $\frac{3}{16}$	$7\frac{1}{4}$ $9\frac{1}{4}$ $11\frac{1}{4}$
Rustic and Drop Siding.......... (Shiplapped)		4 5 6 8	$\frac{9}{16}$ $\frac{3}{4}$	$3\frac{1}{8}$ $4\frac{1}{8}$ $5\frac{1}{16}$ $6\frac{7}{8}$
Rustic and Drop Siding........ (D & M)		4 5 6 8	$\frac{9}{16}$ $\frac{3}{4}$	$3\frac{1}{4}$ $4\frac{1}{4}$ $5\frac{3}{16}$ 7
Flooring..................... (D & M)	1 $1\frac{1}{4}$ $1\frac{1}{2}$	2 3 4 5 6	$\frac{5}{16}$ $\frac{7}{16}$ $\frac{9}{16}$ $\frac{25}{32}$ $1\frac{1}{16}$ $1\frac{5}{16}$	$1\frac{1}{2}$ $2\frac{3}{8}$ $3\frac{1}{4}$ $4\frac{1}{4}$ $5\frac{3}{16}$
Ceiling..................... (D & M and Shiplapped)		3 4 5 6	$\frac{5}{16}$ $\frac{7}{16}$ $\frac{9}{16}$ $\frac{11}{16}$	$2\frac{3}{8}$ $3\frac{1}{4}$ $4\frac{1}{4}$ $5\frac{3}{16}$
Partition..................... (D & M and Shiplapped)		3 4 5 6	$\frac{3}{4}$	$2\frac{3}{8}$ $3\frac{1}{4}$ $4\frac{1}{4}$ $5\frac{3}{16}$
Dressed and Matched........... (Tongued and Grooved)	1 $1\frac{1}{4}$ $1\frac{1}{2}$	4 6 8 10 12	$\frac{25}{32}$ $1\frac{1}{16}$ $1\frac{5}{16}$	$3\frac{1}{4}$ $5\frac{1}{4}$ $7\frac{1}{4}$ $9\frac{1}{4}$ $11\frac{1}{4}$

Note: In all Tongued and Grooved Flooring, and Tongued and Grooved and Shiplapped Ceiling, 5/16″, 7/16″ and 9/16″ thicknesses, the tongue or lap is 3/16″ wide, with face widths 3/16″ wider than listed.

All other machined material 11/16″, ¾″, 1″, and 1½″ thick, tongue is ¼″ wide in tongued and grooved lumber, and the lap is ⅜″ wide in shiplapped lumber, and ¼″ and ⅜″ wider respectively than face widths listed.

TABLE OF BOARD FEET
Actual Length in Feet

Nominal Size Inches	10	12	14	16	18	20	22	24
1 x 2	$1\frac{2}{3}$	2	$2\frac{1}{3}$	$2\frac{2}{3}$	3	$3\frac{1}{3}$	$3\frac{2}{3}$	4
1 x 3	$2\frac{1}{2}$	3	$3\frac{1}{2}$	4	$4\frac{1}{2}$	5	$5\frac{1}{2}$	6
1 x 4	$3\frac{1}{3}$	4	$4\frac{2}{3}$	$5\frac{1}{3}$	6	$6\frac{2}{3}$	$7\frac{1}{3}$	8
1 x 5	$4\frac{1}{6}$	5	$5\frac{5}{6}$	$6\frac{2}{3}$	$7\frac{1}{2}$	$8\frac{1}{3}$	$9\frac{1}{6}$	10
1 x 6	5	6	7	8	9	10	11	12
1 x 7	$5\frac{5}{6}$	7	$8\frac{1}{6}$	$9\frac{1}{3}$	$10\frac{1}{2}$	$11\frac{2}{3}$	$12\frac{5}{6}$	14
1 x 8	$6\frac{2}{3}$	8	$9\frac{1}{3}$	$10\frac{2}{3}$	12	$13\frac{1}{3}$	$14\frac{2}{3}$	16
1 x 10	$8\frac{1}{3}$	10	$11\frac{2}{3}$	$13\frac{1}{3}$	15	$16\frac{2}{3}$	$18\frac{1}{3}$	20
1 x 12	10	12	14	16	18	20	22	24
1¼ x 4	$4\frac{1}{6}$	5	$5\frac{5}{6}$	$6\frac{2}{3}$	$7\frac{1}{2}$	$8\frac{1}{3}$	$9\frac{1}{6}$	10
1¼ x 6	$6\frac{1}{4}$	$7\frac{1}{2}$	$8\frac{3}{4}$	10	$11\frac{1}{4}$	$12\frac{1}{2}$	$13\frac{3}{4}$	15
1¼ x 8	$8\frac{1}{3}$	10	$11\frac{2}{3}$	$13\frac{1}{3}$	15	$16\frac{2}{3}$	$18\frac{1}{3}$	20
1¼ x 10	$10\frac{5}{12}$	$12\frac{1}{2}$	$14\frac{7}{12}$	$16\frac{2}{3}$	$18\frac{3}{4}$	$20\frac{5}{6}$	$22\frac{11}{12}$	25
1¼ x 12	$12\frac{1}{2}$	15	$17\frac{1}{2}$	20	$22\frac{1}{2}$	25	$27\frac{1}{2}$	30
1½ x 4	5	6	7	8	9	10	11	12
1½ x 6	$7\frac{1}{2}$	9	$10\frac{1}{2}$	12	$13\frac{1}{2}$	15	$16\frac{1}{2}$	18
1½ x 8	10	12	14	16	18	20	22	24
1½ x 10	$12\frac{1}{2}$	15	$17\frac{1}{2}$	20	$22\frac{1}{2}$	25	$27\frac{1}{2}$	30
1½ x 12	15	18	21	24	27	30	33	36
2 x 4	$6\frac{2}{3}$	8	$9\frac{1}{3}$	$10\frac{2}{3}$	12	$13\frac{1}{3}$	$14\frac{2}{3}$	16
2 x 6	10	12	14	16	18	20	22	24
2 x 8	$13\frac{1}{3}$	16	$18\frac{2}{3}$	$21\frac{1}{3}$	24	$26\frac{2}{3}$	$29\frac{1}{3}$	32
2 x 10	$16\frac{2}{3}$	20	$23\frac{1}{3}$	$26\frac{2}{3}$	30	$33\frac{1}{3}$	$36\frac{2}{3}$	40
2 x 12	20	24	28	32	36	40	44	48
3 x 6	15	18	21	24	27	30	33	36
3 x 8	20	24	28	32	36	40	44	48
3 x 10	25	30	35	40	45	50	55	60
3 x 12	30	36	42	48	54	60	66	72
4 x 4	$13\frac{1}{3}$	16	$18\frac{2}{3}$	$21\frac{1}{3}$	24	$26\frac{2}{3}$	$29\frac{1}{3}$	32
4 x 6	20	24	28	32	36	40	44	48
4 x 8	$26\frac{2}{3}$	32	$37\frac{1}{3}$	$42\frac{2}{3}$	48	$53\frac{1}{3}$	$58\frac{2}{3}$	64
4 x 10	$33\frac{1}{3}$	40	$46\frac{2}{3}$	$53\frac{1}{3}$	60	$66\frac{2}{3}$	$73\frac{1}{3}$	80
4 x 12	40	48	56	64	72	80	88	96

MOLDINGS

Mouldings are used to soften and ornament square edges and right-angle joints, to hide joints and to add depth to flat faces. There are 8 basic traditional forms borrowed from Greek and Roman classic architecture; they are: Ovolo; Cavetto; Torus and Astragal; Scotia; Roll; Beak and Fillet; Cyma Recta; Cyma Reversa. These forms, used singly and com-bined, produce an endless variety of molding forms for architectural embellishment and picture frames. (See Fig. 2.)

Modern designers use molding sparingly and of simple form, or none at all. Eighteenth century American architecture produced some of the most beautiful and complex molding forms, inspired by Greek and Roman classic architectural profiles. The choice of molding depends on what

pe home you have, and what your
ersonal taste may be.

For architectural purposes, lumber
rds stock traditional and combined
aditional molding forms, both in
ftwoods and hardwoods. They are
ocked in many sizes and for every
nceivable purpose in an almost end-
ss variety from ¼″ quarter round to
″ crown molding. Space permits
ention of only three of the most
mmonly used forms: Quarter
ound, Half Round, and Cove. Lumber yards also stock Rounds which
are not moldings. They are used
when stock dowel-lengths (36″) are
not long enough, and for curtain and
clothes poles, usually made from
North Carolina Pine, and Redwood in
the softwoods; and Ash in hardwood.
Diameters run from ½″ to 2¾″, softwood; from ⅞″ to 1¾″, hardwood.
Moldings are fastened either with finishing nails, set and covered, or flat-
head wood screws, countersunk and
covered.

CHAPTER 4

PLYWOOD

Natural lumber is temperamental. It reacts unfavorably to temperature and moisture changes, and the wider and thinner the board the greater its tendency to twist and warp. Wide dimensioned lumber is also difficult to obtain and costly because a wide board must come from a large tree, and fewer pieces are obtainable from that tree. Moreover, the grain pattern of natural lumber is limited. Thus, although natural lumber is absolutely essential to every type of wood construction, it has inherent disadvantages in its thinner and wider sizes.

To overcome these disadvantages, plywood as we know it today was developed. The idea stems from the ancient practice of veneering a wood surface to achieve patterned grain effects — the early Egyptians have left us some beautiful examples of veneered cabinet work. Modern manufacturing techniques are a vast improvement over these early efforts, as we now build houses out of plywood.

Plywood is natural wood in thin sheets and strips glued with plastic resins under heat and tremendous pressure, in such a manner that the grain of each layer runs at right angles to that of the next layer. On a weight for weight basis, plywood is stronger than steel, its great strength due to its cross-grain construction which distributes strain in two dire[c]tions and eliminates splitting.

GRAIN EFFECTS

Beautiful and unusual grain effe[c] are possible with plywood because the methods used in cutting the t[o] veneer, which are basically of thr[ee] types: Rotary Cut; Flat Sliced a[nd] Quarter Sliced. There are also vari[a] tions in flat and quarter slicing.

Rotary Cut

Rotary Cut means peeling the l[og] on giant lathes, similar to peeling t[he] skin of a potato. This produces t[he] "wild grain" usually seen on fir p[ly] wood because the peeling proce[ss] follows the annual rings of the l[og] It has the advantage of producing [ex] ceptional widths.

Flat Sliced

Flat Slicing is done with the l[og] being first cut in half. Each half [is] then sliced by a razor-sharp blac[de]

Fig. I. Rotary cut.

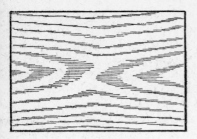

Fig. 2. Flat slicing.

similar to slicing a potato for potato chips. Flat-sliced veneer has a striped grain effect at the edges, changing to a larger, wild grain toward the center. Walnut is often cut in this manner.

Quarter Sliced

Quarter Slicing, an expensive method, is done similarly to flat slicing, but the log is quartered before slicing. This technique produces grain in straight stripes running the length of the veneer, due to cutting approximately at right angles to the annular rings. Quarter slicing is used for almost all of the finer imported and some domestic woods where a definite striped effect is wanted. Mahogany and Vertical-Grain Cedar are examples.

GRADES OF PLYWOOD

There are two veneer-types of plywood: Softwood and Hardwood, and basically two grades: Interior Grade and Exterior Grade. The Interior Grade is highly moisture resistant, but not waterproof, and should not be used where unusually damp conditions exist. Exterior Grade is bonded with phenolformaldehyde resin and is absolutely waterproof—and so is excellent for exterior use where exposed to the weather, and for boat building.

Softwood and hardwood veneer plywood is also graded as Sound 1 Side and Sound 2 Sides, with further qualifications omitted here because they are somewhat confusing to the average layman. As a rule, Sound 1 Side is fine for all practical purposes where only one face will show or is required to be flawless. In furniture making, however, where two surfaces are exposed to view, sound veneer of the same species is obviously required on both surfaces—and is proportionately higher in cost.

Striated Surface

In recent years special patented treatments of plywood surfaces have been developed, capable of being combined in numerous ways for decorative effects. One such surface is "striated," producing a parallel striping in relief, the length of the panel. Used vertically, horizontally, or combined with mitered or butt joints in squares and other forms, it is quite "modern" and attractive for both interior and exterior use. The striations are mechanically produced resulting

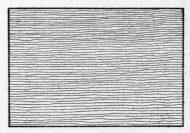

Fig. 3. Quarter slicing.

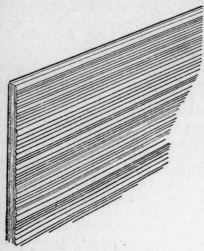

Fig. 4. A "striated" plywood surface.

in irregular-width beading which, in fir plywood — most often used — visually destroys the wild grain characteristic of rotary slicing. There have also been developed patented methods of applying board-width plywood to interior walls which require little or no skill to install.

Laminated and Lumber Cores

Hardwood veneer plywood in the ¾" thickness is obtainable in both laminated core and lumber core. The lumber core is usually fabricated from solid basswood or poplar in strips edge glued, resulting in edges which do not require facing and hold screws, dowels and splines very well. Facing plywood edges, laminated or lumber core, is a matter of personal taste—to disguise the fact that plywood has been used. These edges if well sanded, and filled with water-mix wood putty when necessary, are rather decorative. Lumber core is being gradually discarded due to scarcity of material. It will probably be supplanted eventually by a new, superior wood product of resin-bonded, compressed wood chips which is now obtainable in ⅜" and ¾" thicknesses for paneling, furniture, doors and other structural purposes. It has no grain, but the glass-smooth surface of light tan or redwood color is beautifully mottled, producing something new in furniture and paneling-surface patterns.

USES

Plywood is used extensively for furniture, interior cabinets, counters, paneling, shelving, sub-flooring and structural girders. For exterior work it is used for sheathing, roofing, finished wall treatments and outdoor furniture. In fact, many contemporary architectural designers specify that the entire home, excluding structural members, such as sills, studs, joists and rafters, be built of interior and exterior-grade plywood.

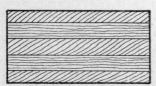

Fig. 5. 5-ply laminated core.

Fig. 6. 5-ply lumber core.

PLYWOOD SIZES AND VENEER SURFACES*
Thicknesses—Inches

Product	⅛	¼	5⁄16	⅜	½	⅝	¾	1³⁄16	Striated 5⁄16	Striated ⅜	Usual Panel Size 48″ x 96″
SOFTWOODS											
Douglas Fir		X I-E	X I	X I-E	X I-E	X I-E	X I E		X I	X E	X
California Pine		X I		X I	X I	X I	X I	X I			X
Idaho Knotty Pine		X I					X I				X
Sitka Spruce		X I		X I	X I	X I	X I	X I			X
Cedar		X I									X
HARDWOODS											
Maple		X I		X I			X I E				X
Oak	X I	X I		X I	X I		X I E				X
Walnut	X I	X I		X I	X I		X I E				X
Birch	X I	X I		X I	X I		X I-E				X
Southern Gum	X I	X I		X I	X I		X I		X I		X
American Elm		X I									X
Philippine Mahogany		X I		X I			X I		X I		X
African Mahogany	X I	X I		X I	X I		X I-E				X
Korina	X I	X I		X I			X I-E				X
Prima Vera	X I	X I					X I-E				X
Duali		X I		X I	X I		X I	X I			X

The woods listed in the accompanying table refer to the veneer face of the plywood. "I" means Interior Grades; "E," Exterior Grade. Hard and softwoods come in a variety of cuts and grain patterns; also in several kinds of wood in the same family group.

* Note: Panel sizes in some woods are also sold, but not stocked everywhere, in the following sizes (inches): 36 x 72, 84, 120, 144, 168, 192; 48 x 72, 84, 120, 144, 168, 192. Gum Striated also comes in squares (inches): 12 x 12, 16 x 16, 24 x 24, 48 x 48.

CHAPTER 5

WOOD JOINTS

There are many methods of joining two or more pieces of wood. Some of these are easy to make and others require considerable craftsmanship (Figs. 1 and 2). All joints, however, require care when laying them out. The marking gauge, try or combination square, T-bevel and a sharp knife for marking, are necessary for accurate layout.

The simplest method of joining two pieces of wood is the Plain Lap, (Fig. 2). You just lay one piece over the other and screw, nail or glue, or both. It is as strong as the fasteners used to attach it, and is one of the most-used framing methods in house construction.

The Butt Joint (Fig. 2) is another method used oftener than other types, particularly in house framing. As a joint for only two pieces of wood, it is the weakest of all, being simply one end-grain piece butted against the face of another. Since end grain, for joining purposes, is the weakest part of a piece of wood, the joint is no stronger than the characteristics of the end grain. Nails pull out easily in end grain, and few glues hold well because it soaks up the glue. Screws hold best if large and long enough. A combination of glue and screws makes the butt joint strong enough for most purposes where pulling strain is not excessive. In house fram-

ing, butt joints are mostly toenailed, strengthening the joint. For cabinet work, butt joints are usually reinforced with corner glue blocks, if they are hidden.

A Half-Lap Splice (Fig. 2) is used to lengthen two pieces of wood when the faces must be flush. It is a stronger joint than that made by laying one piece over the other, as the shoulders, if they fit properly, act as somewhat of a lock, preventing any pivoting tendency. The laps should be long enough to have adequate bearing surfaces.

An End Half Lap (Fig. 2) is used for window, screen door and other frames. It is a strong corner joint if properly fitted, preventing any pivoting or slipping tendencies. It does, however, expose end grain at both corners. A half-lap splice and an end half lap are easily made by gauging the work with a marking gauge and sawing out the laps, preferably with a back saw. Be sure to saw on the waste side of the line, otherwise the laps will be oversize by the thickness of the saw.

The Mitered Half Lap (Fig. 2) is used on corners to hide one end-grain face, and makes a neat 45-degree angle joint on the flat-face surface. It is used for frames of various kinds, excluding picture frames, but is not quite as strong as the half lap, lacking

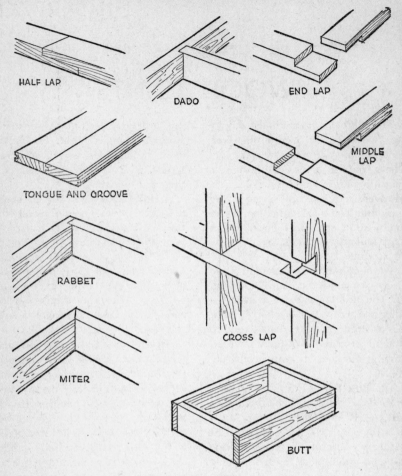

HALF LAP

DADO

END LAP

TONGUE AND GROOVE

MIDDLE LAP

RABBET

CROSS LAP

MITER

BUTT

Fig. I. Wood joints.

the same amount of joining surface. To make a miter half lap, gauge the work and first saw the miter on one piece to a depth of half the thickness. Then saw out the lap to the miter cut. The other piece can be made as a straight lap and then mitered — use your miter box.

Cross Half-Lap joints (Fig. 2) are used for joining two crossed pieces

with flush faces. Each piece i₅ notched or dadoed half its depth o₅ width. This joint adds strength to the pieces, locking them together. For the cross half lap, saw to a depth of half the thickness of the stock and remove the wood between the cuts with a chisel.

The Middle Half Lap (Fig. 2) i₅ used to join bracing members be-

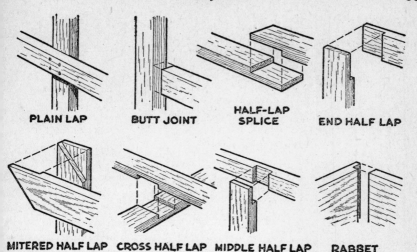

PLAIN LAP   **BUTT JOINT**   **HALF-LAP SPLICE**   **END HALF LAP**

MITERED HALF LAP   **CROSS HALF LAP**   **MIDDLE HALF LAP**   **RABBET**

Fig. 2. Wood joints.

ween frames, forming a strong T-joint. To make a middle half lap, saw ut the end lap and chisel out the iddle lap, as for a cross half lap.

A Rabbet (Fig. 2) means cutting ut one piece to receive flush the edge f the other. It is used a lot for rawers, cabinets and the like, con-ealing one end-grain edge, and pre-venting a twisting tendency of the joint. The backs of most cabinets are joined this way, the end grain facing the back. The rabbet on an end piece is another saw job, but to make a rab-bet on a long piece requires a bit more doing. It can be done with a back saw, but the rabbet plane will do it easier and more accurately. If you must use a saw, clamp a strip of wood on the work, to guide the saw, and clamp another strip to the saw for a depth gauge. The edge can be cut the same way with an improvised guide strip, or a chisel can be used to re-move the waste, and the face of the rabbet planed smooth. See Fig. 3.

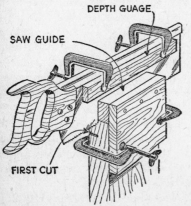

DEPTH GUAGE

SAW GUIDE

FIRST CUT

Fig. 3. Rabbet on long piece.

DADOES

The Dado (Fig. 4) is a groove, either across or lengthwise with the grain to usually receive the butt end of another piece. This joint provides a

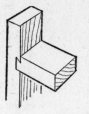

DOVETAILED DADO

Fig. 6.

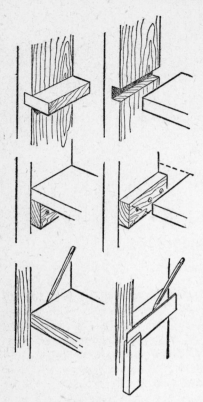

Fig. 4. The dado.

ods, and where fasteners cannot b
used. The only alternative for shelve
between uprights, is to butt join ther
against the uprights and use support
ing pieces framed under the shelve
and against the uprights—more fre
quently used than dadoing. A dado i
made by sawing its sides to the dept
required, and then removing th
waste with a chisel, or much mor
easily with a combination plane c
router. Use the piece to be fitted i
the dado as a marking guide and the
square the lines with a square.

A Stopped Dado does not exten
to the edge of the piece. This require
the fitting piece to be notched out t
butt against the receiving piece. Sinc
a joint shows in either a full o
stopped dado, the extra work re
quired for the stopped dado seem
hardly worthwhile just to hide tw
additional short joints. When makin
a stopped dado, first remove a portio

supporting ledge for the fitting piece
and, in best practice, is used for
shelves and the like where downward
pressure is exerted. It also permits
gluing without other fastening meth-

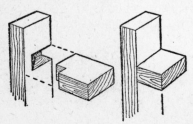

Fig. 5. Stopped dado.

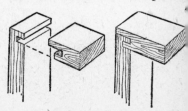

Fig. 7. End dado.

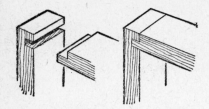

Fig. 8. The dado and rabbet.

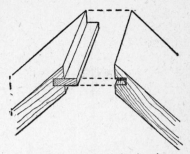

Fig. 10. Mitered and splined.

of the stopped end with a chisel before sawing the sides with a back saw. The dado is, of course, marked out before any cutting is done (Fig. 5).

The Dovetailed Dado (Fig. 6) adds additional strength to the common dado. It is a difficult joint to make with hand tools, and for all practical purposes, the common dado is quite adequate.

An End Dado locks the two pieces, a decided improvement over the rabbet, but here again, for ordinary purposes it is hardly worthwhile going to all the trouble to make this joint by hand (Fig. 7).

The Dado and Rabbet joint works as well as the end dado and is not difficult to make, requiring only a groove in one piece, and a rabbet in the other. Like the end dado, it is much stronger than a plain rabbeted joint. It is made like a single dado and a single rabbet (Fig. 8).

MITER JOINTS

A Miter joint is a 45-degree-angle joint which hides end grain on both pieces (Fig. 9). It is the only joint possible on picture frames and moldings of all kinds where molding contours continue around corners. The edges of fine furniture are always mitered, but it is a very weak joint without some reinforcing adjunct, as only edge-grain surfaces are in contact. For long miter joints, gluing strips are usually used, if hidden. This joint requires accurate cutting as the slightest variation in angle between joined pieces results in a poor joint, or an off-square angle. Mitered pieces are fre-

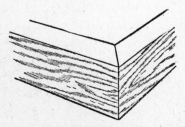

Fig. 9. The Miter joint.

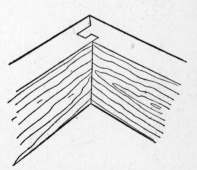

Fig. 11. The lock miter.

quently "splined," (Fig. 10); the miter edges grooved to receive a narrow strip or spline. Another method is to use a "feather," which is similar to a spline, but wider and thinner, the grooves usually only the thickness of the saw kerf. Where mitered pieces, such as moldings and the like, are framed against other material, these reinforcements are not necessary.

The Lock Miter joint requires no reinforcing, but obviously is not worth attempting on long edges, with hand tools (Fig. 11).

DOVETAIL JOINTS

A Single Through Dovetail joint (Fig. 12) is the easiest of dovetail

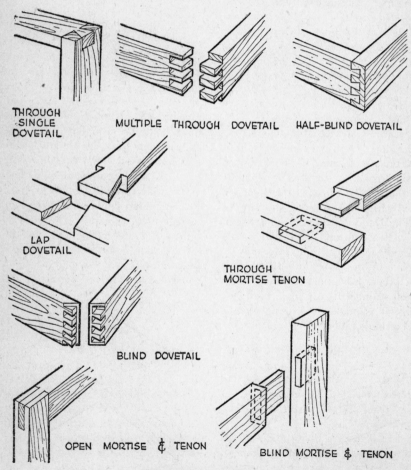

Fig. 12. Dovetail joints.

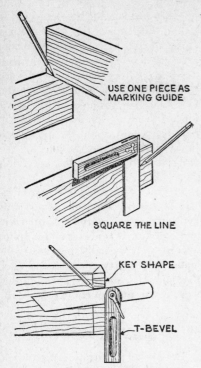

USE ONE PIECE AS
MARKING GUIDE

SQUARE THE LINE

KEY SHAPE

T-BEVEL

Fig. 13. Making dovetail joint.

most of the strain against the contents of the drawer when pulled out, this dovetail is of sound value. It requires extreme care in laying out and cutting, as the meshing pieces must fit accurately. It is not a "must," however, as a rabbeted drawer front, *glued and screwed*, will work as well and can be accomplished with no particular woodworking skill.

The Blind Dovetail (Fig. 12) is an extremely tricky job of woodworking, as the dovetail is hidden by the mitered shoulders of the dovetail. It is used in the finest cabinet work where the craftsman really wishes to show his skill.

When making dovetail joints, use one of the pieces as a marking guide for the depth of the pins and sockets, and square the line with a square. The key-shaped pins and corresponding sockets are best laid out with a T-bevel which is set for the desired angle, and turned over to mark the opposite angle or key shape. The sockets and pins are sawed with a back saw, and the bottoms of the sockets cut with a chisel (Fig. 13).

A Lap Dovetail (Fig. 12) is a locked middle half lap of top-quality craftsmanship. It is as easy to make as the other, mostly with the saw, requiring very little extra time to lay out.

The Through Mortise and Tenon (Fig. 12) is a superior T-joint possible only with stock thick enough to make a strong joint. The mortise is a square or rectangular hole which receives a shouldered tongue or tenon. It is frequently pinned with a wood peg, and was the most commonly used method

joints to make. It is a locked joint (in one direction), but as seven joints show on the combined corners, there is not much reason for making it unless extreme pulling stresses occur against the locked side.

The Multiple Through Dovetail joint (Fig. 12) is a series of single dovetails of small dimensions. With modern glues and other methods of fastening, this joint is hardly worth the effort save in the satisfaction of accomplishing a craftsmanlike job on a corner joint.

A Half-Blind Dovetail (Fig. 12) is used for drawer fronts in fine cabinet work. Since the drawer front receives

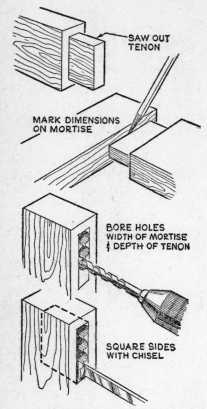

SAW OUT TENON

MARK DIMENSIONS ON MORTISE

BORE HOLES WIDTH OF MORTISE ¾ DEPTH OF TENON

SQUARE SIDES WITH CHISEL

Fig. 14. Making a mortise and tenon joint.

of framing eighteenth century houses and barns (Eastern Braced Frame Construction) which, after 200 or more years, are still as sound in the joints as when originally framed!

The Blind Mortise and Tenon (Fig. 12) is the same as the above, with the mortise and tenon extending only part way into the wood. When assembled it looks like an ordinary butt joint. To make a mortise and tenon joint, first saw out the tenon. Then use it to mark the dimensions of the mortise. Bore a series of holes the width

of the mortise and to the depth of the tenon, and square the sides with a chisel. If you plan to pin the tenon, first bore the hole for the pin through the mortise. Insert the tenon and mark the location of the hole. Remove the tenon and bore the hole *just off-center* toward the shoulder. Then, when the joint is assembled and the pin driven in, it will draw the shoulder of the tenon tightly against the receiving piece (Fig. 14).

An Open Mortise and Tenon (Fig. 12) is another type of corner joint with greater locking powers than the end half lap. It is also used for splicing instead of the half-lap splice. Well-made frames of various kinds, other than picture frames, are joined in this way. Use a saw and chisel to make it.

DOWEL JOINT

The Dowel joint transforms a weak joint into a strong one. Dowels come in stock diameters from ⅛″ to 1″, all 36″ long, usually made of hardwood (Fig. 15).

Lumber yards, and many hardware stores stock dowels in the more popular, smaller sizes. Some stores also stock short lengths of spiraled dowels made especially for gluing.

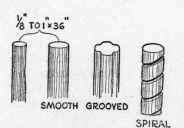

⅛″ TO 1″×36″

SMOOTH   GROOVED

SPIRAL

Fig. 15. Dowels.

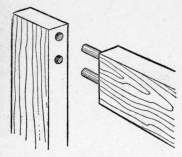

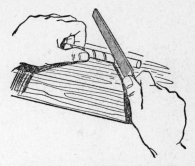

Fig. 16. Glue fills grooves for better adhesion.

Fig. 17. Cutting spirals in a dowel.

The reason for the spiral is so that glue can fill in the grooves for better adhesion (Fig. 16). A dowel which is to be glued should *not* fit the hole tightly, otherwise when joining the pieces, the glue is squeezed out. A sliding fit is best, and if the dowel is not spiraled when purchased, cut spirals in it with the corner of a file by holding the file at an oblique angle and turning the dowel as you file (Fig. 17). Shallow grooves are sufficient. A dowel should be slightly shorter than the depths of the holes.

There are other, more complicated wood joints made, all stemming from the basic ones described. Most of them require the skill of a master craftsman, or the use of power tools. Modern glues, being stronger than wood itself, together with screws, have to a great extent replaced most of the intricate wood joints of the cabinetmaker's art—at least where the amateur craftsman is concerned. It is, however, a matter of pride and joy forever to make a perfect dovetail joint, and for this reason well worth trying. If you have ever had the opportunity of examining a drawer of a cabinet made by an eighteenth century craftsman, you will agree that the almost paper-thin pins of his dovetail joints are a lasting tribute to his incredible skill with saw and chisel.

CHAPTER 6

PROTECT YOUR TOOL INVESTMENT!

It cannot be said too often that tools are no better than the condition in which they are kept. Assuming that you have invested a considerable amount of hard-earned money in a collection of top-quality tools, it is only good judgment to protect your investment by adequately and safely storing your tools. In this way you not only insure the life of tools, but when you need a particular one, you will know precisely where it is.

PORTABLE TOOL BOXES

A portable tool box is a handy device for transporting tools whenever and wherever you need them. If your available storage space is limited, the portable tool box can also take the place of a permanent cabinet. The portable boxes suggested are intended for this purpose; they can be stored in a minimum of space, and will protect your tools. Several of these will be needed to reduce size and carrying weight, and a smaller additional portable box with removable, compartment trays, is fine for keeping nails, screws, bolts, and other small hardware.

The dimensions of the boxes depend on the equipment you have and, as overall sizes of tools vary, the di-

mensions shown in the illustrations (Figs. 1 & 2) are only suggestions, based on housing 26″ handsaws and other tools of average size. Before beginning construction, measure the over-all dimensions of your tools so they will fit in a minimum of space. To keep the weight down as much as practical, ¾″ Idaho White or Sugar Pine is good and easily workable for the ends, sides and handles; 7/16″ stock for the partitions and trays, and ½″ fir plywood is best for the top and bottom pieces because of their widths. For the "pockets" and latches which secure the various tools, use ¼″ tempered hardboard (a dense, highly compressed fiberboard) or fir plywood. Use flat-head wood screws to frame the various members and countersink them either flush, or slightly deeper than flush and cover the heads with either water-mix wood putty or plastic wood, sandpapered smooth.

First cut out all the pieces and then arrange your tools and mark the location of latches and pockets. These should be raised just enough for a snug fit of the tools. Secure them with flat-head screws through both face and separating strips. Latches should be pivoted on round-head wood screws with a thin washer between

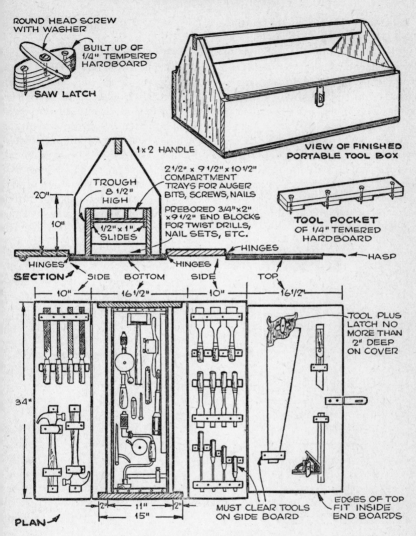

ROUND HEAD SCREW
WITH WASHER

BUILT UP OF
1/4" TEMPERED
HARDBOARD

SAW LATCH

VIEW OF FINISHED
PORTABLE TOOL BOX

1 x 2 HANDLE

TROUGH
8 1/2"
HIGH

20"

10"

1/2" x 1"
SLIDES

2 1/2" x 9 1/2" x 10 1/2"
COMPARTMENT
TRAYS FOR AUGER
BITS, SCREWS, NAILS

PREBORED 3/4"x2"
x9 1/2" END BLOCKS
FOR TWIST DRILLS,
NAIL SETS, ETC.

TOOL POCKET
OF 1/4" TEMERED
HARDBOARD

HINGES

HINGES

HASP

SECTION

SIDE

BOTTOM

HINGES

SIDE

TOP

10"

16 1/2"

10"

16 1/2"

34"

TOOL PLUS
LATCH NO
MORE THAN
2" DEEP
ON COVER

2"

11"

2"

15"

MUST CLEAR TOOLS
ON SIDE BOARD

EDGES OF TOP
FIT INSIDE
END BOARDS

PLAN

Fig. I. Portable tool box.

head and latch. Hinge the sides and top with three, 1½"-long, narrow, cabinet butt hinges with tight pins, each piece hinged in the center and at both ends. Frame the bottom to the end pieces, and the partitions to the bottom and end pieces. Also attach with screws the pre-bored blocks for twist drills, and nail-set and countersink shanks in Box No. 1.

Locate the hinges on the bottom piece and attach. The handles fit tightly into slots on the end pieces and are anchored with two flat-head screws driven in the end-piece edges. With the top and sides closed, locate the screw hooks and eyes, one at each end for each piece.

Removable trays for Box No. 2 are butt-joined on all surfaces, glued if you wish, and nailed with 2d finishing nails, set and covered. You can fit each compartment either separately crosswise, or half lap the strips lengthwise and crosswise.

TOOL CABINET

A tool cabinet (Fig. 3) is more desirable than a tool box so far as space to properly store each tool within arm's reach is concerned. Moreover, as it is a fixed storage space, its weight is not a matter of concern as with the portable box. If you are so situated that a small workshop is not practical, you can still enjoy the knowledge that your tools are well taken care of and easily accessible by making a tool cabinet which you can attach to the inside of a closet door. If you have

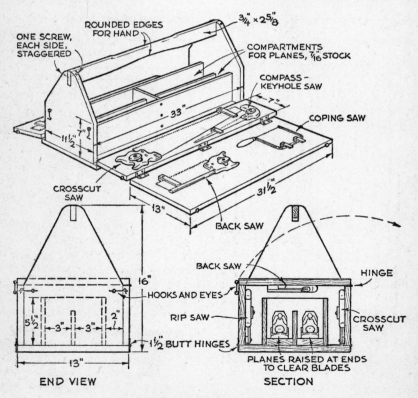

Fig. 2. Portable tool box.

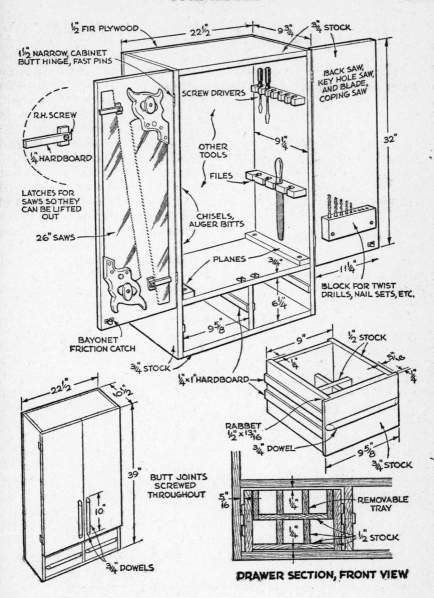

½" FIR PLYWOOD

22½"   9¾"   ¾" STOCK

1½ NARROW, CABINET
BUTT HINGE, FAST PINS

BACK SAW,
KEY HOLE SAW,
AND BLADE,
COPING SAW

R.H. SCREW

SCREW DRIVERS

¼" HARDBOARD

OTHER
TOOLS

9¼"

32"

LATCHES FOR
SAWS SO THEY
CAN BE LIFTED
OUT

FILES

CHISELS,
AUGER BITTS

26" SAWS

PLANES   ¾"

BLOCK FOR TWIST
DRILLS, NAIL SETS, ETC.

11¼"

6¼"

BAYONET
FRICTION CATCH

9⅝"

¾" STOCK

¼" × 1" HARDBOARD

9"   ½" STOCK

1"   5/16

22½"   10½"

RABBET
½" × 13/16"

¾" DOWEL

9⅝"   ¾" STOCK

39"

BUTT JOINTS
SCREWED
THROUGHOUT

5/16

¼"   REMOVABLE
TRAY

10"

¼"   ½" STOCK

¾" DOWELS

DRAWER SECTION, FRONT VIEW

Fig. 3. Tool cabinet.

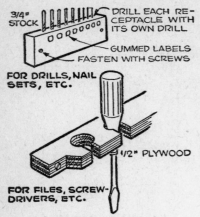

3/4" STOCK

DRILL EACH RE-CEPTACLE WITH ITS OWN DRILL

GUMMED LABELS
FASTEN WITH SCREWS

FOR DRILLS, NAIL SETS, ETC.

1/2" PLYWOOD

FOR FILES, SCREW-DRIVERS, ETC.

Fig. 4. Twist-drill holders.

space for a workshop, the same cabinet can be mounted over your workbench.

Since this project is not intended to be a "show-piece," there is no need to make mitered, rabbeted and dadoed joints—with one exception—the drawer fronts should be rabbeted. Stock lumber is used except for the back which, because of its width, is ½" fir plywood. All other cabinet material, except the ¾" hardwood-dowel pulls, is ¾" and ½" Idaho White or Sugar Pine. Pockets and latches are ¼" tempered hardboard or fir plywood. The center partition for the drawers will have to be planed ¼", the stock size being 6½", and the drawer components ripped to size. Use either resorcinol resin, urea resin or casein glue for all joints before screwing them with flat-head wood screws. Since the screws are driven immediately after applying the glue, clamps are not necessary. Glue is not absolutely essential, but as there are a number of end-grain joints and con-

siderable weight stresses, a stronger, more permanent job will result by using glue. Countersink all screws on the outside of the cabinet slightly deeper than flush and cover the heads with water-mix wood putty or plastic wood.

The dimensions are based on 26" hand saws and for tools of average overall size. Even though you are not completely stocked with every tool the cabinet will accommodate, it would be wise while you are at it, to make it large enough for future expansion of your tool collection. The cabinet is equipped with two drawers with removable trays for screws, nails, and small hardware.

After cutting the various pieces to size, arrange your collection of tools similarly to those suggested in the drawings, keeping in mind future additions. An easy way to establish the locations after experimenting with arrangements, is to trace the outline of the tool with a pencil directly on the wood surface. Since tools vary in thickness, each one will have to be custom fitted for pockets and latches which should receive the tool snugly. Attach all pockets with flat-head screws, countersunk flush, through the face and separating strips, and all pivoting latches with round-head wood screws with washers under the heads.

Make twist-drill holders out of ¾" stock, boring each receptacle with the drill it is supposed to contain (Fig. 4). Do this also with the auger-bit holders which, in this case, are bored for the diameters of the tapered shanks. It is a good idea to use gummed labels marked for each drill size for quick selection. Nail sets, countersinks and tools of similar type can be stored in the same manner. Attach these various holders with flat-head screws, one at each end of each holder being sufficient. Files, screwdrivers and chisel holders can be made from ½" fir plywood bored with holes of smaller diameter than the handles, and slotted to pass the tangs, blades and sockets. Lumber stock for these are apt to split, unless hardwood is used.

Drawer and door pulls (Fig. 5) are made from ¾" hardwood dowels. To make these, file the contacting surface of the dowel slightly flat, bevel the edges at the end after beveling the ends, and attach with flat-head screws from the inside of the doors and drawer fronts, countersinking the screw heads flush. Two screws for each pull are sufficient.

Framing

To frame the cabinet, mark the center of each butting edge with a line on the outer face to each member against which the piece butts, as most of the screws are driven from the outer face of the cabinet. Also mark off, evenly spaced, the locations of the screws along the line, and bore lead holes for them. Fit the joining piece; insert a screw at each end and tap it lightly with a hammer to locate the smaller lead hole in the joining edge. Bore these smaller holes; assemble the members, and drive the two screws part way in, just enough to hold the piece. Then continue boring the small lead holes for the remaining screws. Bore all screw holes

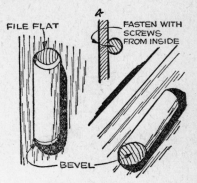

Fig. 5. Drawer and door pulls.

in this manner and then assemble the cabinet pieces, starting with the back and framing each member with glue applied to the edge, then screwing it, one piece at a time. Wipe off excess glue immediately with a clean cloth wrung out in cold water. Attach the doors with 1½"-long, narrow cabinet butt hinges with tight pins, recessing the leaves flush. Fit bayonet-type friction catches, one for each door.

It is best to make the drawers after the cabinet is assembled, so that any slight inaccuracy can be allowed for. Make the trays from ½" stock nailed with 2d finishing nails, set and filled. The easiest way to make the compartments is to cross lap and glue them, framing the ends against the drawer sides with glue and 2d finishing nails (Fig. 6). Make the drawer slides and guides from ¼" tempered hardboard, and attach with small, flat-head screws countersunk flush. When the cabinet is finished, sandpaper all surfaces smooth, *slightly* rounding all sharp corners. The cabinet should be either stained, given a few coats of clear lacquer, painted or enameled.

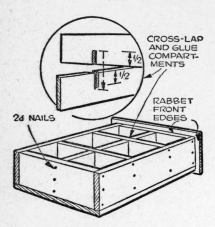

CROSS-LAP AND GLUE COMPARTMENTS

RABBET FRONT EDGES

2d NAILS

Fig. 6. Drawer compartments.

WORKBENCH

If you have a bit of space which you can allocate to the "maintenance and building department" of your home, by all means do so. Lacking a cellar, perhaps your garage or attic will allow space that will hold a small workbench with a few feet in front of it. A workbench is an invaluable piece of furniture for woodworking and home projects of all kinds. True, you can build almost anything without the aid of a workbench, but that is doing it the hard way, particularly if you are working on small projects which require a vise to hold them. The smaller the project the more the necessity for a workbench.

The ideal workbench is the traditional one with a maple top, two or more inches thick; the narrow maple boards face-glued and bolted together, similar to a maple chopping block. This is a very expensive and difficult job of work, requiring un-

usual bolt lengths, perfect jointing and much clamping.

Another method of making the top for a workbench is to use maple boards, glued edgewise, and glued and screwed to a supplementary top of board lumber. This, too, is expensive and, as maple is tougher than the foundation on which it is framed, any warping tendencies of the maple will warp the entire assembly beyond repair. This method also requires fine jointing of perfect edges, with the added difficulty of producing a flat, smooth surface to the top.

The important factor in a workbench is weight and solidity, and a tough top which will take the beating it must take. The workbench suggested (Fig. 7) is tough and sturdy, but with a ¾" fir-plywood top instead of maple. Plywood, thickness for thickness, is considerably heavier than comparable lumber, due to its structure and, if framed properly, will not warp, bend or vibrate. Moreover, fir plywood is uncommonly tough and offers the advantage of a single, smooth piece for the top without any jointing problems.

Most workbenches have a trough at the back for odds and ends, but experience shows that this is nothing but a catchall for wood shavings, chips, sawdust, and dirt. It is also an invitation to park small tools where they should not be. The trough is eliminated primarily for this reason, and also because it would complicate construction of the top unnecessarily. Provision is made for keeping lengths of lumber on the bottom braces, adequately taking care of the average lumber storage problem around the home. The bench is equipped with two drawers having removable compartmented trays for screws, nails and small hardware. The average height of a bench is about 34", but if you are short or quite tall, this height should be changed to about 6" below your waist line.

Here is your opportunity to show your skill with middle half laps and four dadoes which, as explained in

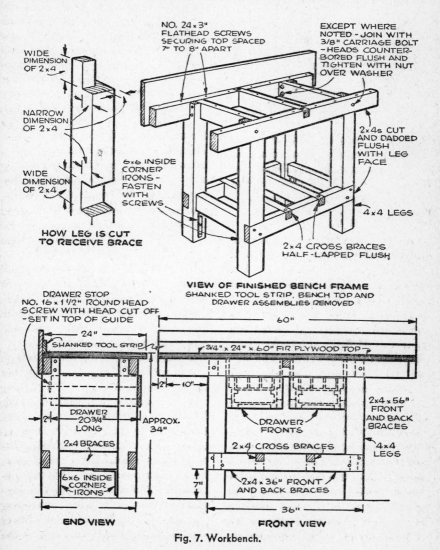

NO. 24 x 3" FLATHEAD SCREWS SECURING TOP SPACED 7" TO 8" APART

EXCEPT WHERE NOTED - JOIN WITH 3/8" CARRIAGE BOLT - HEADS COUNTER-BORED FLUSH AND TIGHTEN WITH NUT OVER WASHER

WIDE DIMENSION OF 2 x 4

NARROW DIMENSION OF 2 x 4

WIDE DIMENSION OF 2 x 4

6 x 6 INSIDE CORNER IRONS - FASTEN WITH SCREWS

2 x 4s CUT AND DADOED FLUSH WITH LEG FACE

4 x 4 LEGS

HOW LEG IS CUT TO RECEIVE BRACE

2 x 4 CROSS BRACES HALF-LAPPED FLUSH

VIEW OF FINISHED BENCH FRAME
SHANKED TOOL STRIP, BENCH TOP AND DRAWER ASSEMBLIES REMOVED

DRAWER STOP NO. 16 x 1 1/2" ROUND HEAD SCREW WITH HEAD CUT OFF - SET IN TOP OF GUIDE

24"
SHANKED TOOL STRIP

60"

3/4" x 24" x 60" FIR PLYWOOD TOP

2' 10"

DRAWER FRONTS

2 x 4 x 56" FRONT AND BACK BRACES

DRAWER 20 3/4" LONG

2 x 4 BRACES

6 x 6 INSIDE CORNER IRONS

2"

APPROX. 34"

2 x 4 CROSS BRACES

4 x 4 LEGS

7"

2 x 4 x 36" FRONT AND BACK BRACES

36"

END VIEW

FRONT VIEW

Fig. 7. Workbench.

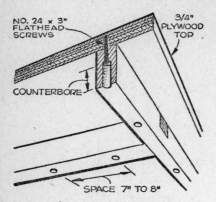

Fig. 8. Top of workbench is removable.

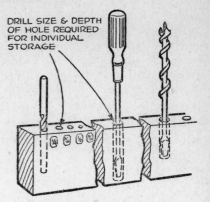

Fig. 9. Strip for small shanked tools.

Chapter 5, are not hard to make, requiring only careful layout and a bit of sawing and chiseling. Remember to always saw on the waste side of the marked line for tight joining.

Legs and Framing

The legs and framing for the bench are Douglas-fir lumber: 4"x4" (3⅝"x 3⅝") for the legs, and 2"x4" (1⅝"x 3½" or 3⅝") for the bracing and top supports. The tops of the legs are cut back to receive the 2x4s flush. The bottom front and back braces are dadoed flush, while the center cross braces are half lapped flush. The bottom end braces are butt-joined with 6"x6" inside corner irons. All framing except for the corner irons is done with carriage bolts, counterbored for flush fitting heads, and tightened with nuts over washers. This results in a rigid frame which can be *disassembled* either completely, or with the ends left intact. The top, too, a ¾" panel of fir plywood, is removable, being secured to the frames with screws counterbored and driven from the underside of the frames (Fig. 8). From time to time bolt nuts will have to be tightened, and if the demountable feature of the workbench is of no importance, apply resorcinol resin glue to all joints before bolting, and nothing will loosen them.

Screwed to the backboard of the top is a strip ¾"x2⅝"x60" for twist drills, countersinks, nail sets and any shanked, small tool. Bore holes in this strip, using the size twist drill it is to receive, and holes of the correct diameters for the other tools, such as screwdrivers and auger-bit shanks. Use gummed labels marked with the size of each drill for easy selection of the size you want (Fig. 9).

To support the two drawers, screw ¾" plywood to the cross braces. For the drawer guides and slides, maple or oak is best, screwed to the braces and drawer sides. Drawer stock can be ¾" white pine or plywood, but the drawer bottoms should be ¼" tempered hardboard for added strength. The drawer sides, front, back and bottom are butt-joined and framed to

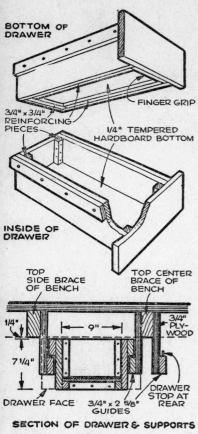

BOTTOM OF DRAWER

FINGER GRIP

3/4" x 3/4" REINFORCING PIECES

1/4" TEMPERED HARDBOARD BOTTOM

INSIDE OF DRAWER

TOP SIDE BRACE OF BENCH

TOP CENTER BRACE OF BENCH

3/4" PLYWOOD

1/4"

9"

7 1/4"

DRAWER FACE   3/4" x 2 5/8" GUIDES

DRAWER STOP AT REAR

SECTION OF DRAWER & SUPPORTS

Fig. 10.

Make sliding trays, about ½ the depth of the drawer, out of ½" lumber stock for the sides, ends and compartments, and ¼" hardboard for the bottoms. Cross lap the compartments with glue and frame the trays with glue and 2d finishing nails (Fig. 11).

Woodworking Vise

A Woodworking Vise is an essential adjunct to the bench. This can be purchased and attached to the bench with screws, or you can save a con-

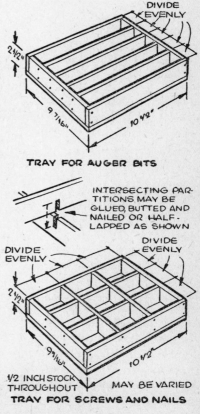

DIVIDE EVENLY

2 1/2"

9 7/16"

10 1/2"

TRAY FOR AUGER BITS

INTERSECTING PARTITIONS MAY BE GLUED, BUTTED AND NAILED OR HALF-LAPPED AS SHOWN

DIVIDE EVENLY

DIVIDE EVENLY

2 1/2"

9 7/16"

10 1/2"

1/2 INCH STOCK THROUGHOUT

MAY BE VARIED

TRAY FOR SCREWS AND NAILS

Fig. 11.

ach other with screws through ¾"x¾" orner reinforcing pieces and ¾"x¾" pieces for the bottom. Make drawer tops by driving a No. 16 x 1½" flathead wood screw into each drawer guide 1⅞" from its end, letting the head project about ⅜". Then cut off the head with a hacksaw or other metal-cutting saw. The drawer fronts require no pulls as they project below the bottom for finger grips. See Fig. 0.

siderable amount of money by buying a Bench Screw, which is the motivating power of a vise, and make your own (Fig. 12). Two pieces of ¾" fir plywood screwed together make efficient and strong jaws, and all that remains to be done is to bore a hole through both jaws and the 2x4 extension, slightly larger than the diameter of the screw with an expansive bit, and attach the screw assembly.

You can also make a Bench Stop for the vise out of a ¾" hardwood dowel, glued (Fig. 13). Bench stops hold

short lengths of lumber for planing sanding and the like, two being required; one on the vise and the other let into the bench top. Holes are bored at intervals through the bench top to accommodate various lengths of lumber. The commercial bench stops are adjustable for height (thickness of lumber), but are designed for thicker bench tops. You can easily make these which will work as well. Since your homemade ones are not adjustable make three, using ¾", ½", and ¼" material for the stops, glued with

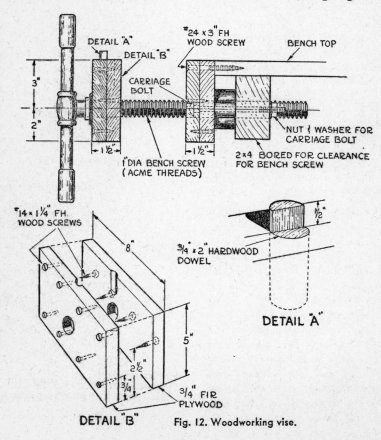

Fig. 12. Woodworking vise.

resorcinol resin glue to ¾" hardwood dowels. The holes in the bench to receive these stops should be just large enough for a snug, sliding fit. You can use the same diameter bit as the dowel diameter, and then carefully enlarge the hole slightly with coarse sandpaper wrapped around a dowel of smaller diameter.

A well-equipped woodworking bench has two vises, one at the left end, and one at the opposite end, its jaws facing the length of the bench. This vise, when there are two, is used in conjunction with bench stops to accommodate long pieces of lumber. You can make two of these vises alike with two bench screws for less than half the cost of one complete, commercial vise of good quality.

Bench Hook

There is one other valuable addition to your workbench equipment which comes in handy for all sorts of woodworking jobs, such as chiseling out dadoes, sawing dadoes and the like. This is the Bench Hook which is

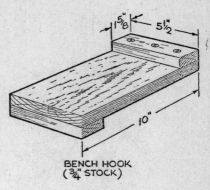

BENCH HOOK
(¾" STOCK)

Fig. 14.

simply a piece of lumber with a stop screwed to the bottom at one end and a stop screwed to the top at the other end (Fig. 14). Make several of these from ¾"x5½"x10" stock, with stops of ¾"x1⅝" stock. In use, the bottom stop butts against the front edge of the bench top, and the lumber to be worked butts against the top stop. Use two bench hooks for long pieces of lumber.

SAWHORSES

Sawhorses are the age-old portable workbenches of the carpenter and, up to the present day, no better substi-

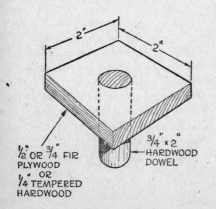

½" OR ¾" FIR
PLYWOOD
OR
¼" TEMPERED
HARDWOOD

¾" x 2"
HARDWOOD
DOWEL

Fig. 13. Bench stop for vise.

Fig. 15. Sawhorse.

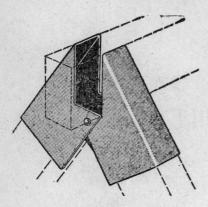

Fig. 16. Sawhorse demountable frames.

tute has been invented for cross-cutting and ripping lumber of any length. They are also invaluable for cutting plywood panels which at best are awkward to saw. Carpenters on a construction job will make a miter box and nail it to the top of a sawhorse ready for any mitering job that presents itself. At least two sawhorses are needed, and for large panels of thin plywood, a third is a good idea to support the middle.

Use 2x4 lumber for the legs and cross piece, and ¾″ fir plywood or ¾″ lumber stock for the end braces or gussets. Douglas fir is a good, tough wood to use. There are two ways of positioning the cross piece; edge or face on top. The face gives more surface on which to work and is preferred by some craftsmen. It offers less bevel surface for the legs, but as

they are end braced, this disadvantage is offset. However, the edge on top is the commonest method of framing (Fig. 15), and if you want a wider work surface, you can nail a 6″ board on the 2x4.

The height of a sawhorse depends on the user's height, and ranges from 18″ to about 24″. It should be low enough for comfortable sawing when the knee is used to hold down the piece — 20″ is about average. Length is optional, but 36″ is a good overall dimension. Spread of legs is important, so that the horse does not rock — 18″ between outer edge of legs is about right. For a horse with a spread of 18″, and 20″ high, the angle of the bevel of the legs is 22 degrees, which you can mark off with your T-bevel adjusted with the use of a protractor, or if you have a protractor head on your combination square, use the square. The easiest way to make the bevel is to saw it. Use flat-head wood screws to assemble the horse, for rigid framing. Fir plywood, ¾″, makes the strongest gussets.

If you do not have space to store sawhorses, you can buy metal frames into which the 2x4s are clamped without the use of screws. These demountable frames do not make as sturdy a sawhorse as a homemade one, but they are adequate enough with the added advantage that they can be disassembled and stored in a small space (Fig. 16).

CHAPTER 7

HOW YOUR HOME IS BUILT

If you are living in a house contructed of lumber, it will have been framed in one of the three basic methods commonly used in this country. These are to some extent dependent on the locality, age, and quality of its construction. The three basic types of framing are Eastern or Braced, Balloon, Western or Platform Frame.

If your house is very old and situated in the East, particularly New England, where lumber was used as the principal building material, chances are that your house is held together by a method historically known as the Eastern or Braced Frame. This type is also known as the Barn or Old-fashioned Frame. Eighteenth and many nineteenth century houses and barns were built to stand forever; consequently, they were mortised and tenoned and pinned with oak pins. Principal framing members were half lapped and pinned, and oak, one of the most durable woods, was extensively used.

Specifications for modern Eastern Braced Frame (Fig. 1), construction call for posts at all corners and opposite all bearing partitions. Frames must have drop and flush girts, mortised and tenoned, and pinned with oak pins. Posts must be tenoned into

sills, and studs must be framed into sills, and all braces cut and spiked into posts, sills and girts. Sill splices must be scarfed where their lengths

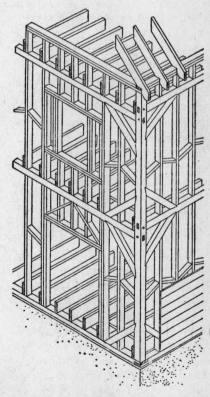

Fig. 1. Eastern braced frame houses were built to stand forever.

115

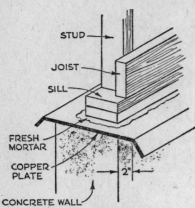

STUD

JOIST

SILL

FRESH
MORTAR

COPPER
PLATE

2"

CONCRETE WALL

Fig. 2. An effective termite shield must extend around the periphery of the foundation wall.

exceed 20 feet. Openings must be trussed and all plates must be halved at the corners and pinned.

Obviously, this type of construction is the strongest and most rigid. It takes the longest to erect, and is the most expensive — so expensive today that it is rarely employed except in deluxe custom-built houses. There are variations in bracing methods and treatment of plate and roof rafters.

EASTERN BRACED FRAME

Sill: Solid 4x6″ and usually larger. It rests on the foundation wall and is anchored to it by bolts set in the foundation wall when it is built. The sill's job is to transfer loads and wind stresses from the frame to the foundation wall. It also forms the base to which the posts, studs and floor joists are framed. Sills are set in stiff mortar for better bonding to the foundation wall, and leveled where necessary with small stone chips.

In some later-day houses, where termites are present, shields of non-corrosive metal were first embedded in mortar, soldered around the bolts, or filled with asphaltic mastic, and the sill then embedded in mortar on top of the shields. Termite shields (Fig. 2), must be a continuous, unbroken metal course around the periphery of the foundation wall, and should extend on both sides about 2″ and bent down to a 45-degree angle. This seems to discourage termites — the most destructive enemies of wood — from boring in and eventually pulverizing the wood.

Sills in homes that are termite infested or otherwise seriously damaged by decay, are dangerous to the entire structure. There is nothing you yourself can do about this. It requires an expert in the technique of replacing sills, which means first jacking up the house to replace them. As you can appreciate, this is no job for an amateur.

Porch supports quite frequently fall heir to decay from dampness and termites. If the porch is a one-story type and does not support rooms overhead, you will be able to repair it yourself if *local building codes permit*. Use 2x4s or larger timber, depending on the porch, to temporarily brace and support it, making sure that the temporary supports and bracing are adequate and on sound supporting surfaces. If posts or other framing members are tenoned into sills and the like, cut off the tenons and spike the existing framing to the replaced material and, if stronger joints are necessary, add corner irons or other fasteners.

The new material should be cre-
osote-treated or zinc-chloride-treated
lumber. It is best when using treated
lumber to have it cut to the correct
size, and bored if necessary, before
treating which should be pressure-
tank applied to be effective. If you
have to cut lumber after treatment,
you must thoroughly soak newly cut
surfaces with preservative. When replacing sills that require splicing,
solid lumber should be half-lap
spliced at least 12", and built-up lumber lapped at least 2 feet. Joints
should be made over one of the anchor bolts if at all possible (Fig. 3).

Posts: 4x6", 4x8" and often larger.
They are placed at all corners of exterior walls and also at points where
load-bearing partitions intersect them,
and where two or more girts would
otherwise be joined together. Posts
are full height, from sill to plate and
in old houses are tenoned into both
sills and plates. Girts are also tenoned
into the posts. A house that requires
a new post or posts — which rarely
happens—is indeed in a sad state of
disrepair.

Girts: 4x6" and larger. In old
houses girts were large and strong
enough to support entire floor loads,
size of lumber having been of no particular concern. Builders just used the
largest timber necessary to do the job.
Later-day builders, using this type of
construction, employed studs to take
up some of the load, reducing girt
dimensions considerably. The girt's
primary function is a horizontal tie
holding the frame together laterally.
It also supports part of the floor load,
and furnishes a tie for the bracing.

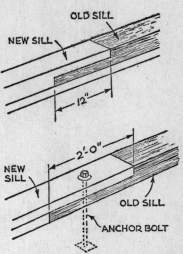

Fig. 3. Half-lap splice new sills for 12".

Girts are either raised or dropped.
Raised girts parallel and have their
top edges on the same level as that of
the joists. This permits the rough
flooring to extend to the girt's outer
edge and be nailed to it, tying wall
and floor together. Dropped girts
(Fig. 4), run at right angles to floor
joists, their top edges on a level with
the bottom of the joists which rest on
the girts.

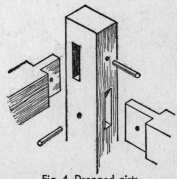

Fig. 4. Dropped girts.

Fig. 5. Built-up plate supporting joists and roof rafters.

The basic reason for raised and dropped girts is to avoid the respective mortises and tenons from coming together at the posts, weakening them. Some old houses have raised

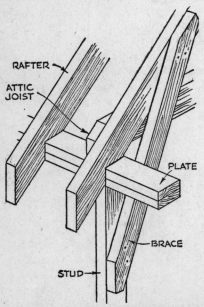

Fig. 6. One method of bracing attic plate.

and dropped girts which support attic floor joists, with posts continuing above them to a plate which supports the roof rafters. Others have only plates which support both joists and roof rafters.

A house that requires new girts is ready to be torn down, there being no conceivable way to remove and replace them short of removing all construction above the offending girt.

Plates: As a rule very old houses have solid plates 4x4″ or larger. Those not so old usually have two 2x4 plates spiked together. (See Fig. 5.) Plates are supported by posts and studs. As a rule they remain in good shape unless considerable roof leakage near them has caused decay, or wind stresses have caused splitting. If this has occurred it can usually be repaired by bracing (Fig. 6), the roof rafter against the stud with knee braces of 2x4s, 1x6s, or iron straps, relieving considerable strain on the plate. Nothing much can be done with hopelessly damaged plates as here, too, the only way to replace them would be to remove joists if they are framed into the plates, and jack up the roof.

Braces: These, to a large extent, characterize this type of construction. Older houses are usually knee braced at a 45-degree angle in pairs of short 4x6″ lumber notched into the posts and sills, and above and below the girts, notched into them and the posts. Newer houses usually have single diagonal braces of 3x4″ and sometimes 4x4″ lumber. They run from sill to girt, and from girt to girt or plate (Fig. 7). Studs are always cut to fit

etween braces, never the reverse. It
quite a job to replace a damaged
race, but it can be done by removing
xterior and interior construction
round it.

Studs: Wall studs, usually 2x4s,
lay an important part in supporting
oor joists, rafter plates and roof
afters. They also form the skeleton
or wall coverings, such as sheathing,
ding materials, plaster partitions,
nd other partition coverings. Wood
ath which was once the sole base for
laster, was first cut in 4-foot lengths
c some 16″ submultiple. This arbi-
ary dimensioning determined the
pacing of studs and joists, although
oists are frequently spaced less and
nore than 16″ apart. There is no par-
cular reason for spacing studs 16″
n centers, structurally, that is. It just
appened and has continued to be the
eneral standard practice. All modern
vall materials are made in stock sizes
f 16″ multiples to conform to the
aditional practice of stud spacing.

raming Openings

Where window and door openings
ccur provision must be made to ade-
uately frame and support loads cared by these openings. Horizontal
aming members which bridge these
penings top and bottom are called
eaders. Vertical framing members
hich support the headers are Trim-
ers, and the short studs between
eaders and the house frame are
alled Cripples.

Window openings are framed hori-
ontally to admit the window frame
roper with enough space between
indow frame and trimmers to allow

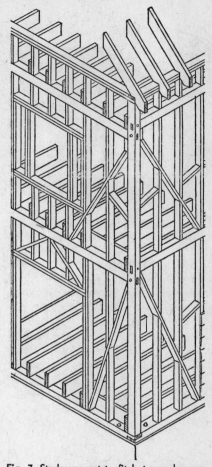

Fig. 7. Studs are cut to fit between braces.

for a pocket in which sash weights of
a double-hung window move up and
down. Vertically the opening is made
large enough for the window frame.
Window sizes are specified in terms
of glass sizes, called "lights" in builder's language. The horizontal opening
size is usually about 11″ over the glass
size to allow for two sash stiles, two
frame thicknesses and two weight

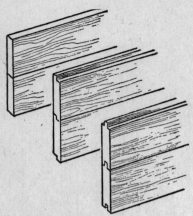

Fig. 8. Sheathing may be square-edged, shiplapped or tongue and grooved.

pockets. Vertically, 11″ is usually allowed over the glass size for three sash rails, window sill, and frame at the top. Casement window openings are determined in a similar manner.

Door openings are determined by overall door-frame dimensions, plus enough additional space to allow for adjustments, blocking, leveling, and door sills for outside doors. The usual allowance is 3 to 4″ horizontally and vertically measured from the tops of floor joists.

Framing for window and door openings must be adequate to support the loads above them. Two 2x4s spiked together are usually employed as headers. Openings wider than 4 feet require either larger dimensioned headers, or trusses. Trusses are usually 2x4s set diagonally between a center cripple and the trimmers, with cripples framed between the diagonals, house framing, and headers. Diagonals transfer the load direction to the trimmers and studs at the side.

Another method of trussing wide openings, where space above the headers does not permit diagonals to the center of the opening, is to frame a short diagonal brace from each lower corner to cripples braced under the plate with additional 2x4s between them. Framing of window and door openings, as described, applies to the three types of house framing – Eastern Braced, Balloon, and Western Platform.

Sheathing

Boards which are nailed to the studs of outer walls form the surface for siding material, and are called Sheathing. On the roof rafters they are called Roofers or Roof Boards and on the floor joists they are Sub flooring. Since the Eastern Braced Frame construction is resistant to sidewise strain occasioned by wind the sheathing is usually applied horizontally. It may be square-edged shiplapped or tongued and grooved (Fig. 8). Ends that are not tongued and grooved are joined only on studs On very old houses sheathing might be any thickness. Modern sheathing is usually 25/32″ or closer to ¾″.

BALLOON FRAME

Balloon framing was developed to reduce the cost of the braced frame and building time. There are two radical differences between the two types of framing. In the Balloon Frame girts are omitted and a Ribband, usually called a Ribbon, takes the place of the girt, and supports the second-floor joists. It runs only at right angles

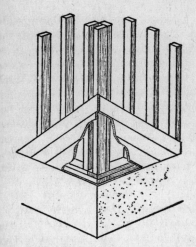

Fig. 9. Sometimes, corners are not braced.

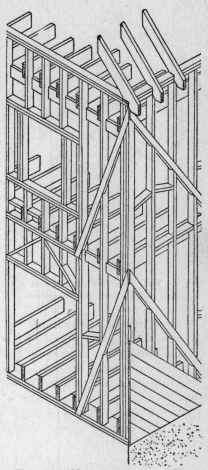

Fig. 10. A ribbon supports second floor joists.

to the direction of the joists. The other difference is that in balloon framing oftener than not there is no bracing. Today most building codes specify bracing at the corners, but originally the structural design omitted these. There are no mortised and tenoned joints (Figs. 9 and 10).

Sill: Usually a single 2x6″ or 2x10″ length of lumber. When it is 4″ thick, it is always double — one 2″ thickness spiked to the top of another 2″ thickness, making it nominally 4″ — actually 3¼″. Methods of laying, anchoring and termite-proofing the sill are the same as that for the Eastern Braced Frame.

Posts: In balloon framing, posts are almost always made of three 2x4s spiked together (Fig. 11), in one of two ways, to allow a return at the inside corners for nailing interior wall surfacing. As in the eastern braced frame, the posts extend as one unit from sill to rafter plate.

Ribbon: A 1x6″ or 1x8″ board which serves the purpose of the girt. It is dadoed into the posts and studs flush on the inner side (Fig. 12), and occurs only on the sides of the frames receiving the ends of second-floor joists, and sometimes attic joists. It is situated so that its top edge is level with the underside of the joists which rest on it and are spiked to the studs.

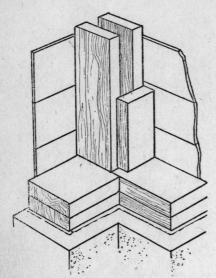

Fig. 11. Balloon-framed posts are usually made of three 2x4's spiked together.

Plates: Two 2x4s spiked together, the under 2x4 is first spiked to the posts and studs and then the top 2x4 is spiked to its mate. Solid 4x4s are never used in this type of construction.

Studs: These are 2x4s which extend as one piece from sill to rafter plate. This method of framing is a distinc-

Fig. 12. The ribband or ribbon is dadoed.

tive feature of balloon-frame construction, and occurs only in this type of framing. At the gable ends, additional studs are framed from rafter plate to marginal rafters. All loads are carried by the studs, each stud carrying part of the load from plate to sill without any lateral distribution taken up by girts.

Openings are framed in a similar manner as for the braced frame, but large openings are oftener than not bridged by oversize headers rather than trussed. This is done because there is no girt at the second-floor level in which to frame diagonal bracing. Some houses, however, have trussed openings by the introduction of an additional header where a girt would normally be. This method, while complicated, is better than a single oversize header which shrinks and swells, and must carry a load without appreciable distribution to the studs.

Sheathing: The balloon frame introduced the practice of diagonal sheathing to compensate for its lack of frame bracing. It was the only way to insure against racking stresses being taken up by the lath and transmitted to the plaster causing it to crack. Diagonal sheathing is a wasteful method of application, and with lumber costing what it does today, modern sheathing is rarely applied diagonally.

It is debatable how much time was saved by omitting the bracing and applying diagonal sheathing. In the non-braced frame, diagonal sheathing runs at an approximate angle of 45 degrees downward from post to

sill at two corners. Diagonally opposite corners are sheathed with the
lumber running upwards, from post
to plate. With the introduction of
bracing in the balloon frame, sheathing was applied horizontally as in the
eastern braced frame, although it was
still general practice until recent years
to sheath diagonally, regardless. Un-
questionably, this method contributes
added rigidity to the structure. It may
be noted here that cracks in plaster
walls do not necessarily indicate that
a house is not properly braced.
Shrinkage and settling of foundations
can also be contributing factors.

Braces: Most of the earlier houses
built by this method were not braced,
but later practice included diagonal
bracing, usually of 1x4″ lumber. This
is dadoed flush into the sill, posts and
studs on the outside, and runs from
sill to the second-floor line; it is repeated to the rafter plate.

Balloon-frame construction is comparatively easy to repair, should some
structural member — excluding sills
and plates — require replacing. Since
outer-wall studs are continuous from
sill to rafter plate, with no interven-
ing heavy timbers framed horizontally, installing new electric wiring or
water pipes does not require cutting
through critical framing. This type of
construction, while light, is strong
enough, but plates and sills are more
prone to damage if contributing
causes exist. The reason for this is due
to the fact that two pieces of lumber
spiked together do not have the structural density of a solid piece, nor the
overall dimensions although they are
nominally the same; a 4x4″ is actually

3⅝x3⅝″, while two 2x4s together
measure only 3¼x3⅝″.

WESTERN OR PLATFORM FRAME

This type of construction is a radical departure from the eastern braced

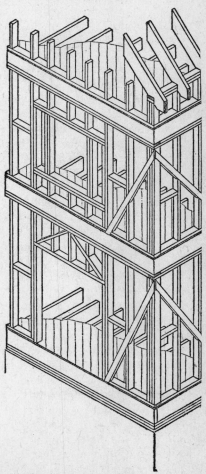

Fig. 13. Western or platform frame.

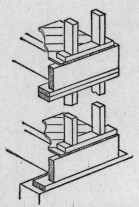

Fig. 14. Joists are framed to headers, and subfloor boards are nailed to joists.

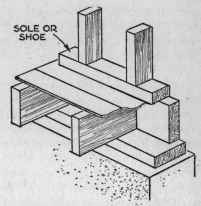

Fig. 15. Soles are spiked through the subflooring to headers and joists.

and balloon frame. Like the balloon frame, it is of lighter construction than the braced frame. It has two new members not found in the other two: the Header and the Sole or Shoe Plate for outer walls. The distinctive feature is that each story forms a platform on which studs for that story are framed, making each story a separate entity. In theory, this type of construction could be carried upward indefinitely. Actually, this idea is limited to the structural possibilities of lumber framing (Fig. 13).

Sills: These are usually the same as for balloon framing: either single or built up. Usually they are single 2x6s, 2x8s, or 2x10s. What has been said for the braced and balloon-frame sill applies here also as to method of anchoring and termite proofing.

Posts: Almost always posts are of the built-up type, as with the balloon frame. They may run as one unit from sill to rafter plate, in which case a 4x4 or two 2x4s are the unit with a 2x4 on each side running from platform

to platform, supporting the plate for that story. More frequently they are three 2x4s running from sill to plate and from sole to plate between each story.

Headers: These are 2″ lumber of the same depth as the joists, which rest on and are framed first directly to the sill (Fig. 14). Joists are framed against the headers and form a sort of box, known as the Box Sill, one of the distinctive features of this type of framing. Building a platform-frame house calls for a different procedure than that of the other two types: joists are framed into the header, and the subfloor boards are then nailed to the joists — forming a *platform* for all vertical structural members. This enables the builder to erect all studs, exterior and interior, up to the second story. This is a decided advantage over the other methods of procedure which call for posts first, then the plates and then the studding, etc.

Soles or Shoes: These are another feature of the platform frame. They are horizontal members, usually 2x4s which support the studs. They are set directly on the subfloor and are spiked through it to the headers and joists (Fig. 15).

Studs: These are 2x4s which run from story to story, as in the eastern frame, but all of the same length. They are framed into the sole instead of a sill, and support a plate for each story.

Openings are framed in a similar manner as for the other two types, except that larger openings are more easily trussed than the balloon frame because the diagonals can be butted against the plate, like the girt in the eastern frame.

Plates: Two 2x4s occur at each floor level, supporting the headers, joists, subfloor and studding for the next story. There are two variations of framing the roof rafters in the platform frame. Plates are framed for the attic floor on which another header and subfloor is framed, with a short section of post and studs supporting an additional plate to which the roof rafters are framed. The other method has only a plate on which rest the joists for the atitc floor, and roof rafters. The attic floor is nailed to the joists and nailing strips attached to the rafters (Fig. 16).

Braces: Originally the western platform frame was not braced. Building codes usually specify let-in bracing as for the balloon frame, and it is common practice now to brace the corners.

Sheathing: Like the unbraced balloon frame, sheathing for the western frame is applied diagonally. This is of

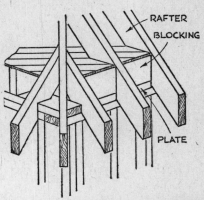

Fig. 16. A plate supports joists and rafters.

greater importance in this type of construction because of an inherent weakness in corner framing when the posts run only one story high. If diagonal sheathing were not used, there would be no vertical tie of any kind. In modern practice, which includes diagonal bracing, sheathing is applied horizontally to reduce waste of lumber, but the diagonal method is still best for the western platform frame, unless posts are continuous from sill to rafter plate.

FIRE STOPPING

In all types of stud-wall construction, hollow "flues" are formed between sill and second floor, and second floor to attic framing. In the balloon frame a flue extends from *sill to rafter plate*. A fire starting in the cellar would be fed by these flues and quickly continue through the entire structure up to the roof. In the very old houses, not much attention was paid to any form of fire retarding. In the eastern braced frame, the girts

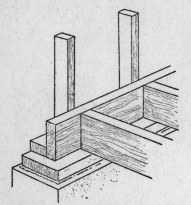

Fig. 17. The T-sill is spiked to the studs.

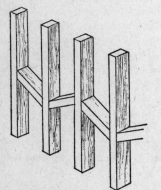

Fig. 18. Draft stoppers nailed in a herring-bone pattern.

ping method. Then the T-sill was designed to shut off drafts at the sill line. The T-sill is a header of the same size as the joists, spiked to the studs, and the joists framed against the header which forms a fire stop (Fig. 17). The sill in this case must be wider than 6".

Fire stopping is somewhat misleading in its meaning, the layman imagining, perhaps, that it means *fireproofing*. Actually, Draft Stopping is more accurate as these methods are fire-retarding barriers, definitely slowing down fire spread. Wood bridging, for all practical purposes, accomplishes the same end as masonry between studs.

General practice of later-day house construction was to frame 2x4 draft stoppers between all studs at a slightly alternating angle, called "herringbone" stopping (Fig. 18). The idea still persists that the herringbone pat-

between each story in some measure acted as fire retarders, but no retarding method was employed at the sill or between floors.

Later-day construction employed bricks laid in mortar from sill to just above the floor line, between the studs. In some instances concrete was poured to the same height between the studs. Also 2x4 bridging between studs about midway between floors was introduced as a further fire-stop-

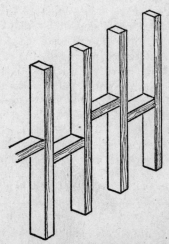

Fig. 19. Horizontal bridging is equally effective.

tern contributes added strength to the wall. Actually, its contribution as a strengthener is negligible, and horizontal bridging (Fig. 19), which requires less time and fitting is equally as effective, with the same slight strengthening factor. Methods of draft stopping and fire retarding in old houses lacking this precaution, will be discussed in Chapter 8.

INTERIOR CONSTRUCTION

Structural methods of constructing partitions and the like are more or less the same in all types of framing, all starting with the floor joists which support the loads.

Joists: Floor joists are supposed to be large enough and of sufficient depth to carry floor loads and prevent deflection from cracking plaster walls. The rule-of-thumb method of determining this is to limit deflection to 1/360 of the span. Most building codes specify the allowable sizes of joists, girders, and rafters for specific loads and spans. Where codes do not dictate sizes, quite often another rule-of-thumb is employed: No. 1 Common joists are equal in span in *feet* to 1½ times their depth in *inches*. No. 2 Common is equal in span in feet to its depth in inches. Both these methods of figuring are based on joists spaced 16″ on centers — an example being:

No. 1 Common, 2x10″ could have a span of 15 feet — 1½ times its depth in inches converted to feet.

No. 2 Common, 2x10″ could have a span of 10 feet — equal to its depth in inches.

Very old houses in rural sections quite frequently have first-floor joists made of heavy timber or small half-logs spaced widely apart. Due to their great age and coincident dampness from cellars — often of stone-wall construction with earth floors — they have decayed to a point beyond safety limits. Replacing them with joists of adequate size spaced 16″ on centers can usually be done without too much trouble. Joists should be bridged for added rigidity, the tendency being for them to bend apart due to load stresses. In later-day house construction joists were bridged with crossed diagonal pieces of lumber 1x2″ or 1x3″ for joists up to 2x10″ inclusive; and 2x2″ or 2x3″ for those of greater depth (Fig. 20). Bridging should occur every 6 to 8 feet of unsupported length of joist.

Creaking and springy floors are generally due to joists inadequately sized, spaced too far apart, not bridged, or all three conditions. Quite frequently 1st-floor joists, while

Fig. 20. Joists should be bridged for rigidity.

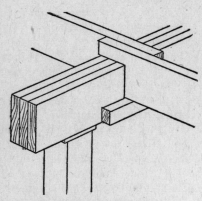

Fig. 21. Built-up girders can run
continuously.

sound, were not designed to carry
modern weight loads of refrigerators,
deep freezers, and the like. Additional joists, or a girder, supported by
posts of wood or hollow steel, can be
added. Girders can be solid timber or
built-up, either being satisfactory.

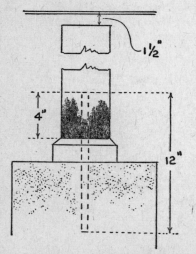

Fig. 22. A metal dowel secures the post to
the footing.

Lumber that is built-up does not
have the same thickness as a solid
piece of the same nominal size, as has
been explained before. Therefore, to
equal the actual thickness of solid
lumber, an additional thickness is required in built-up girders, the lengths
of which should be spiked or lagscrewed together. Such a girder has
the advantage of not checking or splitting nearly as much as is frequently
the case with the larger, solid timbers.
Moreover, solid girders can run only
from support to support, while built-
up girders make possible one continuous piece from wall to wall, thereby
tying the frame closely together.

When replacing or adding joists,
finished flooring must be removed,
but the subfloor is left intact. Where
joists are tenoned into other framing
members in very old houses, saw the
joist off at the tenons, and pry the
joists from the subflooring. Remove
one joist at a time and either cut off
the nails or drive them through the
floor and pull them out. Install the
new joist and nail the subfloor to it
before removing another joist. Solid
bridging or cross bridging can be installed, the ends butting against the
top of the joist being toenailed from
the underside.

Cellar posts supporting first-floor
girders must be clear of any moisture
collecting on the floor; the cellar air
must be dry, and the posts must have
adequate support by way of a footing
of adequate size. A 24x24x12" poured
concrete footing is usual for the average home, regardless of what type
post is used, be it wood or a hollow
steel column. For light loads, small

wood or steel posts, these dimensions can be reduced to about 18x18x12". Extend the footing about 2" above the finished cellar floor, with a ½" diameter x 12" galvanized iron pipe for a metal dowel imbedded in the concrete about 8", and extending about 4" above the footing. This dowel is for a wood post and serves as an anchor (Fig. 22).

Bore a hole in the bottom of the post to receive the dowel and thoroughly coat the bottom with asphalt, tar, or soak it in creosote to prevent possible moisture from the footing seeping in, causing the post to decay. Cut your post about 1½" shorter than the dimension between top of footing and bottom of girder, and use 3" nominal lumber, the width of the post or wider for making wedges. To make them, cut off the lumber about 6" longer than the thickness of the post, scribe a line along the edge diagonally from one corner to the other and saw the block in half, edgewise. Drive the wedges in tightly and spike the post assembly to the girder by toe-nailing. These wedges also form a sort of cap, required if the post is of smaller section than the girder. Quite frequently *slightly* sagging joists can be jacked up in this manner, and often straightened (Fig. 23).

Adjustable Posts

Adjustable hollow steel posts (Fig. 24), with a steel cap attached to a screw, similar to a jack, are relatively inexpensive and made particularly for cellar use, having a base plate which may be bolted to the footing to make certain that they will not move.

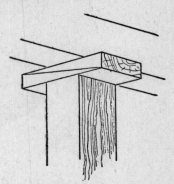

Fig. 23. Wedges can be used to jack-up sagging joists.

Bathroom Joists

You may plan to install an extra bathroom, either on or above the first story level, in which case the existing joists may be too small to carry this additional load. Bathrooms are generally figured to have a dead and live load of from 60 to 70 pounds per square foot, while floor-joist spans are usually planned to support loads from 40 to 50 pounds per square foot. You

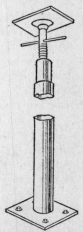

Fig. 24. Adjustable hollow steel post.

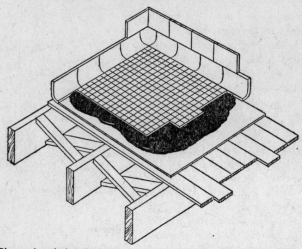

Fig. 25. Plywood nailed to the subfloor provides a smooth firm base for tile.

must therefore add joists, framing them adequately, either on bearing partitions or the outside wall, or both, depending on the location of the bathroom. If your new bathroom floor is to be tile, the traditional method of laying it in concrete or cement — requiring lowered joists to keep the finished floor level with the existing room-floor level — isn't necessary. Tile can now be set in a rubber-base adhesive or cement made for that purpose. All that is required is to make sure that the subfloor is smooth, or better still, ¼" fir plywood nailed over the subfloor and the tile set in the cement on the plywood. The overall thickness of this method of application approximates the thickness of a double floor, so new joists can be added of the same dimensions as the old ones (Fig. 25).

Attic joists in houses of yesterday were frequently spaced farther apart, or of smaller dimensions than other floor joists — the attic being considered at the time of building as traditional storage space only. Expanding the living area to one of these old-fashioned attics will require additional joists to take care of live loads. If your attic is one of these oldtimers and has a floor, it must be removed. After this is done it's a comparatively easy matter to add new joists to support heavier loads — 40 to 50 pounds per square foot and, if a bathroom is contemplated, 60 to 70 pounds per square foot.

Notching Joists

Frequently water pipes and the like must be run through joists. This is a poor practice, but if absolutely necessary, allowable methods are as follows: A notch can be cut in the tops or bottoms of joists, but no deeper or wider than 1/16 the height of the joist. The maximum diameter of a hole bored in a 10" joist is 2½",

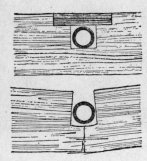

Fig. 26. Correct method of notching joists.

with a maximum distance from the top or bottom of 2". Fig. 26 illus-trates another method sometimes used. The hole should be made only near the top of the joist, and bridged with a block of the same thickness as the joist — otherwise the joist is liable to bend and crack at this point.

Stair Framing

Stair Framing: Openings for stair wells are framed by a combination of Headers and Trimmers. Headers run at right angles to the direction of the joists and are doubled. Trimmers run parallel to the joists, being actually a doubled joist. The headers form the

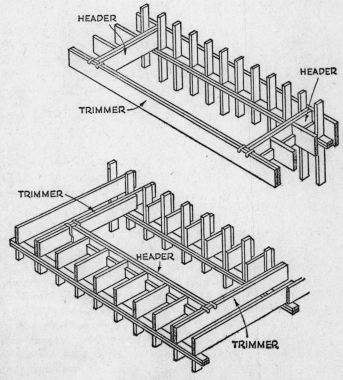

Fig. 27. Right angle and parallel openings.

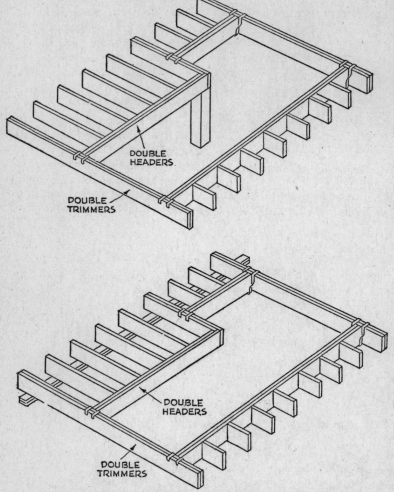

Fig. 28. Two methods of supporting an opening with an angle.

opening at right angles to the joists which are framed to the headers. These shorter joists are called Tail Beams, Tail Joists or Header Joists. This type of construction also pertains to framing around a fireplace. The number of headers and of trim-

mers depends on the direction of the opening in relation to the joist direction; whether or not the stair landing ends at a wall or partition; and whether the opening is a simple rectangle or contains an angle for a stair return. Two examples of rectangular

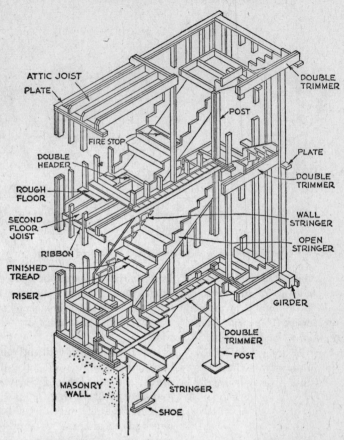

ATTIC JOIST
PLATE
DOUBLE TRIMMER
FIRE STOP
POST
DOUBLE HEADER
PLATE
DOUBLE TRIMMER
ROUGH FLOOR
SECOND FLOOR JOIST
WALL STRINGER
OPEN STRINGER
RIBBON
FINISHED TREAD
RISER
GIRDER
DOUBLE TRIMMER
POST
MASONRY WALL
STRINGER
SHOE

Fig. 29. Typical rough stair framing assembly from cellar to attic.

openings are given in Fig. 27 in which one opening runs at right angles to the joists, requiring one header and two trimmers; the other opening running parallel to the joists, requiring 2 headers and one trimmer.

An opening with an angle is illustrated in Fig. 28 showing two methods of supporting the corner of the angle.

The cantilever method of supporting the angle requires the angle to be fairly close to a supporting partition with joists from an adjacent span which can run out to the header.

Landings are small intermediate floors between floors, designed to break up long stretches of stairs. Landings are usually supported by partition studs to which they are spiked. Sometimes the ends of the landing joists rest on intermediate plates framed to the partition studs. A typical rough stair-framing assem-

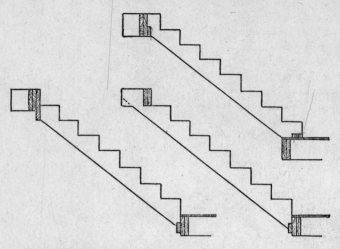

Fig. 30. Three methods of framing stringers to floors and landings.

bly is clearly illustrated in Fig. 29.

Stairs are made up of supporting members called Rough Carriages, Stringers, or Horses. These run from floor to floor, floor to landing, or landing to landing, and are cut to the profile of the underside of the risers and treads. A 3-foot wide stair usually

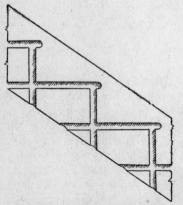

Fig. 31. Stringer framed in position.

is supported by three stringers, one at each side and one in the center. Risers are the vertical dimension of the steps; treads, the horizontal dimension.

Stringers along a wall and partition are nailed to the wall and partition studs, and are either shop manufactured, or built on the premises. Wall stringers manufactured in a shop are grooved or dadoed to receive the risers and treads, with provision for the introduction of wedges to tighten the risers and treads for squeak prevention. Carpenter-built stringers are plain cut.

Rough stringers are framed into floors and landings in a number of ways (Fig. 30). The easiest and perhaps the best method is for the lower end of the stringer to bear directly on the subfloor, the first riser edge rabbeted back to receive a thrust-block strip nailed to the subfloor. This method locks the stringer, preventing it from moving forward. The other or top end is also rabbeted to receive a bearing-block strip nailed to the header or trimmer. There is one disadvantage to this method where stairs are cramped. It reduces head room which may not be adequate because the floor framing extends forward and downward. Moreover, the interior corner of angle turns is difficult to frame this way. Two other methods are also used — particularly where right-angle turns occur: The bottom of the stringer is butted against the header or trimmer and rabbeted to receive a bearing-block strip, while its upper end and top extend under the landing framing. The third method is the same for the bottom, but the top is supported by 1x2" straps.

What has been said about stair-stringer construction pertains only to rough framing. The finished built-on-the-job stair has finished stringers in addition to the rough ones — one for the wall and one for the outside if the stair is open, or two wall stringers if the stair runs between walls, called a Boxed Stair. Methods of fitting a finished wall stringer vary, but two basic methods are equally good. The first method involves considerable woodworking, the stringer being routed out about ½" deep to the exact profile of the risers and treads which are housed in the stringer. The top and bottom of this type stringer takes the angle formed by the intersections of the back of the tread and bottom of the riser. The stringer is framed in position after the rough one has been installed, and the risers and treads fitted into the stringer and nailed together.

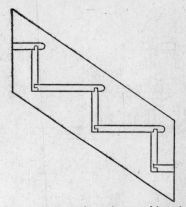

Fig. 32. Risers and treads are rabbeted.

The second method is to cut out the bottom of the finished stringer to conform to the profile of the risers and treads, and fit it over them after they are in place. This requires the ends of the risers and treads to be rabbeted for a close fit (Fig. 32), the nose of the riser butting against the stringer. The top of this type stringer conforms to the angle formed by the risers and treads.

Outside stringers (Fig. 33), are cut to the profile of the risers and treads, the stringer's riser edge being mitered to receive the mitered end of the riser. In good stair construction the tread is rabbeted to fit in a groove in the bottom of the riser (a rabbet-dado

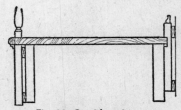

Fig. 33. Outside stringer.

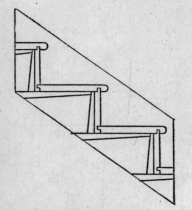

Fig. 34. Wedges can be driven tighter.

joint), and the top of the riser is rabbeted to fit in a groove on the underside of the tread. Treads extend slightly over the riser and the finished open stringer, their edges half-round, called nosing. A small cove or other molding form is nailed under the tread at its juncture with the riser for a finish.

Squeaking Stairs are a nuisance and good only as inspiration for time-battered cartoons about early-morning

RUBBER STRIPS

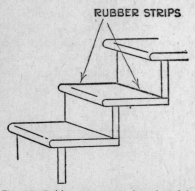

Fig. 35. Rubber strips can be placed between tread and stringer.

home coming. Something should be done about squeaky stairs because the treads are loose and will become looser with traffic. If the stringers have wedges (Fig. 34), and the underside of the stair is accessible, the wedges can be driven tighter. If the more usual made-on-the-job stringer is present, renailing the treads and risers will often correct the trouble. But if the treads and risers are poorly fitted, narrow strips of rubber stair tread can be cut and placed between tread and stringer, and between tread and edge of riser (Fig. 35). This method requires removal of the treads, but the remedy is well worth the effort.

Stair Specifications

If you intend building a new stair, or your present one is poorly designed — that is, too steep for comfortable climbing—one rule-of-thumb method of determining a properly proportioned relationship of tread to riser is as follows: twice riser height plus tread width equals 24″ to 25″. The following combinations for various purposes follow the rule of a total of 24″:

Cellar Stairs: Riser 8″, Tread 8″ (steep)

Back Stairs: Riser 7½″, Tread 9″ (fairly steep)

Front Stairs: Riser 7″, Tread 10″ (easy)

Entrance Steps: Riser 6½″, Tread 11″

Terrace Steps: Riser 6″, Tread 12″

These proportions can of course be varied, but for comfortable use, the

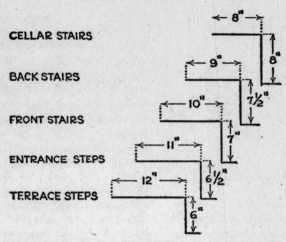

CELLAR STAIRS

BACK STAIRS

FRONT STAIRS

ENTRANCE STEPS

TERRACE STEPS

Fig. 36. Proper relationships between riser and tread.

tread should be wider than the riser is high. This is particularly true today of cellar steps where cellars have been converted into game rooms; for TV and general get-together purposes. For the remodeled cellar, the traditional cellar stair formula is too steep and, if at all feasible, it should be changed to a lesser degree of angle. A riser more than 8″ is too steep for comfort, and less than 6″ is too gradual (Fig. 36).

PARTITION FRAMING

Inside partitions are made usually with 2x4 studs, and in the same manner as outside walls for the western platform frame; that is, they have a shoe or sole, studs and a plate or cap. There are two kinds of partitions: Non-Bearing and Bearing, the latter supporting floor joists overhead. Joists that support bearing partitions are

double, with narrow separating blocks (bridging) between them (Fig. 37). When such a partition is located at

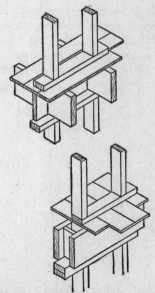

Fig. 37. Separating blocks between joists.

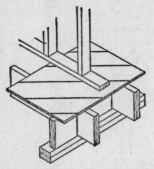

Fig. 38. Solid blocking distributes the load.

right angles to, and near the center of joist spans, all joists are doubled with narrow blocking between them — or the joists are single but deeper than would normally be used. A non-bearing partition running at right angles to the joists does not require extra support, all joists helping to support it. But if it runs parallel to the joists and over one, this one is doubled with narrow blocking between, there being too much stress for one joist. If the partition is located between two normally spaced joists,

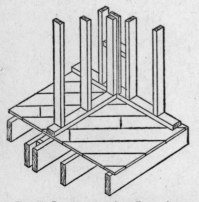

Fig. 39. Partition members framed on subfloor.

longer solid blocking is introduced about every two feet to distribute the load evenly to both joists (Fig. 38).

Partition studs are set up in several ways, the simplest (Fig. 39), and per• haps the best method being to lay the subfloor first as a solid sheet over the entire house area, tying the structure together at that level. Then frame the soles or shoes for the partitions on the floor, and the studs to the soles. Some builders frown on this practice because shrinkage could occur across plate, sole, subfloor and joist, and therefore the stud should rest directly on the joist. This does away with the effect of shrinkage in the subfloor, but makes it impossible to lay the subfloor continuously. If the subfloor is laid diagonally (the usual method), extra blocking is required at the partition point, causing extra waste and labor. And remember that framing lumber should be kiln dried and free from excessive shrinkage.

In western-platform construction, the subfloor is first nailed to the joists, and then the sole is laid and the studs spiked to the sole. Often in balloon framing, when the studs run at right angles to the joists, this same method is employed. Usually, however, in the eastern braced and balloon frame, the partition studs for the first floor are framed on girders, joists, or blocking between joists. Second-floor studs are framed to the plates of the first-floor studs — if partitions set over each other.

Studs are usually spaced 16″ on centers with bridging between them about midway up, which can be herringbone or horizontal (Fig. 40).

Fig. 40. Studs braced with bridging.

The bearing-partition cap is often a 3x4, but usually a doubled 2x4, although a single 2x4 is adequate if the joists rest on the cap, directly over the studs. Non-bearing partition studs are frequently 2x3s, as they function only as a surface for wall coverings. Non-bearing closet partitions are often 2x4s or 2x3s turned facewise

rather than edgewise, to secure added floor space. However, where plumbing waste pipes run in partitions, the studs may be 2x6s, or 2x4s furred out for a wall thick enough to allow for pipe diameters (Fig. 41).

Openings are framed in the same manner as for outside-wall openings, that is, they consist of vertical trimmers supporting horizontal doubled headers. Wide openings are trussed. The usual practice for interior door openings is to make them 1" to 2" larger on each side than the door frames, so that they can be fitted, squared, plumbed and blocked.

Removing Partitions

Non-bearing partitions can be removed when remodeling as, for instance, if two small rooms separated by such a partition are to be made into one large room; or a storage wall

Fig. 41. Studs may have to be furred out to accommodate plumbing.

is to be installed between two rooms. A bearing partition cannot be completely taken out unless adequate support for the joists overhead, such as a girder, takes the place of the partition. It can, however, be remodeled, a few examples being: constructing an opening where none existed; enlarging an opening which is too small; constructing a storage wall between two rooms; converting the partition to a latticed wall to create the effect of spaciousness to two connecting rooms. These various changes in a bearing partition require careful step-by-step procedure, the bearing plate being temporarily braced while remodeling is taking place. Moreover, the finished, remodeled partition must in no way have its load-supporting function impaired. This is not difficult to achieve, as will be described in Chapter 8.

FLOORS

Subfloors

Subflooring, also called rough flooring, as has been discussed previously, is applied either before partition studs are placed, or after the studs are in position. Very old houses were built without subfloors, and before the 20th century, square-edged single floor boards were usually used. Later they were made of tongued and grooved lumber. Eighteenth and early nineteenth century houses were more apt to have random-width floor boards of hardwoods and softwoods, depending on the locality. Thickness varied, but was much heavier than used today, at

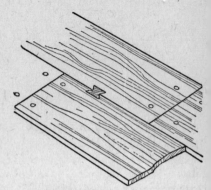

Fig. 42. Hardwood pegs imitate the originals.

times being practically planks with widths up to 36″. Boards were nailed and frequently pegged with hardwood pegs or dowels. In later-day houses simulating these early and beautiful floors, floor boards are usually nailed to a subfloor, with short hardwood plugs inserted to imitate the original pegs (Fig. 42).

A good subfloor is usually made of 1x4″ or 1x6″ stock, and nailed with at least two nails at every joist, with the ends staggered but supported by the joists. There is a considerable difference of opinion on the subject of square edged versus tongued and grooved subflooring, the argument being that tongued and grooved lum-

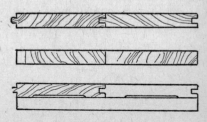

Fig. 43. Opinions on suflooring differ.

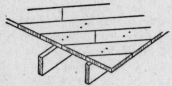

Fig. 44. Subflooring laid diagonally.

ber if dry and exposed to dampness—which is the case oftener than not—swells and buckles, causing uneven floors. This doesn't occur with square edged lumber which should not be fitted too tightly. Thorough nailing is a must for both types (Fig. 43).

Subfloors are usually laid diagonally for two reasons: for the bracing they afford, and because a finished floor is never laid in the same direction as a subfloor; and since the direction of a finish floor quite frequently changes in various rooms, the only way to insure a cross-laid pattern is to diagonal the subfloor (Fig. 44).

Finish Flooring

Finish flooring comes in hard and softwoods, the hardwoods being more durable. If you plan to lay a new finish floor, choice of grain pattern and color, hard or softwood, is purely a personal matter depending a great deal on the style of house, your budget and preference.

Hardwood flooring is the most durable and expensive. It can be bought

Fig. 45. Hardwood ends are tongued and grooved.

in a number of species and many grades, the species oftener used being probably oak. Oak is quarter sawed and plain sawed, but plain sawed is used oftener today because it's cheaper. The hardwoods are Oak, Pecan, Beech, Birch and Hard Maple, and range in thicknesses from 5/16" to 25/32", but not in all species. Face widths range from 1½" to 3¼", and most are tongued and grooved lengthwise and at ends (Fig. 45). Better grades of flooring are also machined hollow on the underside, called Hollow Back, which contributes to a firmer contact with the subfloor, there being less surface effected by uneven-

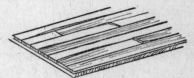

Fig. 46. Finish flooring that has buckled.

ness in the subfloor. Hardwood comes in bundles of random lengths from 2 feet to about 12 feet, the average being about 4½ feet. A limitation of 25% being less than 4 feet is maintained.

Finish flooring should never be laid in a house which is damp due to its having been unheated during vacancy in the winter months—or for any other reason. Kiln-dried flooring will quickly absorb moisture and swell, buckle, twist and fit badly (Fig. 46). Such a floor after drying out would then shrink, leaving gaps between the joints. This precaution, as regards damp surroundings, should be considered when planning to lay a new

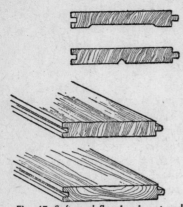

Fig. 47. Softwood flooring is not end matched.

finish floor, even to the extent of *waiting until freshly papered walls have* had a chance to dry out.

Squeaky floors are oftener due to improperly nailed subfloors than to the finish floor, although it, too, can contribute to or be the cause of this nuisance if insufficiently nailed. Before laying a finish floor over a subfloor or an old single-floor, make sure that it is flat and thoroughly nailed. Replace badly damaged parts with new lumber and, if in doubt, nail some more. Be sure to drive in any nails that happen to stick up. In other words, go over the entire subfloor carefully, board by board. Your thoroughness will pay you dividends with a trouble-free finish floor.

Softwood finish flooring is sold in a number of species and grades. You can choose Southern Pine, Douglas Fir, Western Hemlock, Western Larch, Redwood, Southern Cypress, Western Red Cedar, Spruce and Tamarack. The better grades in these woods are hollow back, or scratch

back, flat grain and edge grain—the latter being less prone to slivering and wearing unevenly. However, the flat grain produces a more attractive grain pattern, particularly so in some species. While softwoods are frequently not end matched (tongued and grooved), the best grades are now being matched at the ends also. All have tongued and grooved edges lengthwise (Fig. 47).

Widths vary from 2⅜″ to 5¼″, and lengths from 4 feet to 20 feet, but the thickness for home use is a standard 25/32″. What has been said about precautionary measures for hardwood laying applies also to softwood flooring. The finished floor can be only as good as the subfloor allows.

LAYING A FINISH FLOOR

Estimating Quantities

First you must estimate the quantity of flooring that will be required for a given area; 100 square feet of flooring as it is sold does not cover 100 square feet of area. To get the square area of a room, multiply its width by its length in feet. Then add to the square feet of surface to be covered, the following percentages:

50% for ....25/32″ x 1½″
37½% for ....25/32″ x 2″
33⅓% for ....25/32″ x 2¼″
24% for ....25/32″ x 3¼″
33⅓% for ....⅜″ x 1½″
25% for ....⅜″ x 2″
33⅓% for ....½″ x 1½″
25% for ....½″ x 2″

These figures pertain to a floor laid straight across from wall to wall. Where recesses, such as bay windows

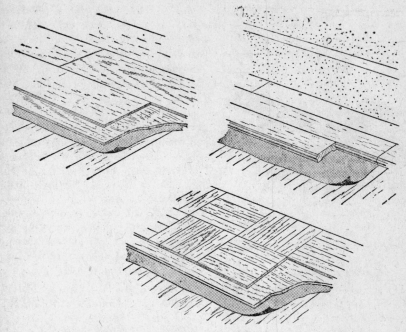

Fig. 48. Building paper should be used to cover the old or subfloor.

and the like occur, additional flooring must be ordered. It is also wise to order 5% additional flooring to take care of cutting and possible damage when laying.

Old floors and subfloors should be covered with a good quality of building paper—15 lb. asphalt-saturated rag felt is excellent. This helps make the floor draft tight, and prevents moisture and dust particularly from a cellar from creeping through. Building paper comes in rolls of 432 square feet. It is inexpensive and provides cheap insurance (Fig. 48).

Finish flooring is "blind nailed," that is, the nails are driven at an angle of approximately 45 degrees into the edge of the strip, in the corner where the tongue and square edge meet. The groove of the next strip hides the nail heads. Use 8d wire casing nails or cut flooring nails for lumber 25/32" thick, and 6d nails for the thinner types of flooring. The nails are set with a nail set, and should be driven every 10" in 25/32" flooring, and not more than 8" apart in the thinner varieties. Cut nails are less apt to split hardwood (Fig. 49); they punch rather than spread the fibers.

To lay the floor, start at the wall line, having removed the base shoe (molding at intersection of baseboard and floor) and the baseboard. Also remove doorway thresholds, if any.

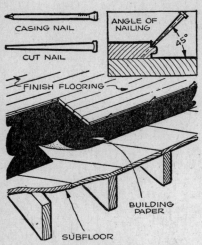

Fig. 49. Cut nails punch the fiber.

The edge of the flooring which faces the wall should be roughly on a line with the baseboard face (Fig. 50), so that when the shoe is nailed to the subfloor, the shoe hides the edge of the floorboard. Nailing the base shoe to the subfloor is the best practice as then, if the baseboard and floorboard

shrink, the shoe is not affected and will conceal the crack. Other methods of nailing the base shoe, such as: framing it to the baseboard, or framing it to the floorboard, result in cracks showing either at the floor line, or at the baseboard line, if shrinkage occurs.

If a shoe is not used, then the edge of the floorboard should be under the baseboard about half its thickness. This first strip of flooring is laid with the grooved edge facing the wall and is face-nailed along that edge. It is a good idea also to toenail the tongue edge, that is, blind nail it. The ends of the strips should be cut to fit the end walls in the same manner as for the side walls, allowing at least ½″ on all sides for expansion (Fig. 51).

The tongue of one strip fits into the groove of the next strip and should fit snugly, but not too tightly. Professional floor layers nail 3 or 4 strips and then drive them against each other tightly. This technique in-

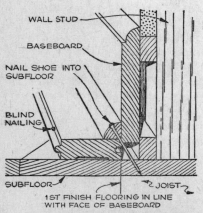

Fig. 50. Nail the shoe to the subfloor.

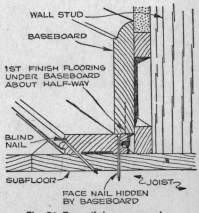

Fig. 51. Toenail the tongue edge.

sures the boards being tight but not too much so. The way this is done usually is to use a square-edged board and a mallet to set the strips. A better method is to plane off the tongue of a piece of tongued and grooved strip, and use the grooved edge to engage the tongue of the floorboard being driven. By this method, there's no chance of damaging the tongue, often the case when a square-edged board is used (Fig. 52).

Since hardwood flooring comes in random lengths, mix the short lengths in with the longer pieces over the entire floor area. Always use long lengths for openings and doorways. Short and cut pieces can be used advantageously in closets. Doors quite frequently must be taken off if the new floor is higher than the old one. The bottoms of doors can be planed to accommodate the new floor.

Floor Finishing

Finish flooring must be scraped or sandpapered to remove scratches and dirt and to smooth out any unevenness of laying. Hand scraping, which according to some authorities produces the most beautiful finish, was once the only method for finishing floors. This, however, is quite a chore, and power sanding machines now usually do the work. These can be rented from most hardware stores. Recommended procedure with a sanding machine is to traverse the floor several times, working the first traverse across the grain and the second lengthwise with the grain. Work with No. 2 sandpaper on the first traverse, and No. ½ on the second

traverse. No. 0 or 2-0 is used on the third and fourth traverse. Manufacturers of hardwood flooring agree that a really fine floor must have four or five sandings with varying grades of sandpaper, as suggested. A final sanding or buffing is accomplished with No. 4, 5 or 6-0 sandpaper. Sanding machines cannot get into corners or close to edges. These should be either hand scraped or sandpapered, the latter being preferable since there's a marked difference in texture between a sanded and hand-scraped finish.

After the sanding has been completed, the floor is swept absolutely clean—*don't use water*—and immediately one of a number of liquid finishes is applied. If this cannot be done the same day, the final sanding should be left for the next when a liquid finish of some sort can be applied. Manufacturers do not recommend using varnish or shellac on fine hardwood floors.

Old floors so badly worn as to be quite uneven in spots are not good bases for a finish floor. Much patch-

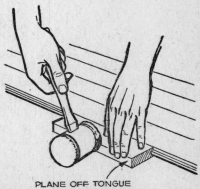

PLANE OFF TONGUE

Fig. 52. Use a planed tongued board.

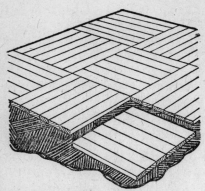

Fig. 53. Prefinished flooring can be cemented.

ing, planing and leveling is necessary —and frequently even these methods aren't enough. A covering of ¼″ or ⅜″ fir plywood, depending on how deep the hollows are, is then the only way to supply a good foundation for the finish floor. Building paper should be laid between the old floor and plywood. The use of plywood as a covering for old and worn floors is also the solution if you plan a finished floor of linoleum, linoleum tile, rubber, cork or of other compositions.

PRE-FINISHED FLOORS

There are several hardwood floors on the market which are pre-finished, requiring none of the sanding operations necessary with regular flooring wood—if care is used to protect them while laying. These floors are mostly oak of various types and colors, and come 3/16″ and ¼″ thick. There are two types of flooring: Squares made up of narrow strips glued at the factory, either in straight courses or in a "basket weave" pattern and broad board about 9″ wide which comes in

random lengths from 4 to 8 feet. The flooring isn't nailed, but cemented to the sub-base with a rubber-base cement, furnished by the manufacturer, in the same manner as laying composition tile, and similar flooring material (Fig. 53). Recommended procedure is that the floor after it is laid should be rolled with a 200 lb. roller which complicates things somewhat, unless you have access to such a roller, or can rent one from a floor-laying concern.

Subfloor

The subfloor must be perfectly smooth, even more so than for regular flooring material, and plywood should first be laid, with building paper under it, if the subfloor or old floor is at all uneven.

For Radiant Heat

This type of hardwood flooring has been processed at the factory to change the cell structure of the wood so that it won't curl or warp under normal conditions, as would be the case with untreated hardwood as thin as 3/16″. A ¼″ pre-finished hardwood flooring that has been baked to counteract the effects of radiant floor heating has recently been developed. This also is cemented to the sub-surface, usually the concrete floor slab used in radiant floor heating installations.

Cost Comparison

There is some saving in these types of finish floor over the regular hardwood floor, as the flooring does not require sanding if precautions are taken to protect it while laying. It is, however, very much thinner than usual 25/32" flooring.

FLOOR REPAIRS

Finished floors in good surface condition which have been used for a number of years, frequently develop cracks between edges more or less over the entire floor. This is usually due to one of the faults of original laying in which the floor, having absorbed moisture when laid, has shrunk. This can be remedied only by taking up each strip and relaying it—quite a chore—but if it is a good hardwood floor, worth the difficulty. Some pieces will inadvertently be damaged when removing the toenailing, and these will have to be replaced with new material. The method of relaying is the same as with a new floor, that is, the strips driven tightly against each other in groups of 3 or 4.

Buckled Strips

Often strips have buckled, due to another fault in original laying—the strip having swelled due to moisture absorption. This more often happens if water has soaked in due to leaks or other causes, the fault not being in the original laying. In this instance you can chisel off the grooved part of a raised strip, being careful not to damage the tongue of its mate. This enables you to remove the strip without splitting the tongue. Remove the mate so that you can extract the bent nails, replace it tightly and re-toenail. Take a new strip and chisel off the

bottom lip of the groove so that you can fit the strip over the tongue of the other. Toenail this from the face, setting the nail below the surface. Do the same to the adjoining grooved piece and fill the set depressions with plastic wood.

Worn Random-widths

You may have a badly worn random-width single floor dating from the eighteenth century, which you cherish. It would be sacrilege to cover this rarity with a new hardwood floor, that is, if the original floor is sound—they usually are unless exposed to the weather. Machine sanding can quite often level the floor enough, if it is a thick floor. If it is not, don't use a power sander. Carefully hand scrape as smooth as possible and be satisfied with a few bumps and hollows which, in a floor of this kind, have a certain charm. Often a hopelessly uneven floor of this type can be saved by removing the boards and turning them over and refinishing them. Wide cracks which have appeared in some of these old floors can be filled with crack-filling material, a number of which are on the market. First clean out the dirt thoroughly and then fill.

Springy Floors

Springy floors due to over-widely spaced joists, can be replaced by plank floor boards which are 2" thick and of varying widths. These in themselves are to a great degree self-supporting. However, the joists underneath them must be strong enough to sustain the added weight. Plank flooring is comparatively new in home construction, and is part of the Plank and Beam system becoming increasingly popular with many home owners. In this system the plank floor, supported by widely spaced beams of considerable depth and thickness, serves as the ceiling of the room below it.

NEW FRAMING METHODS

In "modern" house construction where wood is the principal material, changes in traditional framing have been introduced to meet the new requirements of the modern form, such as, very wide spans in rooms, cantilevered overhangs of flat roofs, corner windows and the like. Pre-fabricated modern houses have produced new methods of framing exterior and interior walls which, due to old and antiquated building codes, are not permissible in all sections of the country. These obsolete codes are being gradually revised to keep pace with modern science which has produced new building materials never dreamed of when building codes were first introduced to regulate the safe use of solid lumber.

The so-called flat roof so frequently used in modern architectural design is nearly always a form of "shed" roof with very little slope. In theory, an absolutely flat roof will shed water, but in practice it's impossible to construct such a roof without the presence of pockets where water would collect. Some modern roofs are designed for just this purpose, that is, to form a shallow reservoir to contain water for cooling purposes. This, of course, entails extraordinary measures to prevent leaks and to take care of the added load.

Framing Openings

In the modern house, small and medium-size openings are framed in the same manner as the traditional house, but very large openings require heavier framing to carry loads and prevent excessive deflections. The simplest, easiest and least expensive way to do this is to employ a single or built-up girder of sufficient dimensions to carry the load. There is a drawback, however, to this method: any shrinkage occurring in the girder will cause settling of the superstructure and cracks in the plaster partitions. To overcome any possible tendency of this sort, trussed spans of various types of construction, similar to bridge spans, are used.

One such type involves the use of a header supported by a series of doubled studs at each end. Verticals are spaced across the span and rest on blocking framed to the girder. The verticals support blocking framed to a plate. This assembly is further braced by diagonals between the verticals, framed to girder and plate. In effect, the plate for the joists and studs overhead is supported by the combination of verticals, blocking and diagonals which distribute the load evenly throughout the entire assembly. Vertical metal tie rods or long bolts are usually required to help distribute the load, as spikes alone are usually not enough.

Another method is to construct a built-up girder of considerable depth.

Here, a plate or flange is used top and bottom, with cripples or stiffeners spaced across the span. Sheathing is nailed diagonally to the plates, one side in opposite direction to the other. The disadvantage of this construction is that the overall thickness of the girder is greater than a normal 2x4 stud wall, even if 2x3s are substituted. Moreover, some settlement shows in this type of girder.

The third and perhaps the most satisfactory method is to use plates and ½″ fir plywood instead of the sheathing, with the surface grain of the plywood running diagonally from each upper corner downward, two panels meeting at the center of the span. If, in addition to nailing, the panels are also glued with a synthetic resin glue, the whole assembly becomes extremely rigid and load sustaining. This method, using nominal 2x3s for plates and stiffeners, results in an overall thickness of the same dimensions as a 2x4 stud partition. The various types of girders mentioned are usually hidden in a finished stud wall or partition.

Framing joists to the built-up girder is done in several ways: on top of the girder, which limits the depth of such a girder because of opening heights; or framed to a header which is lagscrewed to the girder, in which case the girder can be of any depth necessary for extremely wide spans, as for example, from the top of a lower window to the bottom of an upper window.

Corner windows frequently found in modern houses, present a problem different from the traditional method

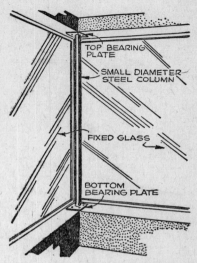

ig. 54. A steel column supports the corner.

of framing. A steel column of small diameter, with top and bottom bearing plates, is usually introduced as support (Fig. 54), in place of the traditional wood corner post. The

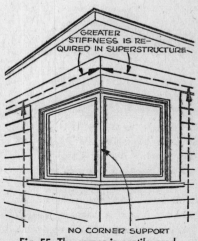

Fig. 55. The corner is cantilevered.

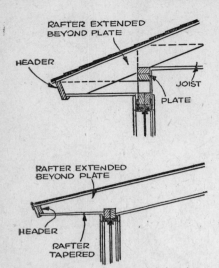

RAFTER EXTENDED
BEYOND PLATE

HEADER

JOIST

PLATE

RAFTER EXTENDED
BEYOND PLATE

HEADER

RAFTER
TAPERED

Fig. 56. Rafters extend beyond the plate.

window is sometimes carried around the column, leaving it exposed, or the column is concealed by the corner window frame which serves two windows. When a steel column is not used, a wood post of larger dimensions takes its place. For small corner

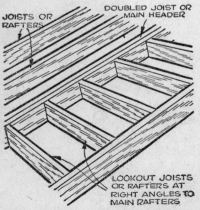

JOISTS OR
RAFTERS

DOUBLED JOIST OR
MAIN HEADER

LOOKOUT JOISTS
OR RAFTERS AT
RIGHT ANGLES TO
MAIN RAFTERS

Fig. 57. Continuous overhangs have lookouts.

windows, the corner is frequently cantilevered, omitting a support. A great deal of stiffness in the superstructure is necessary with cantilever construction, as its tendency is to deflect considerably. This stiffness is extremely necessary due to the heaviest loads being usually found at the corners of a house (Fig. 55).

Modern houses very often have roof overhangs to shade picture windows. These are framed in a number of ways: one being the extension of joists or rafters beyond the plate, to which an outside header is framed. The joists, rafters and header are frequently tapered to permit the low winter-sun's rays to penetrate windows. If the overhang continues around the house, "lookout joists" or rafters are framed at right angles to a doubled joist or main header on the sides parallel to the direction of joists or rafters (Figs. 56 and 57).

Often you will see large expanses of roof supported by widely spaced posts of small dimensions or diameter. Construction here calls for girders, usually built up, supported by the posts, with intermediate joists or rafters framed to the girders. The outside header must be strong and stiff enough to support the extensions without sagging. This precludes tapering the joists or rafters unless the top of the header, full width, is raised above the tops of joists or rafters. This is also frequently done to conceal the small amount of slope to the usual shed-type roof, creating an effect of the roof being perfectly flat.

Another radical departure from the traditional method of framing walls and floors is often employed in the modern house. It is called "stressed cover" or "stressed skin" construction. Most houses using this method are "shop" built, known as pre-fabricated. Wall and floor sections are delivered to the building site, ready to be raised and framed in place. Many modern, custom-built houses also employ the stressed-cover idea, it being fabricated on the job.

Stressed-cover construction usually consists of a panel made up of studs or joists which are covered with plywood on both sides. A stressed-cover floor is usually made up of 2x6″ joists spaced 2 feet on centers. A ½″ or ⅝″ plywood panel covers one side which is the subfloor, and a ⅜″ plywood panel covers the other side which is the ceiling. The panels are glued to the framing with synthetic resin glue and nailed with 6d or 8d nails about 6″ on centers. Walls are made the same way, usually with 1x2″ studs spaced 12″ on centers and covered on the outside with ⅜″ plywood which is the sheathing, and on the inside with ¼″ plywood. There are, of course, variations in this type of construction. These walls and floors when glued and nailed are remarkably strong and rigid, with the loads they carry mostly taken up by the plywood. The face grain of the plywood usually runs at right angles to the direction of the joists in floors, affording maximum stiffness to the joists. Face grain on the plywood for walls always runs vertically. As has been mentioned before, some building codes up to the present don't permit this type of construction, only

because it wasn't dreamed of when the codes were formulated. Basically it is sound, rigid construction.

FINISHED PARTITIONS

Lathing Materials

Partitions in most houses and particularly those of years back are made up of studs, lath and plaster. Lath may be wood, metal or plaster board, with wood predominating in the older houses. Plaster must have a foundation into which it can lock, and wood lath was designed for that purpose. Wood lath is made from spruce, white pine, cypress, or woods free from tendencies to stain which might bleed through the plaster. Two grades, Nos. 1 and 2 wood lath are acceptable. The standard size is ¼″ thick, 1⅜″ wide and usually 4 feet long, although No. 2 may often be ¼x1¼″. Originally lath was split from boards, but is now sawed rough purposely so that the fibers give added anchorage for the plaster. Wood lath is nailed at right angles to the studs and floor joists, and spaced not less than ¼″ nor more than ⅜″ apart. Where two ends meet, a space of ¼″ is left between them. Lath on walls is laid about 5 to 7 courses and the joints then broken, and 5 to 7 more laid and the joints again broken, so that a continuity is broken to prevent a crack, should one occur, from running the entire height of a room. Ceiling laths are usually laid with broken joints occurring every 4 courses. It is common practice today to reinforce corners where the lath abuts, with a narrow strip of light metal lath bent

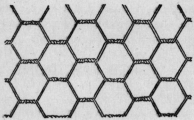

Fig. 58. Wire lath.

at right angles. This procedure prevents cracks from occurring at these

Fig. 59. Metal lath.

points. Moreover, lath that abuts a masonry wall is similarly reinforced for the same reason.

Wood lath must be well seasoned, otherwise excessive shrinkage would occur, yet, if lath is dry and plaster is applied, they quickly absorb the

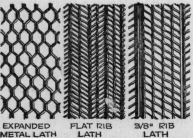

EXPANDED   FLAT RIB   3/8" RIB
METAL LATH   LATH   LATH

Fig. 60. Expanded, flat rib, and rib lath.

moisture, swell and break the plaster keys formed by the spacing. Therefore, the day before plaster is applied, wood lath is thoroughly wetted to permit it to take up the proper amount of water and to evaporate the excess. This procedure conditions the lath so as to prevent excessive swelling and shrinking.

Metal Lath was introduced to take the place of wood lath and has a number of advantages over the latter. It is fire resistant and readily lends itself to formed shapes. There are three basic types of metal lath: woven wire known as Wire Fabric or Wire Lath; punched metal sheets called Metal Lath; and punched and expanded metal sheets termed Expanded Metal Lath (Figs. 58, 59, and 60).

Wire Lath is a woven wire fabric of black or galvanized iron wire with a 2½ mesh per inch. This can be used on spacings up to 12" on centers. For wider spacing than 12", V-rib stiffeners are introduced, spaced 8" apart.

Metal Lath which is a punched and stamped sheet is used considerably as a portland-cement plaster ground for the application of ceramic tile, being the stiffest of the metal-lath group. It is also quite frequently used for ceiling work.

Expanded Metal Lath is sold in plain and stiffened sheets which are classified as Expanded Metal Lath, Flat Rib Lath, and ⅜" Rib Lath, the latter being a combination of expanded metal and ribs of a total thickness of ⅜" from the top side of the lath to the outer edge of the rib.

Metal lath is attached to wood with 6d nails or 1¼", 14 gauge wire staples spaced 6″, with tie wires of about 18 gauge. Some modern houses have suspended ceilings for various reasons, in which case metal lath is always used. Ribbed metal lath is applied with the ribs running at right angles to the studs or joists.

Wall Coverings

Plaster Board of various kinds has in recent years taken the place of wood and metal lath in dwelling construction. It is less expensive, can be applied much easier and quicker, and offers considerable saving in plaster materials. Most of these plaster-board laths have a solid core of gypsum covered with heavy fiber sheets to which plaster adheres better than to any other fabricated product. These boards usually have grooved edges lengthwise, into which the rounded edges of the mating board fit, leaving a slightly grooved joint for added plaster-locking at these joints. The ends are usually cut square.

Gypsum-core boards are as a rule ⅜″ thick, over which ½″ of plaster is usually applied. They range in width from 16″ to 24″, and are 32″ to 64″ long. Some types are plain faced and others are perforated over their entire surface with ½″ holes, for added plaster locking which mushrooms on the back side. Gypsum-core plaster boards are fireproof, which is yet another advantage this material has over other lathing materials.

Plaster boards are nailed lengthwise at right angles to studs or joists with 3d flat-head wire nails spaced about 6″ on studs, and 3″ on the edges. All joints are broken or staggered. At inside corners and where the material abuts masonry walls, the practice is to add narrow bent strips of light metal lath to prevent cracks in the plaster at these points. Wood blocking must be provided between studs and joists for electrical outlet boxes and other attachments, as for any lathing material.

Fiberboard of various makes, in large sheets, is also used as a base for plaster, and attached to studs and joists in the same manner as gypsum-core boards.

The relative adhesive power of plaster to various lathing materials, determined by the Bureau of Standards, is as follows:

On Punched Metal Lath 1.6
On Wood Lath 2.1
On Fiberboard 2.3
On Woven Wire Lath 2.4
On Expanded Metal Lath .. 4.3
On Gypsum-core Lath 6.0

Baseboards

A plaster partition in most houses of yesterday is usually finished with a Baseboard and a Sub-Base or Base Shoe at the floor line, and a Picture Molding near the ceiling. Where the ceiling and walls meet there's usually a Ceiling Cove Molding, or a Cornice of some form. In many old houses this cornice is quite elaborate, made up of a number of molding forms with walls and ceiling joined by a sweeping cove. This type of cornice was molded entirely of plaster, fabricated on the job when the finish-coat of plaster was applied. Some houses have Chair Rails to protect the plaster from contact with the backs of

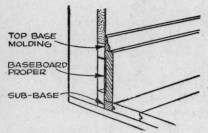

Fig. 61. Three-piece baseboard.

chairs, and many houses have Wainscoats in some rooms, particularly in dining rooms, part way up from the floor.

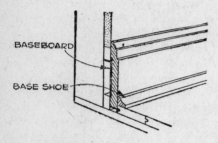

Fig. 62. Two-piece baseboard.

Baseboards, also known as mopboards, skirting or skirting boards, may be ornate or plain and consist of three parts, two parts, or a single

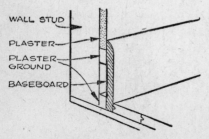

Fig. 63. One-piece baseboard.

piece. Three-part baseboards usually have a sub-base, baseboard proper, and a base molding on the top edge of the baseboard. The sub-base, having a tongue, is put down before the finish flooring is laid, the groove of the floorboard receiving the tongue of the sub-base. Usually plaster grounds for the baseboard, which are strips of wood of plaster thickness nailed to the studs, are found at the floor line for the sub-base, and another just below the top of the baseboard (Fig. 61).

Two-piece baseboards consist of a base shoe and a baseboard, the top edge of which is frequently shaped to a molding form. The plaster grounds are located at the bottom of the baseboard and below its top edge (Fig. 62).

A single baseboard is usually plain faced with a rounded edge at its top instead of molding (Fig. 63). It rests on the sub-floor where a plaster ground is nailed, the other ground being placed just below the top edge of the baseboard. Baseboards are usually hollow back so that they have a minimum of bearing surface on the plaster, insuring a snug fit, and are usually nailed through the plaster grounds to the studs. Sub-bases are nailed to the subfloor, and base shoes should be nailed to the sub-floor also. At inner corners, one baseboard is usually butted against the wall, while the other piece is coped with a coping saw to fit the profile of the butted piece. Outer corners are always miter joints. At door openings, baseboards are butted against the casing, or plinth block edges.

Picture Moldings are narrow width

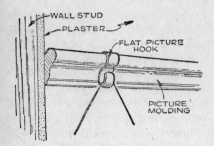

Fig. 64. Picture molding.

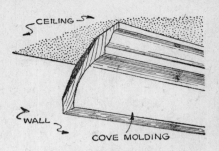

Fig. 65. Cove molding.

wood molding of various forms with a bead top over which standard flat picture hooks fit (Fig. 64). Moldings are always nailed through the plaster to the studs—or should be—particularly if they are supposed to support heavy pictures. Modern-day methods of hanging pictures, employing a special hook with a needle-pointed nail, have largely supplanted the old picture hook, exposed wire and picture molding. These hooks are made in many sizes for varied sustaining loads, but they have one disadvantage in that they leave a hole in the plaster when removed and, in brittle plaster of long years standing, quite frequently chip it out around the hole.

Should you have a picture molding which you plan to remove, carefully consider the work entailed. You will inevitably damage the plaster when removing the molding, and will have considerable patching and repairing to do, besides refinishing the wall to hide the picture molding line. Quite frequently, even repainting will not altogether conceal the original location of the molding.

Ceiling Coves, other than those of plaster, are wood moldings nailed through the plaster (Fig. 65).

Cornices are usually made up of three pieces of molding, or built up of three molding forms with a box supported by blocking nailed to the studs and joists.

Chair Rails are flat strips of wood, usually with a molding form for the two edges (Fig. 66). Plaster grounds are located just below the top and above the bottom edge of the rail which is usually hollow back. Sometimes if windows are at a height where the normal apron is in line with a chair rail, the chair rail runs continuously across the window under the stool, in place of an apron. The old-fashioned chair rail is of little

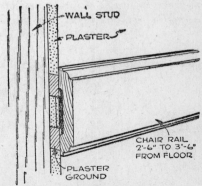

Fig. 66. Hollow back chair rail

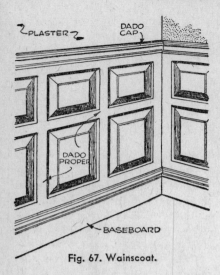

Fig. 67. Wainscoat.

Wainscoating is usually made of wood which, in the old days, was solid panels with molding edges, either recessed or raised. Later-day dadoes were quite frequently flat panels of plywood with molding nailed to the surface. Other wainscoating material used is hard plaster, cloth, linoleum and similar material in sheet form. In wainscoat construction there's a plaster ground at the dado cap, and generally furring strips—the thickness of use now that the modern trend in furniture calls for low-backed chairs, but here again, to remove a chair rail means considerable repair and plaster work. However, if a wall is to be entirely refinished, and the chair rail has ceased to serve its purpose, removing it is worthwhile, should you desire an unbroken wall surface.

Wainscoats are both old and modern, the difference being generally in their treatment. Some old wainscoats were and are masterpieces of wood carving and paneling, an art which reached perfection in simplicity and beauty of proportions during the eighteenth century in America. The lower portion of a wall, if it is of different material than the upper part, is called a Wainscoat; the material of which it is made is called Wainscoating. The surface above the baseboard is the Dado, and the finished top edge of the dado is the Dado Cap (Fig. 67).

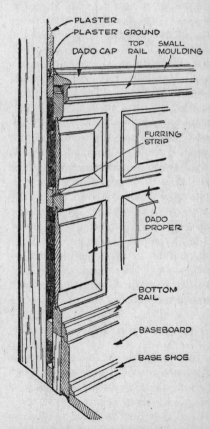

Fig. 68. The wainscoat is fastened to furring strips of the same thickness as the plaster.

the plaster—to the subfloor, on which the wainscoating is nailed (Fig. 68).

A simple wainscoat consists of a cop rail with no dado cap, the dado proper, and a lower rail or baseboard with the usual base shoe. Another type of wainscoat has a top rail on which a dado cap rests, the cap finished off with a small molding; the wainscoating; and a lower rail with the room baseboard added.

Many houses have wainscoats in the dining room made up of panels of plaster with wood strips and molding spaced to form the panels. Here the plaster wall is usually carried down without regard to the wainscoat. The baseboard, vertical strips, bottom and top rails and molding are applied over the plaster, the wainscoat topped by a dado cap wider than usual and grooved to hold ceramic plates. This dado cap is called a Plate Rail. These wainscoats usually run from floor to about 24″ from the ceiling. False ceiling beams of the box type are often part of the architectural design. This type of wainscoat is not difficult to remove, should it be undesirable. The first two types mentioned usually require the plaster wall to be carried down to the floor and entirely refinished.

DOORS

Doors, both exterior and interior, can be classified as of three types: Batten, Paneled and Flush, with a few variations in each type (Fig. 69). The Batten door is made in several ways, the simplest being diagonal boards nailed together as two layers,

each layer at right angles to the other. This type is frequently made as the core for metal-sheathed fire doors.

The usual type of batten door is made up of vertical boards tongued and grooved or shiplapped, held rigid by cross pieces. These cross pieces are from two to four in number, and may or may not be diagonally braced. The cross pieces are called Ledgers and, if two additional pieces forming the sides of the door and corresponding to the ledgers are used, these are known as the Frames. Batten doors can be of any thickness from 1″ to over 2″ stock, but are usually the former. They are, as a rule, used for

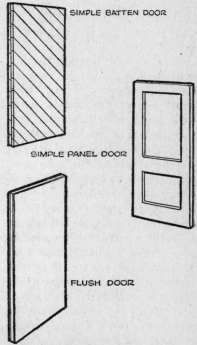

SIMPLE BATTEN DOOR

SIMPLE PANEL DOOR

FLUSH DOOR

Fig. 69. Batten, panel, and flush doors.

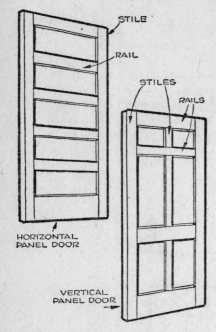

STILE

RAIL

STILES

RAILS

HORIZONTAL
PANEL DOOR

VERTICAL
PANEL DOOR

Fig. 70. Typical panel doors.

cellar doors and outdoor cupboards, being inexpensive and easy to make. They can also be used for interiors of certain period houses, and are quite attractive if well made.

Paneled Doors are made in a variety of panel arrangements, both horizontal, vertical, and combinations of both. A single panel door has for its component parts a Top Rail, Bottom Rail and two Stiles which form the sides of the door. Panels of the horizontal type have intermediate rails forming the panels; and panels of the vertical type have horizontal rails and vertical stiles forming the panels. The rails and stiles of a door are mortised and tenoned, the mortise being cut in the side stiles. This construction is used for every rail joining the stiles. Vertical stiles in a vertical-panel door are tenoned into the horizontal rails, while the rails are tenoned into the side stiles (Fig. 70).

The paneling in doors may be raised or recessed, depending a great deal on the period of the house. Eighteenth century door paneling was almost invariably of the raised type flush with the stile face, with the bevels cut out of the solid wood and having a shallow square shoulder before the bevel began. Any molding form was cut in the solid wood and not attached, as is the practice today.

Top and bottom rails on paneled doors differ in width, the bottom rail being considerably wider. Intermediate rails are usually the same width as the top rail. Paneling material is usually plywood which is set in grooves or dadoes in the stiles and rails, with the molding attached on most doors as a finish.

Fine hardwood doors for interiors are frequently veneered over solid stock. This practice is considered best since hardwoods are very expensive in thick sizes, and have a tendency to twist and warp.

Flush Doors are usually perfectly flat on both sides, but sometimes they are paneled on one side. Solid planks are rarely used for flush doors, unless some authentic-period door is simulated. Flush doors are made up of solid or hollow cores with one or two plies of veneer glued to the cores.

Solid cores are made of short pieces of wood glued together with the ends staggered very much like in brick laying. One, or usually two plies of veneer are glued to the core. The first about ⅛" thick is applied at right angles to the direction of the core, and the other, ⅛" or less, is glued with the grain vertical. Strips, ¾" x door thickness, of the same species of wood used for the panel, are glued to the edges of the door on all sides.

Hollow-core doors have wooden grides or other honeycomb material for their cores, with solid wood edging strips on all sides. Faces of this type door are usually 3-ply veneer instead of two single plies. The hollow-core door has a solid block on both sides for door knobs and to permit the mortising of locks. Flush doors are made for interior and exterior use and are not usually interchangeable, the interior type not being glued with waterproof glue. The honeycomb-core door is for interior use only. There is a general tendency today to manufacture all flush doors with the use of synthetic resin, waterproof glue.

Door Sizes

Thickness of doors varies, depending on the size of the door, but 1¾" is usual. Stock doors are also made 1⅜" and 1⅜" thick, and very wide exterior doors may be 2" or 2¼". Frequently closet doors of narrow dimensions are 1⅛", and all stock doors are made in widths and heights of 2" multiples. Odd-size doors must be made to order, or stock doors cut down.

All doorways have frames to which the door is hung and against which it stops. The frame has three members: two side Jambs and a Head Jamb,

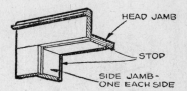

Fig. 71. Frame has two side and a head jamb.

with a Stop as an integral or separate part of the assembly (Fig. 71).

Exterior door frames are rabbeted to receive the door in the same manner as casement windows, with an added member, the Sill which is almost always of hardwood to resist wear. The sill slopes downward and outward, as in a window, to shed water (Fig. 72); it has a threshold which may be an integral part of the sill or attached separately. If the threshold is part of the sill, it's the width of the door thickness and beveled at the front to permit the door to project slightly over it, forming a drip. The back of the threshold has a lip which projects over the finish floor, hiding the joint.

Separately attached thresholds are of hardwood and must be tightly fitted and their underside coated with white lead in oil to form a water seal between sill and finish floor (Fig. 73).

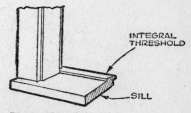

Fig. 72. The sill slopes downward and outward.

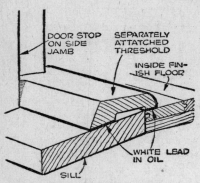

Fig. 73. Separately attached thresholds must be tightly fitted.

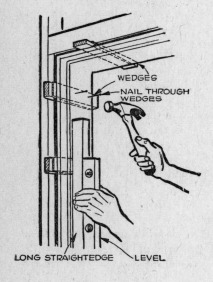

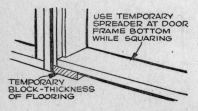

Fig. 74. Wedges are driven tightly to plumb and square the frames.

Interior frames are often set on the subfloor with the finish floor fitted against them, others are set on the finish floor which insures a tight fit between floor and frame. The other method anchors the frame more tightly in position.

Rough framing of doorways, as has been mentioned before, is always large enough in width and height to allow for the thickness of the door jambs, plus an inch of blocking on the top and both sides. This blocking takes the form of pairs of wedges which are driven tightly to plumb and square the frames against the rough framing. When the jambs are plumb and square, they are nailed securely to the rough framing through the wedge blocking with finishing nails which are set and covered (Fig. 74).

Door jambs with integral stops are 1⅛" thick, while those with stops attached separately are usually ¾" thick. The rabbeted type makes a light-tight joint and prevents any illegal attempt of entry by the removal of the stop and the insertion of a knife blade between frame and door edge to push back the lock bolt. Separate stops are usually strips with one molded edge about ½x1¾" firmly nailed to the jambs.

The separate stop makes it easy to change the door's swing from one room to another, requiring only the removal of the stops, reversing them and re-nailing in their new position. This cannot be done with a stop which is part of the jamb. Few houses have this type of rabbeted jamb, but should you find this to be the case in your house, and you wish to change the direction of swing of a door, the easiest method of doing it is to cut the door down to fit the thicker portion of the jamb and add new stops. A door should have a clearance of 1/16″ at the top and sides, and ¼″ or more at the botom if a threshold is not used. If one is used, about ⅛″ clearance is usual (Fig. 75).

Casings (Fig. 75), are the outside trim of the door frame proper. They are used to set off the doorway and to hide the juncture of the jambs and the rough framing. Casings may be of plain or ornate design, depending on the period when the house was built and the style of architecture. They consist of three basic pieces, two side pieces and a head piece, joined in either of two ways. One method is to miter the corners of the head and side pieces, and the other is to butt the side pieces against the bottom edge of the head piece. The mitered joint looks best, but if the casing should swell or shrink, it opens a crack at the miter. To counteract this, many old mitered casings were joined with added reinforcing, such as, dowels glued, part miter and half lap glued, or mitering the outer surface and mortise and tenoning the back surface.

Most casings have a Back Band which is a narrow molding attached to the outer edges of the casing to blend off the square edge next to the plaster wall. This molding is always mitered, regardless of how the casing is joined.

In some houses with deep walls, a supplementary casing was added to the jambs, called Jamb Casing, and paneled to match the paneling of the

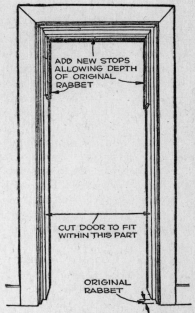

ADD NEW STOPS ALLOWING DEPTH OF ORIGINAL RABBET

CUT DOOR TO FIT WITHIN THIS PART

ORIGINAL RABBET

Fig. 75. To change the direction of swing, cut the door to fit the thicker porton of the jamb.

door or room. Some door casings have a short piece at the base of the side casings, called a Plinth or Plinth Block. These were and are used to form a base for the casing assembly

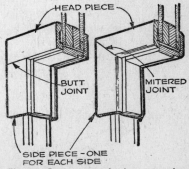

HEAD PIECE

BUTT JOINT

MITERED JOINT

SIDE PIECE – ONE FOR EACH SIDE

Fig. 76. Casings may be butt jointed or mitered.

and a stop for the baseboard, being strictly a matter of appearance and having no structural function. Where plinth blocks are used, the side casing rests on the block which is of slightly thicker dimension and usually of plain design. Today's tendency is to omit the plinth which breaks up the line of the casing.

Blocking in back of door casings is very important to afford good nailing surfaces, and very often a casing and jamb which has gone out of plumb and square is the result of improper blocking, unless the house structure has settled so decidedly as to be the cause.

Truing a door assembly which is badly out of plumb requires the removal of the entire assembly, and replacement with adequate wedge blocking installed to bring it back square and plumb. Doors that bind at the jambs in spots are not necessarily out of plumb due to the frame. You can check the frame with a carpenter's level which has a plumb bubble. Excessive humidity can make doors swell and cause binding. Perhaps the door sags because the hinges are loose due to loosened screws or screw holes no longer able to hold them securely. If the screws have worked out, they can be tightened, but only *after* the door has been removed; the weight of the door can cause the screw-hold threads to strip, particularly in old jambs and doors. Screw holes that are stripped can be plugged with tapered pegs of hardwood driven in and cut off flush, making a sort of expansion device when the screw is re-driven. Plastic wood

can be used, but it requires a longer time to make the repair due to allowing the material to dry thoroughly before re-screwing.

Doors That Stick

Doors that stick slightly due to swelling can be easily sandpapered or planed where the sticking occurs. You can tell where the door binds by the appearance of the edges which are discolored or have the finish worn off, leaving the wood polished from friction. As you carefully sandpaper or plane these spots, rub some blue carpenter's chalk on the jamb section. If the door still binds a trifle, the chalk will be transferred to the door edge, calling for more sanding or planing at that spot. Each time sandpaper or plane off the chalk mark on the door edge, re-chalk the jamb and test the door. The absence of chalk on the door edge tells you the door is clear of the jamb. Remove just enough of the door edge to prevent sticking, because when the door shrinks again a wider space than usual will appear.

Doors that will not close along their entire edge, for some reason other than hinge trouble, should be removed. Hinges should also be removed. Plane down the butt edge of the door rather than the lock edge. Doing this usually requires further mortising of the butt edge to receive the hinge flush.

Doors that are warped—which is unusual in a good door—can sometimes be straightened by placing them on two saw horses with sufficient weight material to flatten the door.

Unless the door is beyond repair a few days of this treatment should produce results.

Sometimes a door shrinks, leaving quite a gap at the lock edge, preventing the latch from engaging properly. To remedy this condition, remove the door and the hinge leaves from the jamb, insert a thin piece of wood or cardboard in the hinge mortise and reassemble. This should set the door out sufficiently for the latch to engage the strike plate.

Often an old door rattles due to the latch fitting too loosely in the strike plate. Removing the strike plate and setting it back from the outer edge of the casing will do the trick. Old screw holes should be plugged as suggested.

Another cause for a door not closing may be due to frame settling, carrying with it the strike plate but not the door. Remove the strike plate and file a larger opening for the latch, or if badly out of place, set the strike plate toward the outer edge of the casing after enlarging the catch opening.

Frequently bit-key locks (the usual type of indoor lock) fail to operate due to the mechanism inside the lock jamming from lack of oil or other causes. It is easy to remove a lock of this sort by first removing the set screw which holds the knob, then pulling out the knob and spindle. Two screws hold the mortised lock assembly which when removed enables you to pull out the lock. This comes apart when a central screw is removed, exposing the "works" which can then be attended to.

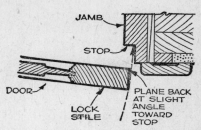

Fig. 77. Plane the lock stile at a slight angle.

HANGING A DOOR

Hanging a new or old door is not difficult if a time-tried procedure is followed. New stock doors have their side stiles projecting at the top and bottom. Saw these off flush. Make sure that the jambs are plumb and square, otherwise you'll have a door that must be fitted out of plumb and square. Plane the hinge stile perfectly smooth and square to an amount that will equal the lock stile when it, too, is planed—the idea being to have the two stiles approximately of equal width.

Then the top rail should be roughly fitted to the top jamb by planing, sawing or both. The lock stile is usually planed at a slight angle back toward the door stop, so that the door clears nicely when opened (Fig. 77). Trim the bottom of the door so as to clear a threshold, if any, by about ⅛″, or if there isn't to be a threshold, the bottom should clear the floor at least ¼″ or more for any rug it may swing over. Allow 1/16″ clearance at the top and sides.

Now fit the door in place *flush with the jamb edge*, using thin wedges of wood driven tightly enough to hold

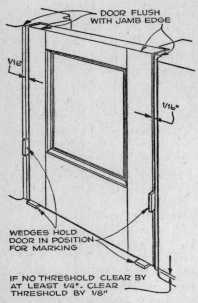

Fig. 78. Wedges hold the door in position.

Mark the locations of the butt hinges with a sharp knife on both the jamb and the door at the same time, so that they align (Fig. 79). Having accurately marked the location of the hinges on both jamb and door, remove the door, and with a square mark the lines of the hinge across the edge. Carefully gauge the depth and width, using a sharp knife. Do the same on the jamb. On all but very thin doors, the mortise on the door edge is cut ¼″ back from the face on the stop side, and the mortise for the jamb is cut 5/16″ back from the stop to allow enough clearance when the door is closed. Cut the mortises with a chisel and attach the separate leaves

the door securely: wedges on each side near where the hinges will be located; and two wedges near the corners at the top and bottom (Fig. 78). Positioning the door in this manner makes possible marking out the location of the loose-pin butt hinges. Although it's common practice to use only two hinges for the average-size door, three hinges are best, insuring a true and free swinging door that won't sag. The distance from the bottom of the door to the bottom of the hinge leaf is usually 10″, and from the top of the door to the top of the hinge leaf about 6″ to 6½″. If a third hinge is added, the centerline of the leaf is of equal distance between the top of the top hinge and the bottom of the bottom hinge.

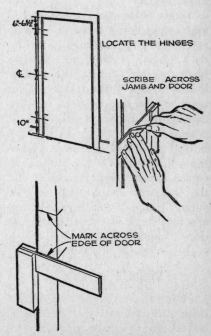

Fig. 79. Locating the hinges.

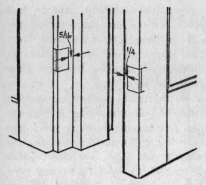

Fig. 80. Mortise the door and the jamb.

lock. To do this, place the lock against the side of the door and mark off the location of the lock. With an ice pick or awl locate at the same time the holes for the knob spindle and keyhole (Fig. 81). Mark with pencil the depth of the mortise which should be slightly deeper than the lock depth to allow for a bit of clearance and the thickness of the face plate. Bore holes through the door for the spindle and the keyhole, using a ¾″ auger bit which is usually large enough. Scribe

of the hinges with screws. Put the door in place with the hinge knuckles meshing and insert the pins (Fig. 80).

If every step was carried out carefully and accurately, the door will swing freely with the proper clearance for the baseboard when the door is swung back against it, and clearing the jambs when it's closed. Should it bind due to a slight inaccuracy, loosening one of the leaves on the jamb and inserting a piece of thin cardboard should rectify the error. Or it may be necessary to mortise one hinge a bit deeper, depending on how much the door binds. If it is at the top corner, the top hinge is recessed and the lower one shimmed, and vice versa. Finally, attach the door stops, allowing slight clearances when the door is closed.

FITTING A LOCK

Fitting the ordinary bit-key lock is done after the door has been hung, and requires a mortise in the edge of the door to receive the body of the

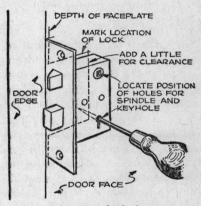

Fig. 81. Locating the lock mortise.

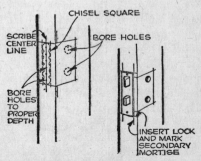

Fig. 82. Scribe a centerline to divide the edge.

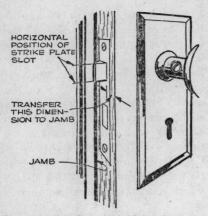

HORIZONTAL
POSITION OF
STRIKE PLATE
SLOT

TRANSFER
THIS DIMEN-
SION TO JAMB

JAMB

Fig. 83. Notice where the latch hits the jamb.

a centerline, dividing the door edge, as a guide for boring the holes for the lock (Fig. 82). Bore holes in the door edge for the mortise, using an auger-bit size the thickness of the lock and with a depth gauge attached. Clean and square the sides of the mortise with a chisel, and then insert the lock to locate a secondary mortise for the face plate. Chisel this out carefully for the face plate to fit just *slightly*

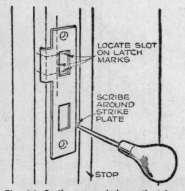

LOCATE SLOT
ON LATCH
MARKS

SCRIBE
AROUND
STRIKE
PLATE

STOP

Fig. 84. Scribe around the strike plate.

deeper than the edge-face of the door. Insert the lock, securing it with screws driven through the face plate. Insert the knob spindle and attach the knobs, and screw on the escutcheon plate for the keyhole.

To locate the strike plate for the latch, the door must be in a closed position. Locate the horizontal position of the slot on the jamb by observing where the door latch touches (Fig. 83). Open the door and carefully measure the distance of the latch from the face of the door. Transfer this dimension to the door jamb. Place the strike plate over the marks and scribe the outline of the plate which is mortised flush. Set the plate and mark the openings in it for the latch and bolt, then remove it and cut the openings out with a chisel to clear the latch and bolt. Finally screw the strike plate in position (Fig. 84).

WINDOWS

Windows are classified as Double Hung and Casement (Fig. 85). There are basically two types of casement window: the Outswinging and the Inswinging type; and these may be hinged at the sides, top or bottom.

The Double-Hung Window is made up of two parts, an upper and a lower sash, which slide vertically past one another. This window has some advantages and disadvantages. Screens can be located on the outside of a double-hung window without interfering with its operation, and ventilators and window air conditioners can be placed with the window mostly closed. However, for full ventilation

Fig. 85. Windows are classified as double hung (left) and casement.

of a room, only one half of the area of the window can be utilized, and any current of air passing across its face is to some extent lost to the room.

The casement window which opens out—the way a casement should open for the most efficient water tightness when closed — requires the window screen to be located on the inside with some device cut into its frame to operate the casement; or the window screen must be hinged and swung up to operate the window.

Inswinging casements, like double-hung windows, are clear of screens, but they are extremely difficult to make water tight, particularly so if there's a driving rainstorm. That is why most casement windows swing out. Casements have the advantage of their entire area being opened to air currents, with the added advantage of catching a parallel breeze and slanting it into a room.

Casement windows in many modern houses are swung from the top, or are made up of comparatively narrow panes of glass, each pivoting on a horizontal plane outward, similar to a series of shutters. These two types allow for ventilation of a room even though it's raining (Fig. 86).

Picture Window

A basically different type of window was introduced along with modern house design, commonly known as the Picture Window. This type is

Fig. 86. Top pivoted windows allow rooms to be ventilated when it rains.

Fig. 87. The modern picture window.

not movable, being a fixed sash with a single pane of plate glass, or a sash containing two panes of plate glass separated by a narrow sealed air space. They are sized much larger than the conventional type of window, extending across the entire front, side or back of houses (Fig. 87).

Since these windows are fixed, a number of devices — other than air conditioners — have been introduced to obtain natural-air circulation through rooms (Fig. 88). Adjustable louvers are built in walls above and below these windows. Some fixed window spans have casement windows above them, hinged at the top, and others have casements at the sides. The picture window, due to its size and weight, requires unusually heavy rough framing to carry the span

and load, with the frequent addition of small diameter steel columns to support the spans. It is unwise to locate these windows where the sun can shine directly on them during the summer months, resulting in blinding glare, and excessive heat radiation. This is primarily the reason for large roof overhangs in modern houses. This type of window, needless to say, is very expensive—plate glass costing what it does—and storm-breakage insurance is a wise precaution. A picture window without a view is of little value, and in congested areas even of less value, as one is virtually living in that glass house of proverbial fame.

All windows, whatever the type, essentially consist of two parts: the Frame and the Sash. The frame is basically made up of four members: the top piece, called the Head; two side pieces or Jambs; and the bottom piece known as the Sill (Fig. 89).

The sash is the frame that holds the glass, or "lights" in builder's lan-

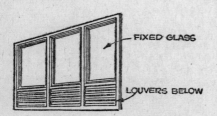

Fig. 88. Adjustable louvers provide ventilation.

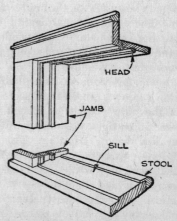

Fig. 89. Window frame members.

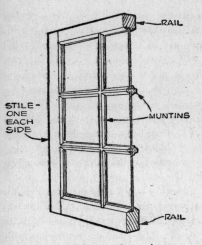

Fig. 90. Window sash members.

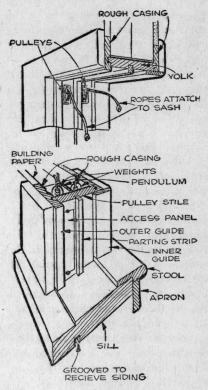

Fig. 91. Box frame.

guage, and is in its simplest form made up of two side pieces or Stiles, and two pieces, top and bottom, called Rails. The smaller vertical, horizontal, or both pieces combined that divide the glass into smaller sizes are known as Bars and Muntins, usually termed just muntins (Fig. 90).

Windows, both double hung and casement, are made of wood, and metal, the metal double-hung window delivered from the factory as a complete unit of sash and frame with balancing devices built in, ready to be fitted into the rough framing. Metal casement windows come as a unit of a frame and sash, but require a wood frame besides, into which they are fitted.

Double-Hung windows are somewhat more involved in their frame construction and operation than the casement. The usual double-hung window frame is known as the Box Frame, being virtually that. Other types of double-hung window frames are simplified and of cheaper construction, known as Simplified Frame and Cottage Frame in which the box-like side pieces, called Rough Casing are omitted.

Box Frame

The Box Frame consists of a top piece or Yoke; two side pieces or jambs called Pulley Stiles, and the Sill. The yoke and pulley stiles are dadoed into the inner and outer pieces (rough casing), forming an open box with the opening toward the studs and headers. The rough casing provides nailing surface to the studs and headers forming the rough opening, lapping them about 1", with the inside rough casing forming the plaster stop. The outside rough casing is also a "blind" stop for the sheathing which should fit snugly against it, with building paper lapping the joint.

The 2" space between the framing studs and the pulley stile, forms the box for counterweights which balance the window sash. The weight box is divided by a thin strip known as the Pendulum which separates the weights for the two sash units. In the stiles near the sill is an opening for easy access to the weights. This opening has a removable strip which is part of the stile and channel for the lower sash (Fig. 91).

Yoke and stile faces are divided by a Parting Strip which is dadoed into them, but removable so that the upper sash can be taken out. The strip forms the center guide for the upper and lower sash, while the outer rough casing, projecting slightly beyond the stiles and yoke, forms the outer guide. The inner guide for the sash is formed by a strip or stop, usually with a molding form on the inner edge. This stop is removable to permit the removal of the lower sash.

At the upper parts of the stiles, two pulleys on each side—one for each sash—are mortised flush with the stile faces for the weight cord or chain.

Sill

The Sill is an integral part of the box frame and slants downward and outward. It usually has one or two ¼" breaks, one occurring at the point where the lower sash rests on the sill, and another near the outer edge to form a seat for window screens or storm sash. These breaks prevent water, dripping on the sill, from being blown under the sash. The underside of the sill, near its outer edge, is grooved to receive the edge of siding material to form a watertight seal.

On the room side of the sill is another piece, the Stool, which has a rabbet on its underside into which the sill fits. The stool edge projects from the sill, forming a horizontal stop for the lower sash. The stool is part of the interior trim of the window, made up of side and head casings and an Apron under the stool. On the weather side are framed finished side and head casings. A Drip Cap rests on top of the outside head casing and is covered with metal flashing to form a watertight juncture with the siding material.

Double-hung window sash come in pairs, one upper and one lower. The bottom rail of the top sash and the top rail of the lower sash are beveled on the inner and outer faces so that they meet and fit snugly when the top and bottom sash are closed. These rails are called Meeting Rails and have a narrower face but are wider than the other rails, extending beyond the parting strip, unlike the other rails and stiles. Meeting rails are rabbeted out around the parting strips to slide freely.

The top rail of the top sash, and the stiles are usually 1⅜" thick for averge-size windows, and 1¾″ for larger sizes. They range in width from 1½ to 2¼″. The bottom sash is the same thickness as the top rail and stiles, but wider: from 2½ to 3¾″, and is develed on the bottom edge to fit the slant of the sill. Meeting rails range in width across the top from 1⅞ to 2⅜″ with a face width of from 1⅛ to 1⅝″. Muntins are usually of the same width as the thickness of the sash, with a thickness from ¾ to 13/16″ and sometimes larger.

All sash, whatever the type of window, is rabbeted on the weather side to receive the glass, glazier's points and putty, excepting the meeting rail for the lower sash of a double-hung window. This is dadoed or grooved to receive the glass. And all sash has a simple molding form cut on the room side, and is usually framed at the corners with an open mortise and tenon, the tenon being cut in the rails. Stiles are grooved on their sliding surfaces partway from the top to receive the weight cord or chain which is knotted in a hole at the end of the groove, or screwed to the stile.

Many very old houses have double-hung windows without sash weights, the frames having been constructed without weight boxes, as for casement windows. Pegs and just sticks of wood were used to keep the window at different positions. These windows usually are difficult to operate because they don't slide smoothly and because their dead weight must be lifted. There have been a number of spring devices invented to convert these windows to counterbalanced ones. One such device is a coiled

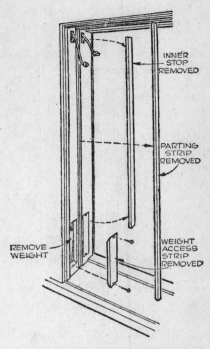

Fig. 92. Remove the parting strip.

spring housed in a metal box which can be attached to the head jamb or side jamb, the window sash being connected to it with a flat metal band. Another type is a spring contained in the grooves in the sash where the cord would normally be. This requires grooving out the sash edge to receive the spring which is also of the counterbalancing type and, in recent years, has been preferred to the weight system by many home owners.

Fixing Broken Cords

When a weight cord or chain breaks it throws the sash out of line, making it practically impossible to

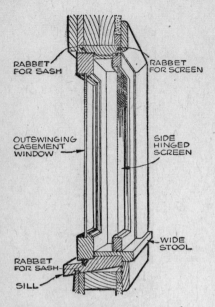

RABBET FOR SASH

RABBET FOR SCREEN

OUTSWINGING CASEMENT WINDOW

SIDE HINGED SCREEN

WIDE STOOL

RABBET FOR SASH

SILL

Fig. 93. Outswinging casement window.

raise or lower it for any distance. There is only one remedy—take out the sash and weight and put in a new cord or chain. This procedure is not a difficult one, as you may have gathered from the foregoing description of the mechanics of a double-hung window. It is wise, while you're at it, to replace all the old weight cords with new ones, preferably of the chain type, the chances being that if one cord has parted, the others are more than likely to part in the near future. And once the sash is out, the rest is easy.

Remove the parting strip which is usually attached with a few finishing nails, the inner stop, and the strip in the pulley stiles giving access to the weights. This strip is usually held in place by a flat-head screw top and bottom. One edge of the strip is usually beveled slightly, requiring the use of a sturdy putty knife to pry the strip. Remove the sash weights and feed the new chain through the pulleys and down into the weight box, and attach the chain to the weights. Then attach to the sash, measuring one of the old cords for the proper length which should be such that the weights hang clear of the sill when the sash are closed. Replacing sash and stops is much easier than removing them the first time after many years of use (Fig. 92).

Casement Windows are considerably less complicated in their construction, being simple frames and sash. The frames are usually made of planks 1¾″ thick with rabbets cut in them to receive the sash. Usually there's an additional rabbet for screens or storm sash. The frames are rabbeted ½″ deep and 1½ or 1⅝″ wide for sash 1⅜ or 1¾″ thick. The additional rabbet is usually 15/16″ or 1-3/16″ wide, depending on whether the screen or storm sash is ⅞ or 1⅛″ thick.

Outswinging casement windows have the rabbet for the sash on the outer edges of the frame, the inner edge being rabbeted for the screen. Sill construction is very much like that for a double-hung window, with the stool much wider and forming a stop for the bottom rail. Casement-window frames are of a width to extend to the sheathing face on the weather side, and to the plaster face on the room side (Fig. 93).

When there are two casement windows in a row in one frame, they may be separated by a vertical double jamb called a Mullion, or the stiles may come together in pairs like a French Door. The edges of the stiles may be a reverse rabbet; a beveled reverse rabbet with battens, one attached to each stile; or beveled astragals (T-shaped molding), one attached to each stile. The battens and astragals insure better weathertightness, the latter being less likely loosened by use. Two pairs of casement sash in one frame are hinged to a mullion in the center (Fig. 94).

Inswinging casement-window frames are like the outswinging type with the sash rabbet cut in the inner edge of the frame. The sill construction is slightly different, being of one piece, similar to that of a door sill, with a rabbet cut for a screen or storm sash toward the front edge, and the back raised where the sash rail seats. This surface is rabbeted at its back edge to form a stop for the rail which is also rabbeted to mesh. (Fig. 95).

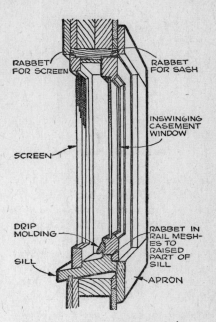

Fig. 95. Inswinging casement window.

Sills in general have a usual slope of about 1″ in 5″ so that they shed water quickly, and are wider than the frames, extending usually to the plaster line and about 1½″ beyond the sheathing. They also form a base for the outside finished casing.

The bottom sash rail of an inswinging casement window is differently constructed than the outswinging type. The bottom edge is rabbeted to mesh with the rabbet on the sill and a Drip Molding is set in the weather face to prevent rain from being blown under the sash.

Fixed Windows are made very much like casement windows without hinges, or the glass may be set in the frames without sash. Where the glass

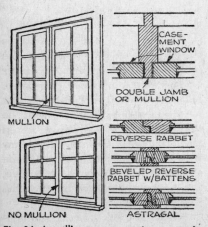

Fig. 94. A mullion may separate casements.

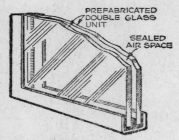

PREFABRICATED
DOUBLE GLASS
UNIT

SEALED
AIR SPACE

Fig. 96. Prefabricated double glass window.

is set without sash, the jambs and sill are rabbeted at the back edges, the glass set in a bed of putty, and flat molding attached to the jambs and sill to hold the glass in place.

A double-hung window frame can be converted into a fixed-sash window by making a single sash for the window and positioning the sash where the former lower sash was. Obviously, with fixed windows, screening isn't necessary but storm sash may be desirable.

Insulating Value of Glass

Double-Glass windows afford considerable insulation. A single thickness of glass is poor insulation against low temperatures, its cold surface radiating discomfort and drafts in a room. Two sheets of glass with an air space between reduce the coefficient of heat transmission from a room from about 1.15 for a single thickness of glass to about 0.45 for two thicknesses.

The oldest form of double-glass installation is the ordinary storm window. The storm window has the advantage of affording insulation and acting as a barrier against high winds.

The disadvantage is the necessity of removing it during the summer months, storing the window, and replacing it with a window screen.

Storm windows are usually made of lighter material than window sash: from ⅞ to 1⅛″ in thickness, but are rabbeted the same as window sash to hold the glass. They are fitted in rabbets cut in frames and sills for casement windows, and to the rough casing and sill in double-hung windows.

A newer method of achieving double glass in a window is to frame a secondary smaller sash into rabbets cut in the regular sash. This secondary sash can be removed if screws are used to hold it in place. The reason for making the secondary sash removable is so that the windows can be cleaned and any condensation which may occur can be removed. Dirt and condensation are bound to occur in time with this type of window, as it's difficult to efficiently seal the air space. This type affords good insulation, and is efficient during the summer months if air conditioning is employed.

The third double-glass method is the installation of prefabricated glass units, usually plate glass, which contain two sheets of glass separated by a narrow, clean air space sealed at the factory. Dirt and condensation cannot occur so long as the seal remains intact. This type of window has almost the same insulating qualities as the other two mentioned, is quite expensive, but does make possible much larger unobstructed window areas (Fig. 96).

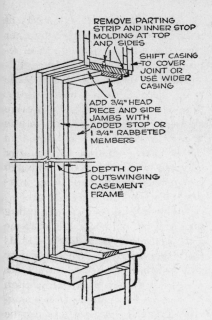

REMOVE PARTING
STRIP AND INNER STOP
MOLDING AT TOP
AND SIDES

SHIFT CASING
TO COVER
JOINT OR
USE WIDER
CASING

ADD 3/4" HEAD
PIECE AND SIDE
JAMBS WITH
ADDED STOP OR
1 3/4" RABBETED
MEMBERS

DEPTH OF
OUTSWINGING
CASEMENT
FRAME

Fig. 97. Double hung to casement.

CONVERTING DOUBLE-HUNG TO CASEMENT

If you prefer casement to your present double-hung windows, it is not difficult to convert the frames to accommodate the new sash. Remove the parting strip and the inner stop molding, and add additional jambs and head which can be rabbeted, or plain with stops attached separately. If the stops are added, the jamb material should be ¾" stock; if rabbeted, 1¾" thick with ½"-deep rabbets. The rabbeted frames afford much better weathertightness, but you can use flat stock and add the stops, coating the contacting surfaces with white lead in linseed oil, or caulking compound before nailing to the frame to insure

weathertightness. A wider inside casing may be necessary unless the old finished casing can be shifted to cover the joint of the new frame without exposing the plaster ground. New sash will of course be required. These can be purchased in stock sizes from lumber yards dealing in mill work, or you can buy the stock already machined with rabbets and molding of any length required. Then you can cut the open mortises for the corners, and assemble the sash (Fig. 97).

To convert casement to double-hung windows requires the rabbets in the frames to be filled in with pieces

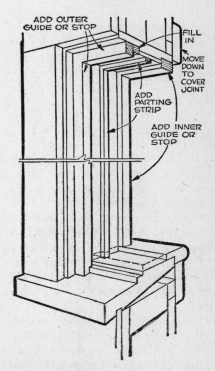

ADD OUTER
GUIDE OR STOP

FILL
IN

MOVE
DOWN
TO
COVER
JOINT

ADD
PARTING
STRIP

ADD INNER
GUIDE OR
STOP

Fig. 98. Casement to double hung.

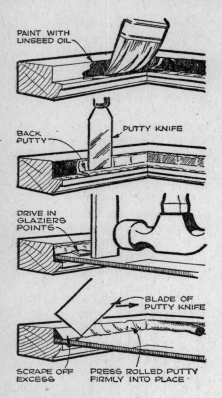

PAINT WITH LINSEED OIL

BACK PUTTY

PUTTY KNIFE

DRIVE IN GLAZIERS POINTS

BLADE OF PUTTY KNIFE

SCRAPE OFF EXCESS

PRESS ROLLED PUTTY FIRMLY INTO PLACE

Fig. 99. Always paint before puttying.

thick enough to form guides for the window sash, with another added to make the parting strip (Fig. 98). The sash will have to be spring-balance equipped as there is no space for counterweights. As with the casement window, the inside casing has to be moved down to cover the joint where the inside stop has been added.

GLAZING

Adding glass to sash is called glazing and must be done carefully to prevent air and water from finding

their way under the glass. Glass should always be about ⅛" smaller than the sash opening, to allow for any distortion in the sash which might break the glass. Before inserting the glass, paint the sash rabbet with linseed oil and then apply a thin layer of putty along the faces of the rabbet to form a bed for the glass (Fig. 99). This is known as back-puttying and is essential to form a seal between glass and wood, which glass alone won't do. Set in the glass and drive glaziers points—which are flat, triangular pieces of zinc—into the sash, allowing a projection of about 3/16" to hold the glass securely. Care must be exercised when forcing these points into the wood so as not to break the glass. A piece of flat, narrow metal, thick enough not to bend and long enough to hold, is a good tool. Place the metal on the point and tap the metal near the point a few times with a hammer. This allows the hammer to clear the glass while tapping. Finally apply putty, which you've rolled into a thick ribbon, by pressing it firmly in place. Then, with a putty knife, scrape off the excess with an even, drawing motion, angling the knife about 30 degrees. This gives a downward bevel to the putty which will shed water quickly. It's important to paint any wood surface, prior to puttying, with linseed oil as an undercoat for the putty, otherwise the wood would absorb most of the oil from the putty, leaving it with no binder. This would cause the putty to soon crack and peel off. Also be sure to get top quality putty which is made of precipitated whiting (calcium carbonate)

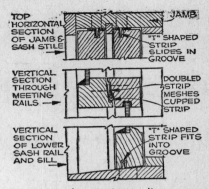

Fig. 101. Weatherstripping needing grooves.

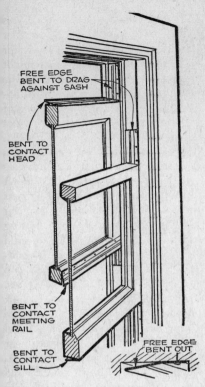

Fig. 100. Flexible metal weatherstripping.

ground in linseed oil with about 5% white lead added. This formula insures a firm adherence of putty to wood and glass, and will not peel or crack off.

WEATHER STRIPPING

No matter how carefully and accurately windows are constructed, in time they allow considerable air infiltration due to shrinkage. Rooms in which we live must have fresh air to some degree for good health and comfort. Moreover, air is required for the proper combustion of fuel in fireplaces and other heating devices. But excessive leakage wastes fuel and causes drafts, and weather stripping is the only way of preventing this.

There are many types of weatherstripping material, but the most efficient are usually of the metal variety. One (Fig. 100), requires no grooving or cutting of sash, being made of thin flexible metal, usually brass or zinc, which is tacked on the frame, the free edge bent so as to drag against the sash. Other types require grooves in

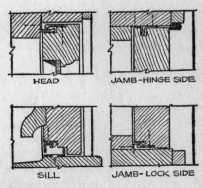

Fig. 102. Spring-contact weatherstripping.

Fig. 103. Careful measurement of screens assures snug fitting, but easy opening.

the sash, and are made in T-shaped strips. The T is formed double or U-shaped, fitting snugly in the grooves, with the flanges tacked to the frame and sill. The U has enough spring to fit snugly and yet allow movement in the double-hung window (Fig. 101).

For Inswinging Casements

Weather stripping for inswinging casement windows is usually a type of metal strip which meshes into or against another metal strip, forming a seal. The sill strip is especially designed to close off the space between sill and rail. Outswinging casement windows are usually equipped with the spring-contact type of weather stripping.

Sponge Rubber

There is also a type of weather stripping for casement windows and doors which is made of sponge rubber of varying thicknesses. It is attached to the frame with a rubber-base cement which is an integral part of the weather stripping. This type is the easiest to apply and quite efficient for the life of the rubber. It is much more obvious than metal types, but makes a tight seal without the possibility of sticking, which happens if metal weather stripping becomes distorted.

SCREENS

Screen sash is usually ¾" stock, but for large windows and doors 1⅛" material is frequently used, or ¾" lumber is braced with a horizontal member. Screen doors are best made of 1⅛" lumber, the top, middle rails and stiles 2¾", and the bottom rail 3¾" wide. Window-screen sash is usually 1¾ or 2¼" wide. The easiest method of attaching screen material is to cut it about 1" wider and longer than the opening, tack or staple it, and cover the edges with a narrow, thin molding attached with brads. Another method is to rabbet the inside edges about ⅜x½", attach the screen in the rabbet and nail a ⅜x½" molding flush with the face of the sash. Both methods have a tendency to stretch the screen material slightly when the molding is applied (Fig. 103).

There are several ways to make the sash, the best being to cut open mortises and tenons for the corners, with the rails tenoned into the stiles. This makes the strongest joint. The other way is to half-lap the corners. Both types of joints are nailed or screwed. Using resorcinol resin glue in conjunction with nails or screws makes a rigid joint which will remain so.

When attaching screen material, start at one end and tack, or staple it with copper staples, holding the material tightly as you nail. Then, hand stretch the screen along the side, working toward the other end and attach, making sure that the weave is parallel to the ends and sides. Finally tack the sides and apply the molding. Another method which works well, if

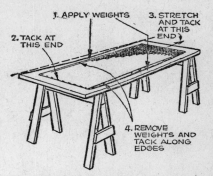

Fig. 104. Method of stretching screen evenly.

there's any doubt in your mind that you won't be able to stretch the screen evenly, is to place the sash on two saw horses, attach the screen at one end and then place weights of even value on the sash at the center. This will bow the sash a *trifle* (Fig. 104). Now lightly stretch the screen and attach at the other end. Remove the

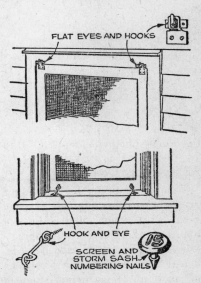

Fig. 105. Hooks and eyes make removal easy.

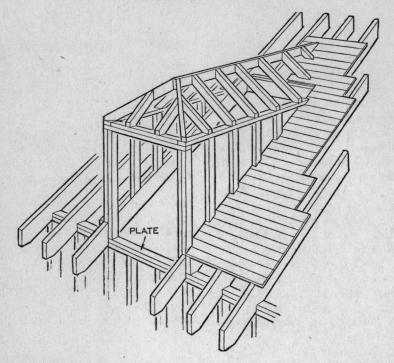

Fig. 106. Dormers are formed when a vertical wall rises out of the roof as an extension.

weights, which brings the sash back to normal, and attach the screen to the sides. Be careful not to bend the sash too much, otherwise it may stretch the screen too tightly, causing it to tear away or hold the sash in a bowed position.

Screening Safeguard

A good idea when screening doors is to screen the lower part with heavier wire mesh, or doubled screening material, if there are children or animals around. This can only be done if the screen door has an additional horizontal bracing rail. For easy removal of a window screen, it should be attached at the top with hooks and eyes made for this purpose (Fig. 105). Hooks are screwed to the face of the casing and the eyes, which are offset for the sash to fit flush, are screwed to the face of the sash. The screen is held in place with two ordinary screw hooks and eyes in the lower rail and sill. Screens, since they are custom fitted to each window, should be numbered, with corresponding numbers on the window frame. Small metal disks with stamped numbers can be purchased at hardware stores; these have lugs which can be hammered.

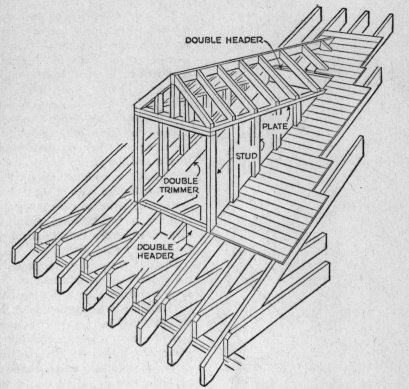

Fig. 107. Double headers make a solid base for studding that is run to the trimmers.

EXTERIOR CONSTRUCTION DETAILS

Basic types of framing have been discussed in some detail, and mention should be made of dormer construction since most houses, particularly those of past years, have one or more of these as part of the roof framing. Whenever a vertical wall rises out of a roof it's called a Dormer, and windows set in this wall are known as Dormer Windows. Dormers may have a gable, or hip-type roof which is framed into the main roof, or a shed-type roof which frequently blends into the roof proper (Fig. 106).

The wall of a dormer may be a continuation of the face of the main wall, or be set back from the face, depending on the type, or period the house simulates. The reason for dormers and dormer windows is to give light and air to an attic which may be finished or planned to be finished for additional living space. Some dormers of the shed-type roof extend almost the entire length of the house, providing almost normal ceiling height.

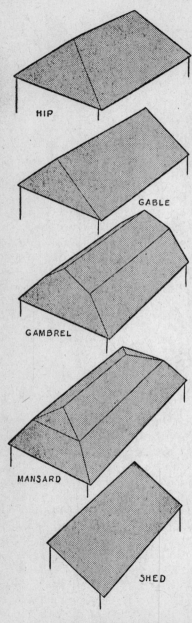

HIP

GABLE

GAMBREL

MANSARD

SHED

Fig. 108. Five basic roof types.

The dormer which is set back from the face of the main wall is framed between doubled trimmers which are part of the roof-rafter framing; that is, a roof rafter at each side of the dormer is doubled, and forms the sides of the dormer opening. A doubled header is framed between these trimmers at the base of the dormer and at a point where the dormer roof frames into the main roof. Main roof rafters are framed into these headers. Studding for the sides of the dormer are framed either to the trimmers or to the rough roof boarding, and carry plates to which the dormer roof rafters are attached (Fig. 107).

Dormers that are an extension of the main wall are basically of the same construction as just described, but without a header at their base, the studding for the face of the dormer being framed to the main roof-rafter plate. The rafters for the roof are framed to a header similarly placed as for the other type, with studs for the sides framed in the same manner.

Some dormers have the wall studs extend to a sole framed to the attic floor. Windows are framed in the same manner as other windows, that is, with trimmers and headers and, if height is limited, the plate may form a part of the top header.

ROOFS

Roofs are basically of five types: Hip, Gable, Gambrel, Mansard, and Shed (Fig. 108). All roofs have some degree of slope which is called the Pitch (Fig. 109), defined usually in one of two ways: by fractions or by ratios.

For example: if a roof slopes in height 4″ to every 12 of its horizontal run, the ratio is 4″ to 12″, called 4-12. The fractional method is based on 24 and not 12. With this system, a ratio of 4-12 is termed fractionally as 1/6 pitch: 24 divided by 4 equals 1/6. To determine the rise in inches of a given fractional pitch, multiply the fraction by 24: 1/6 pitch equals 1/6 x 24, or 4—4″ rise to every 12″ of run—4-12. You can determine the height of a roof at its peak if you know the fractional pitch by multiplying the fractional pitch by the span or width of the house: a house with a 1/6 pitch roof which is 40 feet wide would be 1/6 x 40 equals 6⅔ feet or 6′-8″ from plate to peak. By dividing the measured height of a roof, from plate to peak, by its width will give you the fractional pitch of the roof: 6⅔ feet

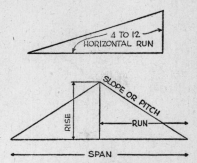

Fig. 109. Factors determining pitch.

divided by 40 feet equals 1/6 pitch.

Roof Framing is made up of various members which are identified as follows: Roof Plate; Ridge or Ridge Board; Hip Rafter; Jack Rafter; Common Rafter; Valley Rafter; Purlin and Collar Beam.

Roof Plates have been described.

The Ridge or Ridge Board is found in all roofs except the shed-type. It

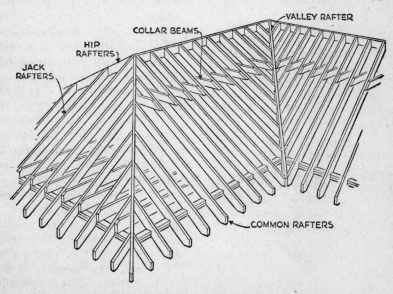

Fig. 110. Jack rafters are framed to the hip rafters and the plate.

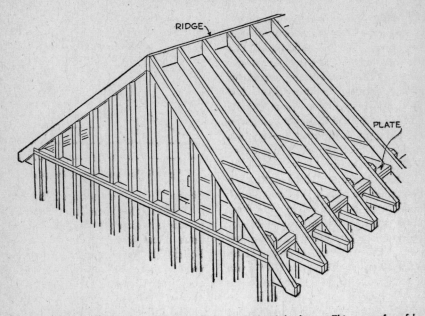

Fig. 111. Ends on a Gable roof are formed by the ends of the house. This type of roof has rafters extending from ridge board to plate.

forms the peak of a roof and is the structural member to which the rafters are framed, forming the lateral tie which holds the rafters together as a unit. In a hip roof, rectangular in form, the ridge board has considerable length, while in the same type roof but square in form, it's extremely short. The lowest part of a roof where the rafter-ends, plate and cornice combine, is known as the Eaves. Where the juncture of the roof and wall occur, there's an ornamental detail called the Cornice which is frequently made up of moldings and boards, with the gutter usually part of the assembly.

Rafters support the loads of the roof, snow and wind. In a Hip Roof

the Hip Rafters run from the corners of the plate to the end of the ridge board, and form the exterior angle where the two roofs meet.

Jack Rafters are framed to the hip rafters and the plate, and are called such because they are shorter than the Common Rafters which run from the plate to the ridge board. The pitch of a hip roof is the same on all four sides (Fig. 110).

A Valley Rafter forms the interior angle where two roofs intersect.

The Purlin occurs in a gambrel roof, being the structural member to which the rafters of different slopes are framed. The juncture of these different slopes is also called the purlin. A Collar Beam is the stiffening

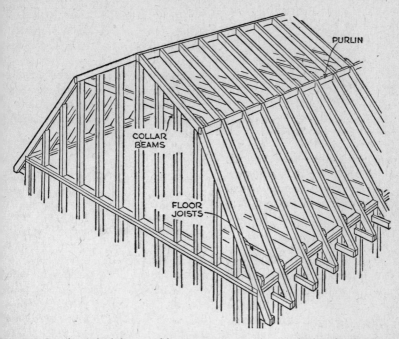

Fig. 112. Popular in both barn and house construction, the Gambrel roof with its two slopes affords additional attic space and storage room.

member for a rafter, bridging it at varying distances below the ridge board. Collar beams are usually the ceiling framing for finished attics.

Hip

The Hip Roof has been described, being a four-sided roof either square or rectangular in form.

Gable

The Gable Roof has rafters from plate to ridge board, the ends of the house forming Gable Ends (Fig. 111).

Gambrel

A Gambrel Roof has two planes of sloping roof on each side of the ridge board; the first slope, from plate to purlin being rather steep, while the second slope, from purlin to ridge board, is much flatter. Barn construction favors this type of roof, as it allows much more storage space under the roof than other types. In dwelling construction it gives more head room for a given space in the attic (Fig. 112).

Mansard

The Mansard Roof was quite the favorite with architects of the late eighteenth and the nineteenth century when they designed "mansions." In principle it is like the gambrel, but with almost vertical sides from plate

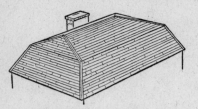

Fig. 113. Varying pitch made the Mansard roof practically another story.

to purlin. From there on it was almost a flat roof. It produced practically an extra story to a house while at the same time it functioned as a roof (Fig. 113).

Shed

The Shed or Lean-To Roof was used principally for small additions to a house and for small storage structures on the property. Today, it is the most popular type of roof for modern dwelling construction. It consists of rafters sloping in one direction, framed to plates at each wall juncture. A tying member is necessary with this type of roof to react against the tendency of wind pressures to push the high side outward. The ties are joists which also are the ceiling support (Fig. 114).

ROOFING

All roofs must be covered with some waterproof material, and shingles being the oldest form, are most used. Shingles may be of wood, asphalt composition, asbestos or slate. Roll roofing is another material more frequently used today than in former years.

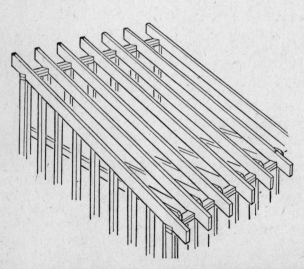

Fig. 114. Joists should not only support the ceiling in the Shed roof. They also act as a tying member to protect the roof from wind pressures acting on it.

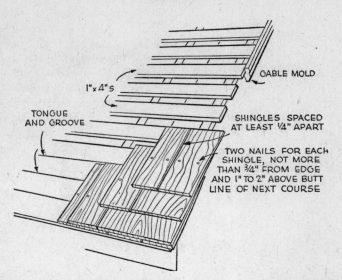

GABLE MOLD

I"x 4" s

TONGUE
AND GROOVE

SHINGLES SPACED
AT LEAST ¼" APART

TWO NAILS FOR EACH
SHINGLE, NOT MORE
THAN ¾" FROM EDGE
AND I" TO 2" ABOVE BUTT
LINE OF NEXT COURSE

Fig. 115. Careful attention to underboarding and the placement of both wooden shingles and shingle nails will insure an overlapping construction that is waterproof.

Wood Shingles

Wood Shingles were hand split or "rived" in the old days and produced the best shingle, because splitting tears the wood fibers while the modern method of sawing them cuts the fibers. This leaves the cells open, making it easier for water to penetrate and cause disintegration. Some of the better grades of wood shingle have a split and a sawed face, the shingle being first split from a thick board and then sawed diagonally through, making two wedge-shaped shingles, each with a split and a sawed face.

Wood shingles are manufactured in three grades: Nos. 1, 2 and 3. Widths vary and are random in a bundle, being approximately 4, 5, 6 and 8", and may be had in lengths of 16, 18, 20 and 24". No. 1 grade is free of defects, is heartwood and edge (vertical) grain. Nos. 2 and 3 have defects above the weather face and may or may not be edge grain. It's poor economy to shingle a roof with an inferior grade of shingle, as edge grain shingles are less likely to warp, and heartwood (center portion of a log) is the most durable.

Application

Wood shingles are usually nailed to 1x4" boards spaced on centers equal to the weather face (exposure) of the shingles, the boards being nailed to the rafters. At the eaves, for the distance of two courses of shingles, close-fitting tongued and grooved roof boards are nailed to the rafters for the starter and first course. Sometimes solid roof boarding covers the entire surface of the roof (Fig. 115).

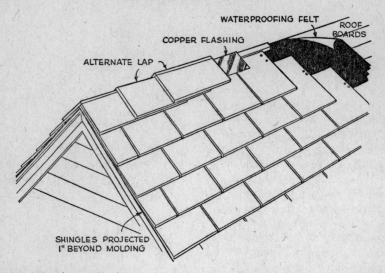

Fig. 116. When laying shingles, staggering the joints is the most effective means of protecting the shingle junctures below from leakage.

The amount of weather face of a shingle depends on its length, slope of roof, and the distance from the eaves to the ridge, the distance being divided into a number of full courses of shingles. An exposure of about 5½″ is average for 16″ and 18″ shingles, the limit being about 7½″ for the 16″ and 8½″ for the 18″ length. A 24″ shingle can be laid as much as 11½″ to the weather, depending on the roof slope. If shingles aren't stained by the manufacturer, and you wish to have color on your roof, dip them when thoroughly dry in a good quality creosote stain about ⅔ their length, and let them dry in a loose pile. Don't soak shingles in stain, just quickly dip them—and never paint a wood-shingled roof, which results in swelling.

Unstained shingles are usually thoroughly wetted with water before laying, and are spaced closely but not tightly together. Dry shingles must have a space between their side edges of from 1/16″ to ¼″ depending on their width, otherwise they would swell, buckle and split when they became wet. Stained shingles, when wet, swell less than the unstained.

Starting Course

The starting course at the eaves is always doubled and extends about 1″ beyond the edge, forming a drip. At the rake (slope-edge of roof) shingles should extend at least ½″ to form a drip. If shingles are laid in a straight line, a chalk mark or a straightedge wood strip is used to keep them parallel to the length of the roof. Other methods of laying shingles are in an uneven line; the ends staggered; or laid with a wavy line, simulating a

European thatch (straw) roof. In the latter method, eaves are sometimes curved downward to further simulate a thatch roof.

Stagger Joints

Joints of each course are staggered from 1½ to 2″ beyond those of the preceding course, so there's no possibility of rain finding its way between two joints and through the roof (Fig. 116). There are a number of methods of finishing the shingle course at the ridge. The simplest is attaching a saddle of two pieces of lumber over the ridge and the shingles. This saddle may have metal flashing under it, over it or none. Another method is known as the Boston Ridge. Here shingles are used for the saddle, but nailed lengthwise to the ridge, and of even width. Alternate shingle edges lap each other along the ridge, and step flashing is placed under each shingle to make the assembly watertight. The way the Boston ridge is usually made is to lay a shingle, extending it somewhat beyond the ridge, and then splitting or cutting it on a bevel even with the edge of the opposite shingle. The same methods used for the ridge are also used for the hips of roofs.

Flashing

Valleys in roofs are handled in one of two ways. Metal flashing is first laid and the shingles then laid over the flashing, stopping short of the center of the valley by 2 to 3″ on each side, that is, the exposed metal valley is 4 to 6″ wide at the top. As the valley descends, it should become wider by 1″ to every 8 feet. This

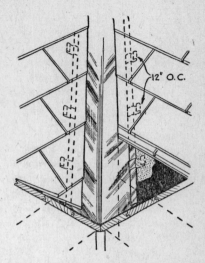

Fig 117 Wider at bottom than at top, open valley construction facilitates water flow.

taper is constructed so as to facilitate drainage as the water rushes down the valley, and to prevent snow and ice jambs. This method of construction is called the open valley. Sometimes the flashing is crimped in the center to form a V-dam when a smaller roof joins a larger one to prevent water from the larger roof running up the smaller one (Fig. 117).

The other method of constructing a valley is known as the closed valley and is more difficult to achieve. The singles are laid across the valley, supported by a board. Step flashing must be laid for each shingle (Fig. 118.) The greatest number of roof valleys consist of metal-flashed open valleys.

Valley flashing should be attached with cleats of metal and never directly nailed to the roof boards. The cleats are about 2″ wide and 4″ long and

are usually spaced 12″ on centers.
They're nailed at one end and the end
is turned over the nail heads. The
other end is turned up and the flashing edge is bent over and under the
cleat end, forming a firmly locked
grip (Fig. 119).

Tracing Leaks

Tracing the source of a leak in a
shingled roof is sometimes difficult
because the source quite frequently
is not where the leakage shows. De-
fective flashing around chimneys and
elsewhere oftener than not are contributing causes. However, damaged
and badly warped wood shingles can
also be the reason. Holes in a shingled roof, large enough for rain to
leak through, can usually be discov-
ered by the daylight which shows
through them. An old stunt is to push
a wire through this hole from the
attic side which will locate the hole
for you when you're scrambling
around on the roof.

There's a curious phenomenon,
difficult to explain, concerning holes
in a wood-shingled roof. There are
some eighteenth century houses
whose original hand-split-shingled-
roofs are so badly damaged in spots
that you can see through them. Yet,
when a severe rainstorm occurs,
not a drop of water leaks through.
Patching such a roof inevitably makes
it leak like a sieve. Don't depend on
this phenomenon—it doesn't happen
too often. An old, badly damaged roof
of any area larger than a few shingles
here and there, must be recovered
with new material, and will be discussed in Chapter 8.

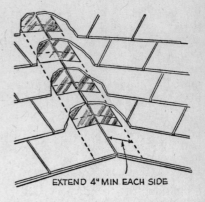

EXTEND 4″ MIN EACH SIDE

Fig. 118. In closed valley construction
shingles are laid across the valley.

Replacing Damaged
Wood Shingles

Replacing damaged wood shingles
isn't difficult. First lift up the offending shingle enough so that you can
rock it sideways and break it away
from the hidden nails—it will usually
split away easily. Replace with a new
shingle which, of course, can't be
blind nailed like the original one. Nail
the new shingle on its face and cover
the nail heads with roofing cement.
When nailing shingles, never force

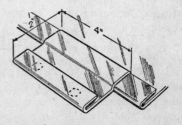

Fig. 119. Metal cleat used to secure valley
flashing to roof.

the nail head into the face of the shingle. This only tears the fibers around the head, or may split the shingle. Zinc-coated, flat-head 3d roofing nails are used, two being required for narrow shingles, and three for wider ones (Fig. 120).

Asphalt Shingles

Asphalt and asbestos shingles, due to some building codes and lower fire insurance rates, have to a large extent replaced the wood shingle. Asphalt shingles are made from an asphalt-saturated heavy felt covered with a layer of colored crushed slate. There are a number of grades of this roofing material, depending on the quality of the asphalt, felt and thickness of the shingle. The best quality is eventually the cheapest.

Types

Asphalt shingles are manufactured as separate shingles in several sizes, and also in strip form. Single shingles are usually 9x12" and 12x16", while strips are about 9" wide and from 18 to 36" long. The latter are slotted about 9" apart to simulate the spacing between wood shingles, and the slots extend about 4 to 5" up from the butt edge. Other shapes include the diamond and hexagonal, both in single and strip form.

Strip Type

When laying the strip type, one course is laid along the end of the slot of the preceding course, the courses staggered similarly to laying wood shingles. Asphalt shingles are relatively thin and of even thickness and

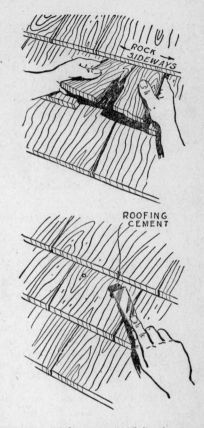

Fig. 120. To replace worn wood shingle, move it sidways, breaking it from hidden nails, and replace, covering nails with cement.

consequently do not produce the distinct shadow line of the thick wood shingle. To give a heavier shadow line, some asphalt shingles are manufactured with an added coating of slate at the butts, and some butts are doubled. Distinct shadow lines on a roof or wall give it a certain character pleasing to the eye as they break up an otherwise monotonous flat ex-

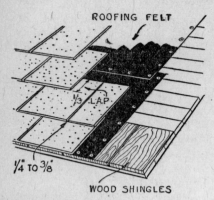

Fig. 121. Spacing should be ¼ to ⅜". Second course laps the first by approximately ⅓ the shingle's width.

panse. However, it is purely a matter of personal taste whether a roof should have a thin or heavy shadow line.

Asphalt Shingle Base

Solid roof boarding is required as a base for asphalt shingles, and since the material is soft and bends easily, either a starting course of wood shingle, or a metal or wood drip strip is first nailed as a support for the shingle so it won't droop over the eaves edge. Roofing felt is laid over the wood shingle or strip, and over the entire roof as a waterproof underlayer. The starter course of asphalt shingle, if it is single, is laid over the wood shingle or strip, but with its long dimension parallel to the eaves. Then the first course is laid over the starter course with ¼" to ⅜" spacing between shingles. The next course is laid with the joints broken, lapping the first about ⅓ the width. This method is continued over the roof (Fig. 121).

Strip asphalt shingles are laid the same way, except that the starter course is laid with its slots pointing toward the ridge. The first course is then laid over the starter, with the slots pointing downward and continued up the roof. The next and succeeding courses are laid with the joints broken as with the single-shingle method. Ridges and hips are made with strips of roll-roofing felt of the same composition as the shingles, or the Boston hip and ridge method is employed whereby separate shingles are bent over and nailed on both sides. These are laid with lapped joints. Flashing for either method isn't necessary (Figs. 122 and 123).

Open valleys are most frequently made with roll roofing instead of metal flashing, and closed valleys are more easily made with asphalt shingles than with rigid wood shingles. When strip shingles are used to make a closed valley, they are usually run into the valley from one side, and up the roof a short distance on the other side in alternate layers. This produces a closed valley which is completely self-flashed (Fig. 124).

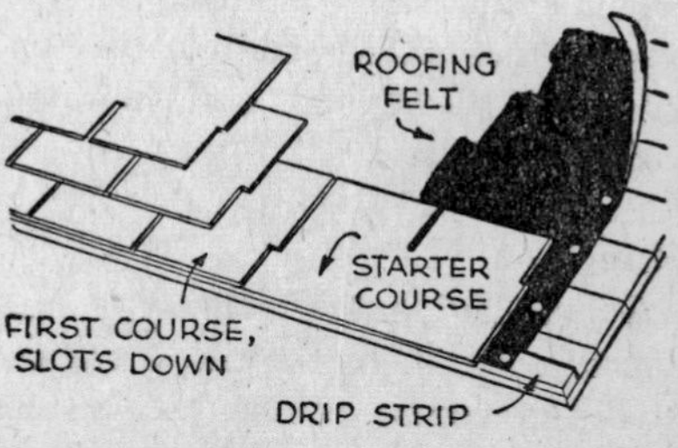

Fig. 122. First course in asphalt shingling has slots pointing downward. Slots on starter course point towards the ridge.

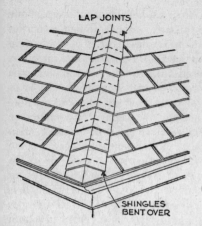

Fig. 123. Bent over shingles replace flashing at ridges and hips.

Roll Roofing

Roll Roofing is also an asphalt-processed material the same as the shingle, being applied in long, overlapping strips. It comes slate coated and uncoated, some types being 32" wide, others 36" wide. It is laid by applying asphalt cement along the edges which are lapped 2 to 3", and 6 to 8" at the ends. It is then nailed along the edges and ends with flat-head roof nails every 2 or 3". Hips and ridges are made with a strip bent over the hip or ridge, and valleys have a strip of roofing instead of metal flashing. At the eaves and rakes the roofing is turned over the edges and nailed on the undeside (Fig. 125).

Slate Surfaced

There is another type of roll roofing which comes 36" wide with a 17" colored, slated surface. This, when laid, forms a double-surfaced roof, the slated surface lapping the unslated. The unslated surface is nailed down first, then cold asphalt cement is applied on this and the next slated

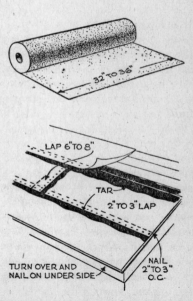

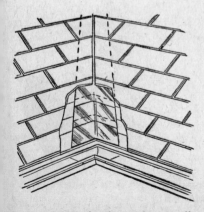

Fig. 124. Strip shingles produce a self-flashed closed valley.

Fig. 125. Roll roofing is lapped 2 to 3" along edges, 6 to 8" at ends.

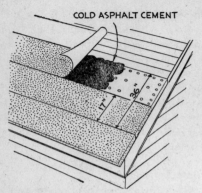

Fig. 126. Roll roofing with a 17" slated surface presents a cemented lated surface to the weather.

ment under pressure, and are, along with slate, the only shingle materials which are fireproof. They are rigid and extremely durable, and manufactured in strip and separate-shingle form. The strip shingle is about 14" x 30" with the butt edge designed to simulate the ends of a number of shingles. The upper edge is triangular.

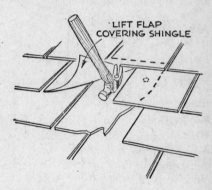
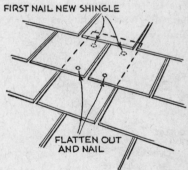

Fig. 127. Replace asphalt shingle by removing offending shingle, then nailing new shingle to shingles above and below.

course is laid down, producing a cemented slated surface to the weather with all nails concealed. Eaves and rakes are handled in the same manner as for other types of roll roofing. Roofing material of the roll type is used chiefly for so-called flat roofs, it being ideal for pitches of as little as 1" to 12", not possible with shingles of any type. It should not be laid in cold weather as it is brittle at low temperatures (Fig. 126).

Asphalt Shingle
Roof Repairs

Repairing an asphalt-shingled roof is easy. First remove the nails holding the damaged shingle by lifting up the flap of the shingle covering it. Remove the damaged shingle and replace with a new one. First nail the new shingle to hold the shingle under it, then flatten out the shingle above it and nail, securing two layers (Fig. 127).

Asbestos shingles are fabricated from asbestos fibers and portland ce-

Single shingles are about 8" x 16" and both strip and separate types are of even thickness. The strip is perhaps the most popular since it is quicker laid, covering the area of about 5 single shingles, but when down creates the illusion of the roof having been laid with separate shingles. There are a variety of colors and several grain textures to choose from, and the shingles come pre-punched for nails. Special starter shingles are required for both types, which also applies to ridges and hips.

Asbestos Shingle Base

Asbestos shingles require a solid roof-boarding base with roofing felt over it but left loose at the eaves. A wood cant strip is first nailed along the eaves, and then a metal drip strip is nailed over the cant strip. A special starter course is nailed over these with a 1″ overhang at the eaves and rake. Then the loose felt is laid over the starter course and the first course of

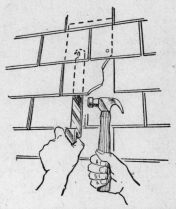

Fig. 129. A slater's shingle ripper cuts concealed nails when it is necessary to remove a single, broken shingle.

less. Ridges, hips and valleys are made in the same manner as with wood shingles, but with special pieces designed for the ridges and hips (Fig. 128).

Repairing Broken Asbestos Shingles

Repairing a broken asbestos shingle requires a slater's shingle ripper — a long-bladed tool having a hook with a sharpened edge at one end and an offset handle at the other. This is slipped under the broken shingle, and concealed heads (Fig. 129), are cut by striking the handle offset with a hammer. A hacksaw blade fixed into a handle, in place of a ripper, can be used to saw off the nail heads. Remove the shingle and replace it with a new one. Drill a hole for a nail through the side joint of the two shingles above the new one and drive a nail flush with the *new* shingle. Then slip a narrow piece of copper strip under these shingles and over

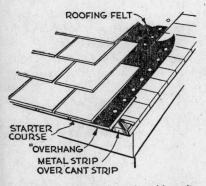

ROOFING FELT

STARTER COURSE
1″OVERHANG
METAL STRIP OVER CANT STRIP

Fig. 128. The layer effect of roof-boarding, felt, and shingles staggered provide proper roof protection.

shingles is laid over the roofing felt. Other courses are staggered with laps of not less than 2″. The weather exposure of the shingles can be 7″ or

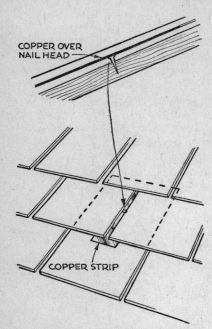

COPPER OVER NAIL HEAD

COPPER STRIP

Fig. 130. The use of a copper strip, such as the one shown, permits replacing a single shingle in its course since it is impractical to nail it as before.

the nail head of the new one. Another method of attaching the shingle is to nail a copper strip in the side joint of the two shingles below the location of the new one, at a point near the butt edge of the new shingle, but clearing the shingle under the nailing point. Slip in the new shingle and bend the copper strip over the butt edge. The copper strip holds the shingle in place (Fig. 130).

Slate Shingles

Slate shingles are the most durable of all roofing materials, and rarely is it necessary to repair them as they'll usually outlast the house. This mate-

rial is also the most expensive and requires much heavier roof framing to sustain the considerable weight. Slate comes with the nail holes prepunched and countersunk, as it is next to impossible to make holes without danger of cracking or damaging the slate. Holes can be drilled into this material with a twist drill, however.

Laying Slate

Slate is laid in a similar manner to wood shingles, but on solid roof boards with heavy roofing felt over them. Average thickness is about 3/16", although slate can be had up to ¾" thick. Lengths range from 10" to 24" in 2" multiples. A cant strip is first nailed along the eaves to start the slate at an angle corresponding to that of succeeding overlapped slates. The starter course is laid with the long dimension of the slate parallel to the eaves line, then the first course is laid over that. It is usual practice to then lay about 12 courses to the weather about 6½", five following courses 5½", and the remaining courses about 4½". Ridges, hips and valleys are laid similarly to wood shingles.

Repairing a broken slate requires the same general procedure as for an asbestos shingle, using a copper strip to cover the heads of nails.

CORNICES

Cornices are basically of two kinds: Closed and Open. The open cornice has exposed roof rafters, or false rafters nailed to the rough ones. Since

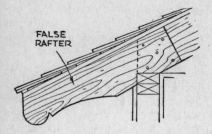

Fig. 131. Since rough rafters contain imperfections they are usually cut off at the plate line; finished lumber is nailed to the roof rafter and extended beyond the wall line.

rough rafters contain imperfections, it is usual practice to cut them off at the plate line and nail finished lumber to the roof rafter a short distance back from the plate, extending the false rafter beyond the wall line. These are often cut to a simple ornamental profile (Fig. 131).

Rafter Ends

The ends of the rafters are finished with a board called the Fascia, and at the building line they are closed off with a board known as the Frieze. Blocking is nailed to the rafter sides for a nailing surface for the sheathing board and the frieze. A molding is usually nailed at the intersection of fascia and roof board, and quite frequently at the frieze also. If the rake of the roof has an overhang, the roof boards are extended beyond the rafter and finished with an edging strip. A Barge Board is nailed to the underside of the boards and finished with a shingle molding. A frieze board finishes the juncture of the roof and wall. There are no rafter extensions on the rake side of the roof.

Closed Cornice

Closed cornices are made in different ways, the simplest being a crown molding nailed to the ends of the rafters which extend a very short distance beyond the plate. Below the molding there is usually a frieze board blocked out beyond the siding material. The rake corresponds in extension to the eaves and is finished in the same manner. Often the crown molding is nailed directly to the siding without the addition of a frieze board (Fig. 132).

Boxed Cornice

A Boxed Cornice in its simplest form consists of the usual fascia board attached to the rafter ends; a Plancia

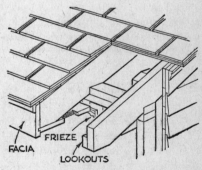

Fig. 132. Closed cornices usually have a frieze board situated below the molding.

which is a board fastened either directly to the underside of the rafters, or to the underside of additional horizontal framing known as Lookouts. The plancia extends from the fascia to the wall, and is dadoed into the fascia just above its lower edge, forming a drip. Sheathing is carried up to

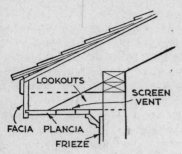

Fig. 133. The plancia is dadoed into the fascia just above its lower edge.

the roof boards, and a frieze seals off the juncture of the plancia and sheathing. The rake of a closed cornice is similar to the eaves, with look-outs nailed to the wall. These support the plancia which is finished with a frieze as for the eaves. Boxed cornices are usually "returned," about the width of the cornice, at the juncture of rake and eaves (Fig. 133).

GUTTERS

Gutters are designed to carry off the rain water shed by the roof and channel it into downspouts or leaders, and thence to sewers or dry wells. There are many kinds of gutters, made of wood or metal, and all must have a slope toward the leaders of not less than 1/16″ per foot. The most elemental type of wood gutter is two boards nailed to form a V. The V must be lined with metal or coated with a waterproof material to prevent the joint from parting and leaking. It is fairly efficient but isn't used on good building construction (Fig. 134).

Wood Gutters

Stock wood gutters are shaped from solid Douglas fir, cedar, red-wood or cypress and are, in effect, a form of large molding serving the double purpose of channeling water and adding a decorative detail to the cornice. The face of the gutter is usually an ogee molding with a semi-circular inner surface. Where the ends are joined they are butted, with a lead or soft copper sheet covering the joint, recessed flush and nailed with copper nails. The metal sheet is first laid in elastic roofing cement. Corners are carefully mitered and the joint covered in the same manner. Where the leader fits into the gutter, the same procedure applies, with a lead spout connection for the leader.

Wood gutters are usually attached to the fascia board, but sometimes are attached directly to the rafter ends. If they are attached to the fascia, they should be separated from the board by ¼″ blocking or with washers to allow an air space which prevents decay at the juncture of the gutter

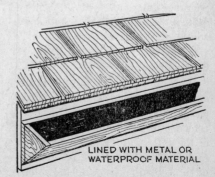

LINED WITH METAL OR WATERPROOF MATERIAL

Fig. 134. The elemental type of wood gutter consists of two boards nailed to form a V.

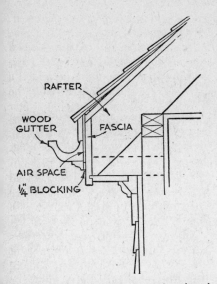

Fig. 135. Gutters should always be placed far enough below the edge of the shingle to prevent water backing up under them.

making successively deeper notches in each rafter, starting with the farthest from the leader. This gutter must be metal lined and the roof well flashed. Since the slope of the roof determines the lower edge of this type of gutter, it is usually quite shallow unless the roof slope is gradual, due to the practical limit permissible of notching roof rafters (Fig. 136).

Pole Gutter

The Pole Gutter extends beyond the roof slope and, while easier to construct than the built-in type, its capacity is even less. It consists of two pieces, one wedge-shaped and the other a straight board or strip. Metal flashing must cover this gutter also, run well under the shingles

and fascia. Gutters should always be placed far enough below the edge of the shingles to prevent water backing up under them, should the gutter become full. The distance between leaders and the high point of gutters should be kept relatively short for appearance sake, otherwise the slope is quite noticeable and destroys the horizontal of the cornice (Fig. 135).

Built-on-the-job

Built-on-the-job or built-in gutters are of two kinds: concealed, or projecting above the roof line. The concealed gutter requires deep notching of the rafters and occurs a short distance up from the eaves. It is made up of three boards nailed to the sides of the notches, and gets its slope by

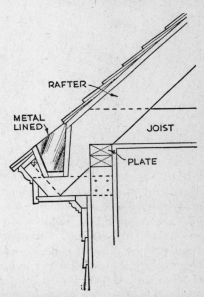

Fig. 136. The concealed gutter is made up of three boards nailed to the sides of notches cut in the roof rafters.

Fig. 137. Pole gutter.

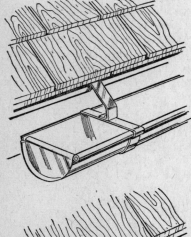

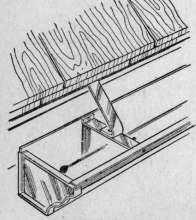

Fig. 138. Metal gutters.

above, and lock into flashing below it. Due to its shallowness, rain water rushing down the roof slope as often as not cascades over the edge of the gutter (Fig. 137).

Metal Gutters

Metal gutters are made of galvanized iron, copper, lead, zinc or tinned steel; and in many shapes, both ornamental and plain. The least expensive and, perhaps the most efficient, is the simple half-round gutter with a turned-over bead. The usual method of attaching metal gutters is by flat straps attached to the roof boards before the shingles are laid. Metal brackets are used for large-size gutters with a heavy water capacity. Metal gutters should be free of the fascia for the same reason that wood gutters should be, but if certain types with square backs are attached directly to the fascia, the backs must be carried well under the shingles to prevent any chance of leakage (Fig. 138).

Leaders

Leaders or downspouts are made of metal, either square ar round, and must be large enough to carry the roof water away (Fig. 139) as it pours. The connection between leader and gutter is usually an S-shaped piece called a Gooseneck. On more ornate types of gutters and leaders, the gooseneck empties into a box called the Leader Box. This has no particular practical function except to be ornamental. Where the gooseneck attaches, there should be a strainer in the gutter to prevent leaves and twigs from entering the leader and cause

toppage there or in the sewer connection. It is usually made of wire
bars spaced close enough to prevent
solid material from entering but not
retard the flow of water. These strainers are usually attached with spring
clamps and can be removed for cleaning (Fig. 140).

SIDING

Siding, which is the finished outside surface of the house, comes in
many forms and a number of materials, wood being the most popular.
Wood siding is sold as Clapboards,
Beveled, Beveled Shiplap, Drop or
Novelty, Board and Log Cabin. Log-
cabin siding is not stocked by many
lumber yards, its use being more or
less regional (Fig. 141).

Clapboards

Originally houses were finished
with clapboards of even thickness,
each lapped over the other. In time
the boards warped, separating from
their narrow contact with each other,
giving the interior very little protection against air infiltration.

Beveled Siding

Beveled siding was then introduced, which is made by sawing a
thick board lengthwise at an angle,
producing two beveled boards, thin
at the top edge and thick at the butt.
This is the most common form of
wood siding and comes in widths
from 4 to 12″. The boards are lapped
about 1″ for narrow widths, and 2″
and over for the wide types. They are
usually nailed at the butt edge and
through the tip edge of the board below. Very narrow siding is quite often

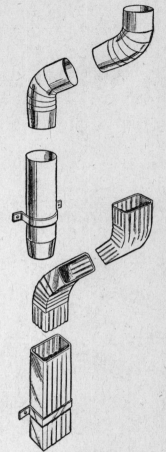

Fig. 139. Downspouts.

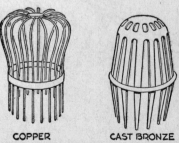

COPPER   CAST BRONZE
Fig. 140. Gutter strainers.

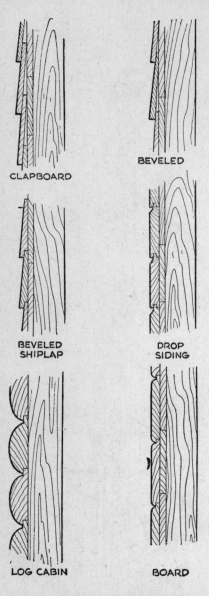

CLAPBOARD

BEVELED

BEVELED SHIPLAP

DROP SIDING

LOG CABIN

BOARD

Fig. 141. Conventional wood siding is sold as Clapboards, Beveled, Beveled Shiplap, Drop or Novelty, and Log Cabin, which is considered a standard in only a few regions.

nailed near its thin edge similarly to shingles. It is nailed to solid sheathing over which building paper has been attached. Window and door casings are first framed; the siding butts against the edges of these. Corners are either mitered, or corner boards are first nailed to the sheathing, and the siding fitted against the edges. Beveled shiplap siding is procurable but not often used, there being very little advantage gained in its use. Beveled siding is easy to repair and replace (Fig. 142).

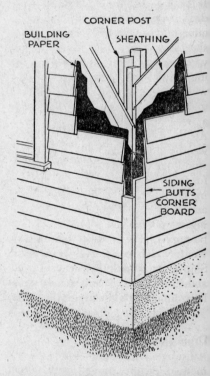

CORNER POST

BUILDING PAPER

SHEATHING

SIDING BUTTS CORNER BOARD

Fig. 142. Narrow siding is nailed to solid sheathing over which building paper has been attached. Siding butts edges of windows and door casings which are framed first.

Drop Siding

Drop or Novelty Siding was originally designed to be used as sheathing and siding combined. It comes in
a wide variety of face profiles and is
either shiplapped or tongued and
grooved. If used as a combined
sheathing and siding material,
tongued and grooved lumber is used,
the tongue up, and nailed directly to
the studs. Sometimes building paper
is first stretched over the studs, but
oftener the paper is omitted (Fig. 143).
It is not good building practice to use
drop siding alone, since it affords a
minimum of weathertightness. When
sheathing is not used, the door and
window casings are set *after* the siding is up. This leaves open channels
where casing and siding contacts, and
makes it extremely difficult to achieve
a watertight window or door head.
At the jambs of these openings a
weatherstop is nailed to the rough
studding, but even so it is possible
for water to creep in through the siding channels. If sheathing is first used
and then building paper, drop siding is an excellent material and can
be applied like beveled siding, after
window and door casings are in place.
Shiplap joints are then usually used,
and the siding becomes a form of
horizontal board covering (Fig. 144).

Drop Siding Corners

Corners are sometimes mitered, but
more often are framed with corner
boards over the siding when sheathing is not used. This method, too,
leaves openings along the edges of
the boards. A better method is to use

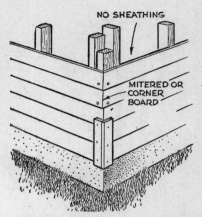

Fig. 143. Novelty siding is often used as a combination sheathing and siding material.

asphalt-saturated felt around the
posts, nail narrow corner boards to
the posts and butt the siding against
the boards, nailing the siding to the
posts. With sheathing, corners are
made as with beveled siding.

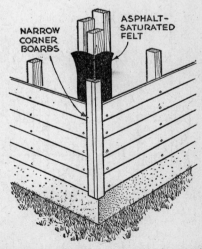

Fig. 144. Place asphalt-saturated felt around posts and nail narrow corner boards to them.

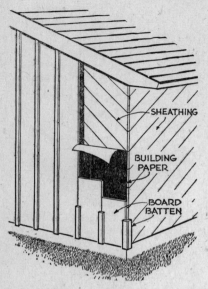

Fig. 145. Proper method of using vertical board and batten over sheathing and paper.

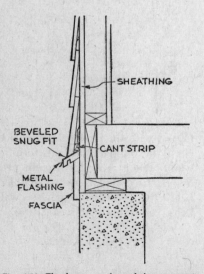

Fig. 146. The bottom edge of the cant strip should fit snugly against the water table.

Board Siding

Board Siding can be either vertically or horizontally applied; square edged, shiplapped or tongued and grooved. Vertical boarding is the traditional method of covering barns. Originally the beams or studs in a barn were spaced very wide apart and vertical boards were nailed to these and the bracing between, as part of the structural support of the roof. Narrow strips of wood were nailed over the joints, making them reasonably weathertight—that is, for a barn. Many modern houses employ the vertical board and batten, but with sheathing and building paper as a base. The modern-day method of applying vertical board and batten is to coat the edges of the boards just before nailing, with white lead in linseed oil and drive them tightly against each other. The battens are similarly coated as are the surfaces they cover. This procedure insures a good watertight seal (Fig. 145).

Horizontal boards are either tongued and grooved or shiplapped, and are usually applied without battens, presenting a solid wall surface. Some modern houses are battened horizontally for the effect of added lowness and length, the battens handled in a number of ways. One such method is graduating the width of the battens from narrow at the top to wider at the bottom of the wall. They have no purpose and are used for decorative effect only.

Water Tables

Water Tables may or may not be part of the siding detail. If used on beveled siding, a fascia board is nailed to the sheathing which extends to the top of the foundation wall, the fascia lapping the juncture of sheathing and wall by about an inch. It should be beveled on the under edge to form a drip, and the top edge of the fascia is also beveled to receive a beveled strip or table which extends beyond the fascia. If it extends much, a molding is attached under it. Metal flashing covers the table and is brought up under the building paper. A cant strip, usually lath, is nailed to the sheathing at the top edge of the table for the first course of siding. The bottom edge of this course should be beveled to fit snugly against the water table. If a water table isn't used, the first course of siding laps the sheathing and foundation-wall line the same as a fascia would lap. A cant strip gives the proper slant for the first course of siding.

Drop siding and vertical or horizontal boarding do not usually have water tables. If they have, the construction is the same as for beveled.

Log Cabin

Log-Cabin Siding is shiplapped, partially round lumber about 2″ thick through its thickest part, and is sold in a number of widths. It is designed to simulate peeled-log construction but does not cross lap at the corners. It is usually applied like drop siding, without sheathing, and is used a great deal for summer-camp construction. If sheathing and building paper are used, log-cabin siding, cheaper than other wood siding, makes a good, weathertight covering (Fig. 147).

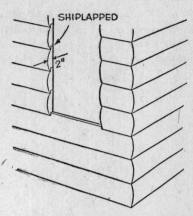

Fig. 147. Log cabin siding is usually applied like drop siding, and is used chiefly for summer camp construction.

Wood and Asbestos Shingles are also used extensively for finished walls of houses, and are applied in very much the same manner as for roofs. Some wood-shingled walls are double-coursed for better insulation and to achieve a deeper shadow line, in which case Nos. 2 and 3 grade shingles are used for the under courses. As they shed water faster on a wall, the feather face is often increased beyond that used on roofs. Corners are not mitered, but are alternately lapped with the shingles trimmed to conform to their slant. A form of water table is made by extending the first course, which is always doubled, below the top of the foundation wall, being furred out with a cant strip.

Asbestos Siding Shingles are of a different size than roof shingles, being usually 12x24″. Waterproof backing strips, furnished with the shingles, are used behind each vertical joint and at the corners. Shingles are nailed with three nails at the top and bottom edge. Water tables are not used with these shingles, the shingle being placed about ⅜" below the top of the foundation wall, and nailed to a cant strip. Courses are alternately lapped as when roofing.

CHAPTER 8

HOME IMPROVEMENTS

Most houses in urban districts, built during the past 40 years, were constructed with adequate firestopping throughout their construction. A lot of older houses were not so constructed, depending on their locality and the building restrictions in force when they were built.

There is not much you can do in the way of installing firestops between floors of these houses unless you remove part of the wall covering near the juncture of the wall or partition, subfloor and joists. If the wall covering is in first-class condition and you are happy with it, it is best left alone, particularly so if you are not sure if there is or is not firestopping at these points. As mentioned before, firestopping means only fire retarding, that is, closing up the natural flues created by conventional stud-wall construction.

Houses with cellars, the ceilings of which are quite often unfinished, can be fire retarded easily at the point of the joists and foundation wall, and since many fires start in the cellar, it is good insurance to install fireproof material if none exists. A finished ceiling of portland cement and expanded metal lath is excellent fire-retarding material, and one of the wallboards, preferably one with a gypsum core, works equally well and

is much more easily installed. Mineral wool, or vermiculite (a form of mica expanded under heat into millions of imprisoned air cells) which comes in "pebble" form, is excellent material for firestopping, besides being a first-class insulating material (Fig. 1).

Methods

There are two methods of firestopping at the sill and foundation wall of a cellar. One method is to fill in the space between sill and subloor with fireproof material and nail ¾" boards between the joists to hold the material in place. The other method, if the still is deep enough, is to fill a space about 2" thick from the top of the foundation to the subfloor, and hold it in place with 2" lumber between the joists.

Partitions over a cellar girder can be similarly filled by removing 6" of wall about 12" from the subfloor, and filling the space between the studs with vermiculite (Fig. 2). The same procedure can be used for partitions on other floors and outside walls, if desired (Fig. 3).

Attics can be sealed off by nailing a ¾"x8" or 10" board to the underside of the roof rafters at the plate and filling the space with vermiculite.

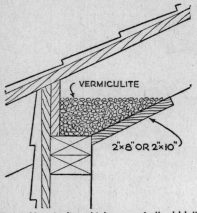

Fig. 1. Vermiculite which comes in "pebble" form is an excellent material for firestopping besides being a first-class insulator.

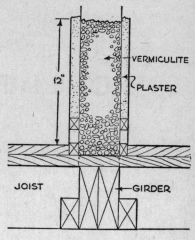

Fig. 2.

An unfinished attic with exposed joists can be thoroughly insulated with this material by pouring it evenly to a depth of about 3" between the joists (Fig. 4). An easy way to level the vermiculite is to make a scraper by cutting out the ends of a board which spans the joists, and of a depth 3" less than the depth of the joists. The cutout ends act as guides on the joists as the board scrapes the insulation evenly. An attic so insulated, in a small one-story house, can save up to 22 per cent in fuel. A thousand square feet 3" thick costs about $70, depending on the locality.

INSULATION

There are numerous forms of insulating material designed for various methods of application. There are basically four types: Loose Fill; Blankets and Batts; Insulating Wallboards; and Bright Aluminum Foil. Except for the latter, these materials act on the principle of an accumulation of quiet or dead air which is the poorest of heat conductors. The bright aluminum foil works on the principle of heat reflection, being in itself an excellent conductor of heat.

Loose-fill insulation is one of the oldest types, exemplified by the old ice houses with their double walls filled with sawdust.

Blankets and Batts

Blankets and Batts are made up of vegetable or mineral-fiber material, and are different from insulating wallboards only in the degree of their compactness or compression. The wallboards have less insulating qualities because of their compression. Solid wood has good insulating properties because of its cellular structure, but thickness for thickness, fiber insulating boards have better qualities because their cellular structure is less compact.

More heat is lost through a roof than through the walls of a house, particularly so if the attic is unfinished and unheated, the warm air rising through the walls into the cold attic and out through the roof. That is why blocking off air circulation at the juncture of the attic joists and the plate, and at the cornice with loose fill contributes a great deal toward preventing heat loss at these points. Insulating the attic joists and the space between the roof rafters, further reduces a considerable amount of heat loss.

Outside-wall insulating materials must have a vapor barrier to prevent the interior warm air from striking the exterior cold air and condensing into trapped water. This holds true also for roof insulation for the same reason. Blanket and batt insulation come with and without integral vapor barriers of glazed asphalt-saturated felt or craft paper. The vapor barrier is always placed facing the interior, and should be as close to the wall or ceiling covering as possible.

Blankets are attached in several ways. One method is to bend over the ends of the blankets and attach them to the studs with wood lath, the blanket being placed midway between the thickness of the wall. This provides an extra dead air space which is added insulation. Another method is to nail the flaps of the vapor seal which extend beyond the blanket to the sides of the studs.

Batt insulation (Fig. 5) is applied in much the same manner, but fills practically the entire thickness of the walls, the vapor-seal flaps being nailed to

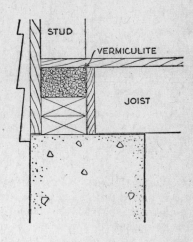

Fig. 3.

the stud edges. Both blanket and batt insulation come in standard widths to fit conventional stud spacing. The advantage of blanket or batt over loose fill in walls is that the insulating material is contained and kept compact, while loose fill may pack in time, leaving an uninsulated space at the top while it has packed too tightly at the bottom—losing some of its insulating properties.

Existing house walls lacking insulation are usually insulated with loose fill blown into openings cut through the exterior sheathing. This must be done by contractors equipped with the necessary equipment. Since this method of insulating provides no vapor barrier, there is the possibility of condensation occurring, although many houses have been so insulated without any apparent signs of condensation.

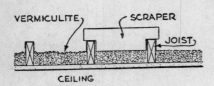

Fig. 4. An unfinished attic with exposed joists can be thoroughly insulated with vermiculite by pouring it evenly to a depth of about 3″ between joists.

Insulating boards are also structural in their purpose, and houses today are more often than not sheathed with fiberboard for the double purpose of insulation and structural rigidity. These differ from interior wallboards only in that they are either saturated or surfaced with asphalt for weather resistance. Their structural strength is about the same as wood sheathing with greater insulating properties. Moreover, they are more easily, quickly and economically applied. They come in ½″ and 25/32″ thicknesses, and in a number of panel widths and lengths. Interior wallboards of fiber composition are particularly effective for remodeling attics, where they serve the dual purpose of supplying a finished wall plus insulation. Even without additional insulation, an attic thus surfaced, will show an appreciable reduction in fuel bills.

Aluminum Foil

Bright aluminum foil which comes in flat and crinkled form is more often used between first-floor joists, where there is no cellar, to prevent the cold air from the ground from being transmitted through the floor. Also used to

some extent between studs in walls, it must form a tight seal where it is attached to the framing members in a similar manner as blanket insulation. This material has about ⅔ the insulating properties of blanket, batt or loose fill.

INTERIOR WALLBOARDS

Modern wall-covering materials of the "dry-wall" type—meaning walls put up without the use of water—are made in a variety of trade-name products, but can be classified roughly as four groups. They are pulp boards; fiberboards of either wood or cane fibers; gypsum-core wallboards; and plywood. Besides these, there are also cork tiles, linoleum, and wood-veneer on fabric.

The four groups come in panels of varying widths and lengths; in tile form, and plank or board form. Some are square edged, beveled square edged, tongued and grooved, and shiplapped; others have recessed edges for the special application of tape and cement to achieve an unbroken wall surface which is then painted.

Wallboards in general were at one time considered only for cheap wall coverings with the conventional wood battens covering the joints in all directions. Today this is not true of these materials. They are still in most cases very economical to install, but they are not condemned to the category of cheapness or makeshift. Many owners of very expensive modern houses prefer such walls to plaster. The problem of joints still exists, with all but the boards that are tape-cemented, but more thought is now given to the handling of wallboard panels and joints so that they may form part of a decorative scheme.

Basically, all wallboards of whatever material are nailed to 1"x2" or 3" wood strips which are nailed to the existing plaster wall. Furring strips are also used on masonry walls in the cellar and on existing ceilings of plaster. The use of furring is for the purpose of obtaining a level flat surface for the wallboard, and to permit the arrangement of wallboard panels for a planned decorative arrangement. This is not always possible if the panels were to be nailed to the existing studding. Wallboards should also be nailed at intermediate points which, between normal stud spacing, would be the blocking between the studs. As this blocking was framed without regard to standard wallboard-panel sizes, it is all the more important to use furring to accommodate wallboard-panel sizes.

Pulp Boards

Pulp Boards are usually 3/16" thick and come in panels 4x8 feet. They need more bracing than the fiberboards, being more flexible, and the insulating properties are less. Some of these boards are manufactured with a pre-painted pebbled surface which takes paint readily, should you prefer another color. They are structurally quite strong and can easily be bent around curves of large radii.

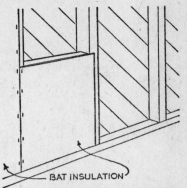

Fig. 5. Batt insulation fills practically the entire thickness of the walls, the vapor seal flaps being nailed to the stud edges.

Fiberboards

Fiberboards are usually ½" thick and come in panels 4x6 feet and longer; in tile form from 12"x12" to 16"x32"; and in plank form from 8" to 16" wide and from 8 to 12 feet long. The tiles and planks have a special type of tongued and grooved edge with a beveled front edge which permits blind nailing. These fiberboards have excellent insulating qualities, having been designed for the purpose of efficient insulation combined with a finished wall surface. They have, however, relatively soft surfaces which mar easily if furniture or other hard objects strike them.

Hardboards

Hardboards are made "regular" and "tempered," the latter having a "skin" which is extremely hard and smooth. Hardboards range in thickness from ⅛" to ¼", and are sold in panel form 4x8 feet and longer. Most of these boards are smooth surfaced, but some brands can be had with a

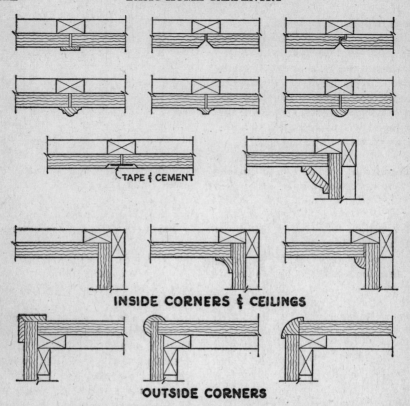

Fig. 6. Joints of wallboards can be finished in a variety of ways, depending on your personal preference and the effect you wish to achieve.

"leather-grain" texture. All are dark-brown in color. The tempered variety also comes in panels grooved in a 4" square-tile pattern, ready to be enameled in whatever color you choose and then varnished with a waterproof varnish, for bathrooms and kitchens. Hardboards make extremely rigid and hard wall coverings, but have little insulating value.

Tileboards

Tileboards are made from ⅛" tempered hardboard in tile patterns, usually 4x4 feet, in a variety of colors which have been baked on, or hot-paint sprayed. These colors are extremely durable and waterproof, and the tileboard is an economical method of wainscoating a kitchen or bathroom. Tileboard is also sold in panel form with horizontal grooves and plain surfaced for the modern effect of wall surfaces above a regular tile-pattern wainscoat, or as wainscoat material.

Gypsum-core wallboards run from ¼" to ½" in thickness and come in panels 4x6 feet and longer. They are made square edged and with recessed edges for tape-and-cement application. Their insulating properties are a bit less than that of the insulation fiberboards, but they are one of the few wallboards that can be treated so as to hide their joints when painted.

Plywood

Plywood is sold in thicknesses from ¼″ to ¾″, and in panels 4x8 feet and longer. It is also obtainable in a special board form with grooved edges which produce a slightly lapped joint. This product is applied with metal clips and produces a planked-wall surface which requires no finishing. The planks are ¼″ thick, 16¼″ wide, and from 6 to 8 feet long. Surfaces are Birch, Knotty Pine, Sliced Oak and Philippine Mahogany. This type of wall can be put up easily, quickly and permanently. Plywood is also obtainable with a striated surface and with the fir grain etched out, the latter producing a novel grain-relief effect.

Joints

Joints of wallboards (Fig. 6) can be finished in a variety of ways, depending on your personal preference and the effect you wish to achieve. There is a special type of plane made, with a form of razor-blade iron, with which you can bevel, groove and shiplap insulation fiberboard cleanly and accurately.

Methods of applying various wallboards depend on the type, but most are nailed to whatever surface is used. Others, such as ceiling tile, are nailed and cemented, while tileboards applied over flat surfaces are cemented, and nailed if applied to furring or framing, the nails set flush in the "joints" and then covered with matching-color "touch-up" paint. Whatever wallboard you choose, it is advisable to follow the manufacturer's directions for applying his particular product. These instructions are furnished on request when you purchase the material from your dealer.

ENLARGING ROOMS WHERE LOAD-BEARING PARTITIONS EXIST

If you have two small rooms separated by a load-bearing partition, and you would like to combine them in some way to achieve added spaciousness, light and ventilation, you can do it by changing the old, solid partition into an open one. Moreover, if there is a narrow doorway in the partition, you can convert it to a wide opening. If no door exists, you can construct a wide opening in the partition. See Fig. 7.

Load-bearing partitions, as mentioned previously, are partitions that carry the joists of the ceiling or floor overhead. These cannot be completely removed unless a girder of equal load-bearing properties replaces the partition and spans the room from

Fig. 7. Two small rooms separated by a load-bearing partition can be converted into one large room by changing the old solid partition into an open one.

wall to wall, or from another partition to wall or partition. Such a girder would necessarily have to be of unusual depth and thickness.

Calculating the dimensions of such a girder to sustain a given load is a structural engineer's job and beyond the ability of the average amateur carpenter. The stud spacing necessary can, however, be utilized as an open decorative effect which will give you airiness, light and ventilation, and the openings between the studs can be utilized to display potted plants and books by introducing spaced horizontal boards between the studs.

First, make sure that no water or soil pipes are hidden in the existing partition. If such exist, the part of the partition containing them must be left as is, since it is a major operation to attempt to remove these pipes and place them elsewhere. Electrical conduits or BX cables and outlets can be removed and provision made for them in other partitions, or in a part of the existing one near the juncture of another partition or wall. Moreover, if BX cable is being used for baseboard receptacles, the cable can be run along the studs at the new location of the baseboard which will cover the cable.

Remove the existing wall covering from ceiling to floor on both sides of the partition, exposing the old studding and plates. Old studs must be replaced with new, clear finish lumber of the same dimensions, since the new studs will be exposed. Removing and replacing the old studs must be done one at a time so as not to weaken the structure. If the old studs are nailed to a plate under the floor joists, saw them off at the rough floor line and nail the new studs to the rough floor with 2x4 blocking between them, also nailed to the rough floor and studs. Toenail the studs with 16d (3½″) common nails. See Fig. 8.

Studs that are nailed to a sole located on the rough floor can be removed by pulling out the nails and nailing new studs on the existing sole.

Enlarging Doorway

An old narrow doorway can be enlarged, or a new large opening installed according to the general method of framing openings in new

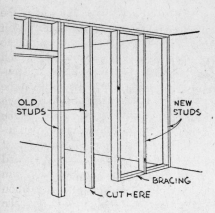

Fig. 8. Removing and replacing old studs must be done one at a time so as not to weaken the structure.

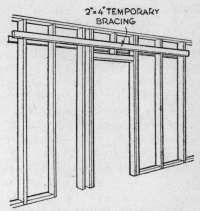

Fig. 9. Before enlarging a doorway temporary bracing is required to replace the studs which are to be cut out.

construction as discussed in Chapter 7. Before enlarging a doorway, however, temporary bracing (Fig. 9) is required to support the studs which are to be cut out for the larger opening. Nail a 2x4 or 2x6 with 20d (4″) nails across the studs on both sides of the partition, slightly higher than the top of the opening-to-be, and extending at least two studs beyond those to be removed. These temporary braces act as temporary headers until the studs have been cut and headers framed in place. Now cut out the studs in the way of the new opening, and remove the trimmers and headers of the old doorway. Replace with doubled headers (2x4s for openings up to 6 feet wide, and 2x6s for openings 8 feet wide), supported by trimmers spiked with 20d spikes to the studs framing the new opening. Truss this new opening (Fig. 10) with diagonal braces at each corner and intermediate cripples (short studs) spaced

evenly between the opening studs. Nail the cripples first (16d nails), and frame 2x4 blocking between them, spiked (20d) to the plate. After this new framing has been well spiked together, remove the temporary braces. An 8-foot opening is the widest you can make; use a 6-foot opening if it will do.

The double studs forming the opening should be covered with ¼″ plywood (Fig. 11) or ¾″ solid stock to hide the stud joints, and the underside of the headers must be covered in a similar manner. Blocking between the studs is necessary for bracing and can be 1″x4″ stock arranged in a symmetrical pattern, or 1″x6″ or 8″ stock can be framed between the studs as shelves for potted plants, books, etc.; (Fig. 12).

Wall Covering

A new wall covering must be used between the ceiling and on a line with the finished underside of the headers of the opening. A wallboard of your choice is best for this and is easily applied. Frame 1"x4" stock between the studs, on a line with the bottom edge of the wall board, closing off the space between the plate and bottom edge of the wallboard. Nail a quarter-round molding at the juncture of the cealing, and the wallboard for a finish at that point (Fig. 13).

As a finish at the base of the open partition, nail 1" stock between the studs at the height of the new baseboard, forming a closed box in which BX cable can be laid for baseboard outlets, if desired. Then nail the new baseboard to this and the studs with finishing nails set and filled. Nail a quarter-round molding, as a base shoe, at the juncture of the floor and baseboard (Fig. 14).

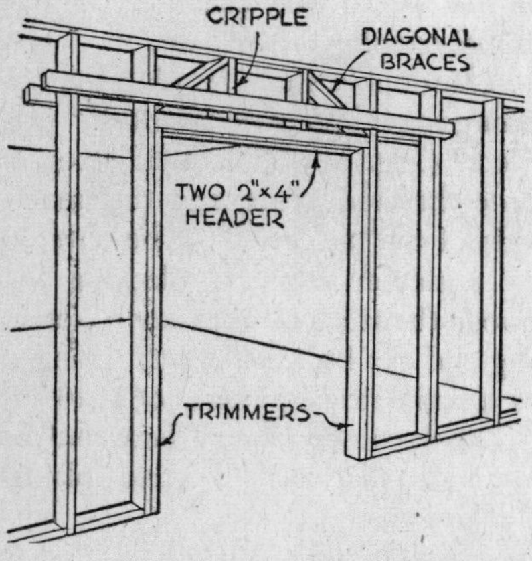

Variations in treatment of the open-partition idea are numerous, depending on the architectural arrangement of your rooms, but the preliminary steps are the same, whatever form the finished partition (Fig. 15), will take. Just make sure that each step is performed carefully, keeping in mind that when you remove a structural member, replace it before removing another. And *always* adequately brace an old opening before removing structural members to enlarge the opening.

Window openings can be enlarged in the same manner as door openings, but when doing this, temporary bracing must be nailed across the top and below the sill line before cutting studs, removing headers and trimmers, and replacing them.

HOW TO BUILD A PARTITION

If you need an additional room and have a large one that can be partitioned, it is easy to do. The partition

Fig. 10. Truss new opening with diagonal braces at each corner and intermediate cripples (short studs) spaced evenly between the opening studs.

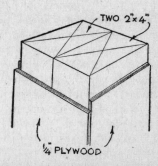

Fig. 11. The double studs forming the opening should be covered with 1/4" plywood to hide the stud joints.

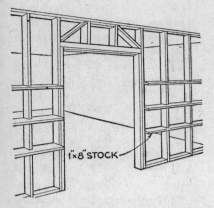

Fig. 12. Stock of 1x8" dimensions can be framed between the studs as shelves for potted plants, books, etc.

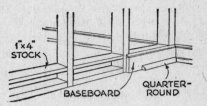

Fig. 14. As a finish at the base of the open partition, nail 1" stock between the studs at the height of the new baseboard, forming a closed box in which BX cable can be laid for baseboard outlets.

can have a door or not. Use 2"x4" lumber for the plate, studs and sole. No. 1 common dimension fir is good.

First, accurately mark out the line of the partition on the existing ceiling and on the floor. This is most easily done with a carpenter's line and blue chalk. The line is chalked, stretched between the walls of the room at the location of the proposed partition — about ½" from the ceiling — and snapped. This leaves a chalk line on the ceiling. Do the same at the floor line. Then nail a plate to the existing ceiling joists through the plaster, using 20d spikes. Nail the sole to the finished floor in the same manner. Now mark out the locations of the studs on 16" centers on the sole, and cut the studs to fit tightly between the plate and the sole. There may be vari-

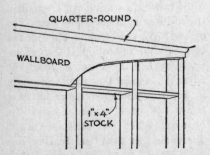

Fig. 13. A new wall covering must be used between the ceiling and on a line with the finished underside of the headers of the opening.

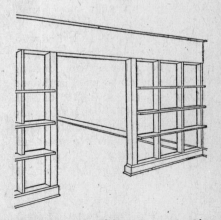

Fig. 15. Variations of the open partition idea are numerous, but the preliminary steps are the same for whatever form the finished partition will take.

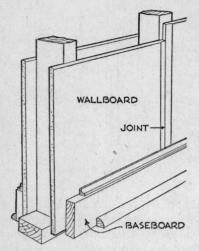

Fig. 16. The wall covering easiest to apply is one of the wallboards. If you desire an unbroken wall surface use gypsum-core wallboard with recessed edges.

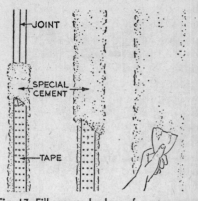

Fig. 17. Fill recessed edges of gypsum-core wallboard with water-mix cement, press perforated fiber tape into the cement, and smooth out nubs of cement that penetrate the perforations.

ations in the floor or ceiling level, so each stud must be custom fitted. Toenail the studs to the sole with 16d nails. Use a carpenter's level vertically to keep the studs plumb, and toenail them to the plate.

If you plan to have a doorway, frame trimmers on each side of the studs forming the opening, making allowance for the finished jambs and blocking—roughly about 1½″ on each side. Frame 2x4 headers between the studs and spike them securely. Frame one or two cripples between the headers and the plate, depending on the width of the opening. Since the partition is non-bearing, the opening for the door need not be trussed.

The wall covering easiest to apply is one of the wallboards (Fig. 16). If you wish to have an unbroken wall surface which can be painted and not show panel joints, use gypsum-core wallboard with recessed edges. Blocking between the studs should occur about midway between ceiling and floor for stud bracing, if this type of board is used, since the board is nailed to the studs horizontally.

To prepare the joints of gypsum-core wallboard for painting over them, first fill the recessed edges with the water-mix cement which is furnished with the wallboard. Then press the perforated fiber tape (also furnished) into the cement. The nubs of cement coming through the perforations are then smoothed out (Fig. 17). After the cement has dried thoroughly, apply another thin coat and feather this out 3″ or 4″ on each side of the channel. When this coat has dried, apply another coat and feather this out 8″ to 10″ on each side of the channel. After 24 hours, sandpaper the cement smooth and level with the wallboard. Then coat the entire wallboard surface with a varnish size recommended by the manufacturer. Apply any type of paint, and you will have a wall with an unbroken surface similar to plaster in effect.

Should you prefer other types of wallboard or plywood, blocking between the studs is advisable for a rigid job. The blocking should be spaced about 24″ to 30″ horizontally between the studs, and the wallboard nailed to the studs and blocking. Forms of wallboard other than gypsum core are usually applied vertically with the joints centering on the studs. These joints can then be battened or otherwise treated.

Wallboard

Wallboard, whatever the type, should be run about ¼″ to ½″ from the ceiling and floor, and covered at the ceiling with a molding, either quarter-round or crown, and at the floor line, covered with a baseboard and base-shoe molding. If BX electrical cable is to be installed in the new partition for baseboard receptacles, stop the bottom of the wallboard about 4″ from the floor, with blocking between the studs at this point as a nailing surface for the wallboard. Run the BX cable along the bottom edge across the studs. Wherever there are receptacles, blocking must be nailed between the studs to support the receptacles. If the wallboard is ½″ thick, the BX need not be notched into the studs, as it is about the same thickness. The baseboard will cover the cable, saving considerable work of notching out the stud edges. Fram-

OLD DOORWAY

Fig. 18.

ing the door jambs and casing is discussed in Chapter 7.

HOW TO MAKE A FLUSH DOOR OUT OF A PANELED ONE

You may desire to modernize your home by replacing your paneled doors (Fig. 18) with the flush type (Fig. 19). You can do this at a fraction of what it would cost you to buy new flush-type doors—which if well made are expensive—by covering the old doors with ¼″ plywood of whatever species of wood veneer you prefer. No basic alteration in the door need be made except to remove the door knobs, plates if any, or the key-

BEFORE   AFTER

Fig. 19. You may wish to modernize the doors of your house by replacing your paneled doors with the modern flush-type. You can do this at a fraction of what it would cost to purchase new flush-type doors.

hole escutcheon plate. The door stops must be set back ¼″ or slightly more, to accommodate the added thickness of the door on the closing side. These are changed after the door has been covered.

First, remove the door. Some door panels have molding around them which extends slightly beyond the stile and rail faces. If these moldings are not flush, remove them so that a perfectly flat surface is maintained over the entire face of the door. Screw nailing strips, of a thickness to be flush with the faces of the rails and stiles, and about 3″ wide, on the paneling between the stiles and rails (Fig. 20). Do this on both sides of the door for added nailing surfaces for the plywood. Two 4x8-foot panels of plywood will be required for each

door. Cut the panels of plywood about ½″ larger than the door on all sides, and nail them with finishing nails spaced about 4″ apart along the edges and along the centers of the intermediate rails or stiles and nailing strips.

Set the nails slightly and cover with plastic wood of the same color as the wood. For a rigid covering job, use resorcinol resin glue spotted at intervals over the back of the plywood. The nails will act as clamps. If glue is used, the paint or varnish of the door must be removed for good adhesion. After the door has been covered on one side with plywood, use a fine-tooth carpenter's saw (11 points per inch) and trim off the oversize of the panel, flush with the door edge, sawing from the face side (Fig. 21).

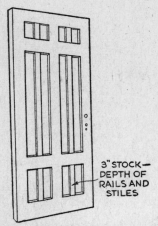

Fig. 20. Screw nailing strips, of a thickness to be flush with the faces of the rails and stiles, and about 3″ wide, on the paneling between the stiles and rails.

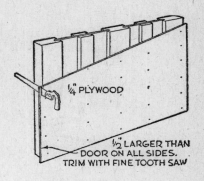

Fig. 21. After the door has been covered on one side with plywood, use a fine-tooth carpenter's saw and trim off the oversize of the panel flush with the door edge, sawing from the face side.

Then cover the other side of the door and trim off the edges. Fill in any ply holes which may occur in the edges of the plywood with plastic wood and, when dry, sand the edges smooth with successively finer grits of garnet paper.

Facing the door edges is not necessary and would entail cutting the door down to allow for the added thickness. By carefully matching the color of the plywood face, and painting the door edges front and back, the plywood facing will hardly show—if at all. A ¾″ hole must be bored in the panels for the door knob and keyhole, after which the knobs are again assembled and the escutcheon plate screwed on. The finished job will look like a modern, flush-type door. Moreover, adding the plywood panels has made your door doubly rigid in construction, and if resorcinol resin glue has been used, it will never warp.

Fig. 22. Narrow door casings make a doorway more modern looking, but this cannot be done unless the old plaster wall is recovered with some type of wallboard.

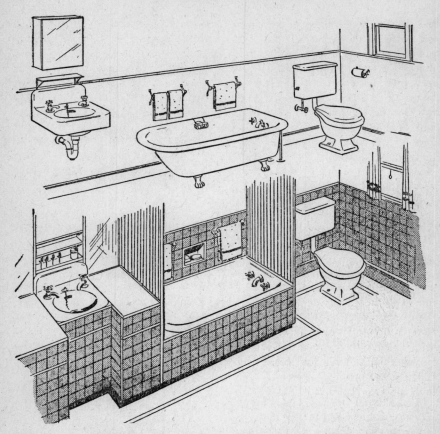

Fig. 23. Old-fashioned bathrooms need not stay that way if a bit of imagination is used to modernize them. The illustration above shows how such modernization can be effected at a fraction of the cost of replacing with modern equipment.

For exterior doors, use on the weather surface a ¼″ plywood which is bonded with waterproof glue—known as Exterior Grade plywood. It may be had in a few of the hardwood veneers, such as Philippine Mahogany, and also in striated form in Fir which, because of the striations, does not show its wild grain. The striated plywood makes a striking door surface, both for interior and exterior use, the interior grade being sold in Fir, Philippine Mahogany, Redwood and Gum. The thickness is 5/16″ instead of the usual ¼″ for the interior grade, and ⅜″ for the exterior grade.

Narrow door casings also make a doorway more modern looking, but the problem here is to cover the space left between the old casing and the plaster stops. This cannot be done unless the old plaster wall is to be recovered with some type of wallboard (Fig. 22), in which case narrow door casings and flush-type doors will definitely improve the appearance of the room and give it seemingly added space.

MODERNIZING THE BATHROOM

Old-fashioned bathrooms need not stay that way for long if a bit of imagination is used to modernize them. The worst offender in an old-time bathroom is usually the bathtub with its four feet. Many bathrooms, in suburban and rural districts, have tongued and grooved wainscoats with layer upon layer of dark-brown varnish over them, and perhaps a wood floor. Not much though was given in the old days to storage space in the bathroom, and the lavatory, tub and toilet were disorganized, with considerable waste space between them.

Fig. 23 illustrates a typical old-fashioned bathroom and shows how such a bathroom can be modernized at a fraction of the cost of replacing with modern equipment. Obviously, the illustration can only offer suggestions since, if you have an old-fashioned bathroom, it is more likely than not that the arrangement differs from that in the drawing. Some bathroom layouts lend themselves even more to

modernization than the one illustrated, particularly so if the bathtub is set between two walls.

A toilet can quite frequently be completely isolated from the other fixtures by a wall around it with a door, if space permits. The main idea in the modern design of a bathroom is to make each fixture as private as possible, affording several members of a family the simultaneous use of the room.

Many bathrooms of yesterday were spacious for no particular purpose. This spaciousness can be used to good advantage when modernizing. Where space permits, a dressing-table alcove can be constructed; floor to ceiling closets and drawer units can be installed; a bathtub can be part of a curtained or glass-door inclosure; and many other efficient innovations can be added to make this room attractive and more useful.

Converting Bathtub

A bathtub off the floor and with feet can be converted into a modern-type easily with a wood frame around three sides of the tube, covered with tileboard. Tileboard can be had in a number of bright colors in square-scored tile, horizontally scored, and plain. Use 1"x2" pine strips for the frame, and 2x2s for the corner posts. Most bathtubs with feet are made from ⅜" formed steel with heavy porcelain enamel fused to the inner and curve-lip surfaces. One end is usually a half-circle while the other or faucet end has curved corners. The lip is curved with a square under edge.

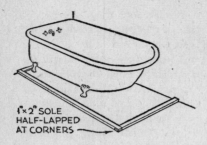

Fig. 24. Nail down the sole to the floor, half-lapping the corners.

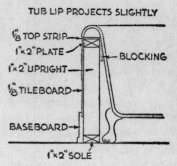

Fig. 25. The uprights may have to be blocked at their back edges near the top of the tub to fit snugly against it.

Build the frame very much as you would build a stud partition, that is, frame a plate and sole with uprights spaced about 12″ on centers. Since the bath tub is curved at both ends, your frame must extend to the longest dimension of the tub and have square corners. The frame must be a little more than ⅛″ shorter at both ends than the length of the tub, so that the ⅛″ thick tileboard face will be a little less than flush with the bottom edge of the lip of the tub. The height of the frame must be ⅛″ short of the under edge of the lip to permit a strip of tileboard to be inserted under the lip and to the edge of the tub.

Nail down the sole to the floor, half-lapping the corners (Fig. 24). Then frame all the uprights and posts to the plate which you also half-lap at the corners. Nail diagonal pieces across the corners flush with the top of the plate to support the top pieces of tileboard. The uprights may have to be blocked at their back edges near the top of the tub to fit snugly against it (Fig. 25). Frame horizontal pieces between the uprights, alternately staggering them so that you can nail them from the upright face side.

The assembled frame (Fig. 26) is then put in place on the soles and toe-nailed to them. Nail the corner posts at the open end of the frame against the wall or, if it is tiled, cement the posts to the tile. If your bathroom floor is already tiled, the soles can be cemented to the tile with a rubber-base cement made for cementing tile to wood and other surfaces, or holes can be drilled in the tile floor with a star drill, and expansion-screw anchors inserted. The sole is then screwed to the floor. The latter method, while it entails more work, is perhaps the best way to attach the sole to a tile floor, although using the special cement and letting it dry for about 48 hours will hold the sole in place permanently.

Tileboard is easily sawed with a fine-tooth carpenter's saw, sawing from the face or finish side. Saw the board along a "tile joint," rather than through part of a tile face. Finishing nails are used when nailing tileboard, and should be driven flush—not set. When nailing tileboard, do not drive

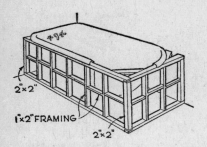

Fig. 26. The assembled frame is put in place on the soles and toenailed to them.

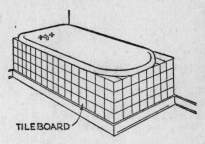

Fig. 27. To apply tileboard, nail and cement the end pieces first, the top edges flush with the top of the frame. The height of the board should be such that a special tileboard base can be nailed or cemented in place, lapping the bottom edge of the end and front pieces.

the nail flush with a hammer because you will probably mar the surface. Drive the nail almost flush and then use a nail set. The nail heads are hidden with touch-up paint to match the color of the board, and are sold by the manufacturer of the board. This paint is also used to touch up any marred surfaces, edges, etc.

To apply the board, nail and cement the end pieces first, the top edges flush with the top of the frame. The height of the board should be such that a special tileboard base can be nailed or cemented in place, lapping the bottom edge of the end and front pieces (Fig. 27). The width of these bases varies with the manufacturer's product, but is usually 3¾" or 4" wide with a rabbet ½" deep to receive the tileboard proper. The front edges of the end pieces should be flush with the frame and sanded smooth. Now cut two pieces of tilboard for the front so that when they are butt joined at the center of the tub, the ends will be flush with the faces of the end pieces. Before applying the front, sand the edges smooth and square, as any sanding done after they are in place will mar the finish

of the adjoining piece. Use cement for the butted edges and, after the board is in place, immediately wipe off excess cement. The exposed edges can then be painted with touch-up paint matching the color of the surface.

After the end and front pieces are in place, cut top strips to slide under the curved lip of the bathtub, having sanded the outer edges of the strips. The front top strip is held in place with cement applied to the top surface of the plate which supports the strip. At the ends of the bathtub, top pieces are cut in a rough curve to loosely fit the contour of the tub, the outer edges forming a square corner and flush with the vertical faces of the front and end pieces (Fig. 28). These top end pieces are cemented to the diagonal braces across the corners and to the plate surface. The edges that are butt joined are cemented. Butt join the top end pieces to the top front strips at a point where the lip of the

Fig. 28. At the ends of the bathtub, top pieces are cut in a rough curve to loosely fit the contour of the tub, the outer edges forming a square corner and flush with the vertical faces of the front and end pieces.

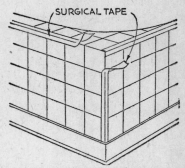

Fig. 29. Another method of covering the exposed butt joints of the tileboard is to use waterproof surgical zinc-oxide tape.

tub will hide them, that is, a little beyond the point where the lip begins its arc at both ends.

Another method of covering the exposed butt joints of the tileboard is to use ½″ or ¾″-wide *waterproof* surgical zinc-oxide tape (Fig. 29). Carefully lap the corners evenly with the tape and press it firmly in contact with the board. Zinc-oxide tape will stick indefinitely if it is fresh and is not deliberately peeled off. This method of covering the joints leaves no exposed edges and makes a waterproof joint. Paint the tape with touch-up paint that matches the color of the tileboard.

Lavatories

Treatment of lavatories is similar to that of bathtubs, if you desire a cabinet-type lavatory. Provision must be made at the front of a lavatory for the removal of the panel of tileboard, so that the plumbing may be reached. This panel should be screwed in place with chromium-plated or plain roundhead wood screws. These can be painted with touch-up paint to match the color of the panel. Cabinet doors can be made up of 1x2 frames to which the tileboard is cemented, the

doors hinged in the usual manner. As tileboard comes in plain as well as scored colored sheets, door and drawer faces can be plain surfaced tileboard of a contrasting color. Very attractive effects can be achieved by this method, and a wide variety of treatments is possible.

If your bathroom does not have a tiled wainscot, the use of tileboard of the same color or another harmonizing color can be used to make a "decorator's" bathroom. Above the wainscot the same material can be used with the tile pattern, horizontally grooved pattern or plain, also in the same or harmonizing color. Tileboard manufacturers make stainless-steel inside and outside corner moldings and caps into which the board slips. Hardboard bases, caps, and insertions where two panels meet, are also available.

Tileboard can be applied with cement directly to a wall surface if the surface is level and even. Slight unevenness can be leveled out with patching plaster, but if the wall bulges badly, furring strips should first be nailed for the tileboard. Ceilings, too, can be covered with a ceiling tile with tongued and grooved interlocking edges which are blind nailed. This tile comes ⅜"x12"x12" in a variety of rainbow colors hot sprayed similarly to tileboard.

Glass Partition

The use of ribbed glass as a partition which is translucent, yet affords privacy, can be installed to separate the various fixtures. This material requires a wood frame. Medicine cabinets which extend beyond the face of the wall can be recessed flush between the studs before the wallboard is applied. This can also be done with soap holders, handholds for the bathtub, tissue holders, etc., replacing the old hanging types. Frameless mirrors and other fixtures can be installed to suit your taste and budget.

A shallow cabinet from floor to ceiling can be installed between the studs, or one stud can be removed to give added width. If you do this, be sure to put double 2x4 headers across the span supported by trimmers, if the partition bears a load. If you need more depth for a cabinet and want to equip it with drawers, extend it beyond the face of the wall besides recessing it between the studs. In this way the floor space taken up by the cabinet is reduced.

Old wood floors can be covered with ceramic tile cemented with a rubber-base cement to a ¼" fir plywood surface which has been nailed to the floor, without appreciably raising the bathroom floor level.

From the foregoing you can readily see that an old ugly bathroom can be modernized for increased efficiency and colorful charm without the considerable expense of new equipment and plumbing installations.

BUILDING A STORAGE WALL

There never seems to be enough closet space in a home, no matter how numerous the closets. This is probably due to our instinctive urge to store all of our possessions for the day when they may become useful again. A storage wall is the answer to the problem of providing extra closet space. An existing partition between two rooms can be used as one wall face of the storage wall, and a new wall built across the room to contain the closet or storage space. A 24" inside depth for the new storage space is about minimum for practical purposes, particularly if the closet is to contain clothes on hangers. A 30" to 40" depth is better if the room from which the space must be taken will warrant shortening by that much. See Fig. 30.

The wall coverings of the existing partition must be removed and from one to two studs removed between every second or third stud. Removing every other stud will give you a space of approximately 32" between stud centers. Removing two studs will approximate 48" between stud centers. The new wall which you build must correspond in stud spacing to the ex-

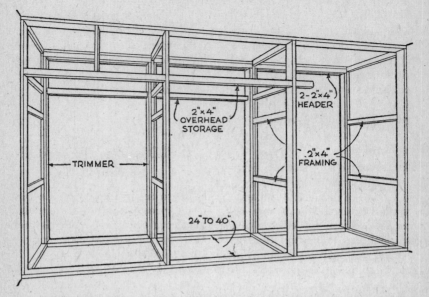

Fig. 30. A storage wall is the answer to the problem of providing extra closet space. An existing partition between two rooms can be used as one wall face of the storage wall, and a new wall built across the room to contain the closet or storage space.

isting one. The procedure is the same as for putting up a regular partition; a plate at the ceiling and a sole at the floor, with studs nailed to both. See Fig. 31.

If the existing partition bears a load, care must be taken not to weaken the span between removed studs, and doubled 2x4 headers set on edge must be nailed to the existing plate, supported by trimmers spiked to the studs which remain. The new partition, being non-bearing, does not require headers or trimmers. The best way to shore up the spans before removing any studs in the existing partition—if it bears a load—is to temporarily support each overhead joist with a 2x4 from the floor to the ceiling on *both sides* of the plate. The 2x4s should be placed as close as possible to the plate, with just enough space between them to allow you work room. The most efficient way to do this is to cut the studs shorter than the ceiling height, and drive wedges between the ceiling and studs for a tight fit.

Then cut out the studs not to be used, spike trimmers to those that remain, and frame headers to support the plate. The headers must be toenailed to the plate, and the trimmers toenailed to the doubled headers. The temporary stud bracing can then be removed.

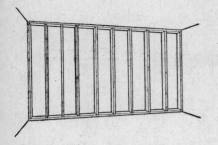

Fig. 31. The new wall must correspond in stud spacing to the existing one, and the procedure is the same as for putting up a regular partition; a plate at the ceiling and a sole at the floor, with studs nailed to both.

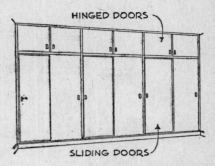

Fig. 32. Usually storage wall closets are designed for cloths with storage space overhead, given access to by hinged or sliding cabinet doors of plywood.

Utilizing Storage Wall

There are many ways of utilizing a storage wall, depending on your particular storage problem. Usually these closets are designed for clothes with storage space overhead, given access to by hinged or sliding cabinet doors of ⅜" or ½" plywood (Fig. 32). Frequently the storage wall is divided so that one half, more or less, supplies storage space for each room. Another variation is to have a dressing-table alcove on one or both sides of the wall —separated by a wallboard thickness —for adjoining bedrooms. These alcoves can be flanked by storage space for both rooms, or one room.

The wall faces of storage walls are usually plywood doors, ⅜" or ½" thick, preferably of the sliding variety for closets, so that no additional space is lost to the rooms by hinged doors. Hardware can be purchased for sliding doors which run on overhead tracks, requiring no floor track, groove or other obstructing device. However, since a sole is necessary in any event, the doors can be run on rollers of the show-case variety. These come in metal strips with the rollers attached. Matching ¼"-thick plywood panels are used to surface that portion of the wall not giving access to closet space, and the studs are also faced with matching ¼" plywood as a finish.

Drawers (Fig. 33) can be made for storage walls of sufficient depth, to supply the needs of both rooms, or if shallow, for one room, replacing the conventional "his" and "her" dressers in bedrooms. Whatever the arrangement, the studs, which are the main framework of the storage wall, must be bridged horizontally at the top, bottom and between these points for added rigidity, and to afford nailing surfaces for wallboards separating the closet space. This framing is also necessary for attaching clothes poles and the like. Additional framing is also necessary—if storage space above the closet doors is intended—to support a floor of ½" or ¾" plywood.

It is amazing what additional storage space is afforded by a 24" storage wall spanning a room, and the variety

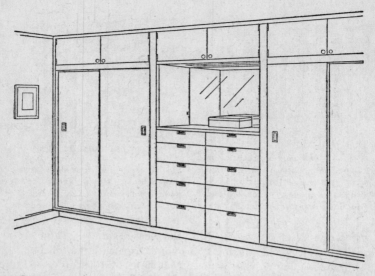

Fig. 33. Drawers can be made for storage walls of sufficient depth to supply the needs of both rooms or, if shallow, for one room.

of arrangements possible with such a wall will not only solve an annoying storage problem, but will result in a modern architectural treatment introducing charm to an otherwise uninteresting room. The storage-wall idea can be used in any part of the house where such a wall is feasible, making possible all sorts of built-in appliances, such as, TV-radio-phono combinations, bookshelves, kitchen equipment, dining services and the like.

A KITCHEN-SERVICE OPENING

One of the most efficient time and step savers is the service hatch, or opening between the kitchen and din-

ing area. Most modern houses designed today are provided with a service opening, its architectural treatment as varied as modern house design. Some openings have sliding doors to close off the kitchen from the dining area when the opening is not in use; others open on a lunch counter used for breakfast and luncheon, and serve the dining area for dinner; still others have a Venetian blind which disguises the opening, making it appear as a window until it is needed (Fig. 34).

The latter idea fits in more readily with an existing room arrangement, although any number of treatments are possible, more or less governed by the architectural features of both kitchen and dining area. The bottom of the opening should be more or less

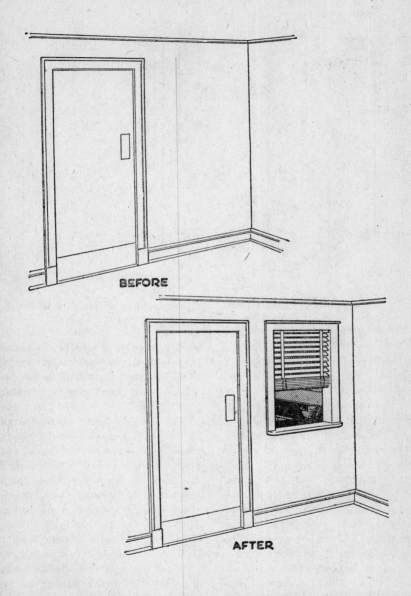

BEFORE

AFTER

Fig. 34. An efficient time and step saver is the service hatch between kitchen and dining area. The one illustrated above has a Venetian blind which disguises the opening as a window until needed.

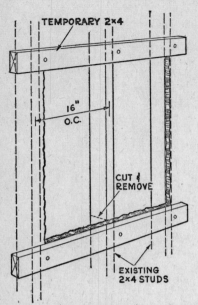

Fig. 35. First brace the proposed opening top and bottom by nailing a 2x4 across the studs in the same manner as for enlarging a window.

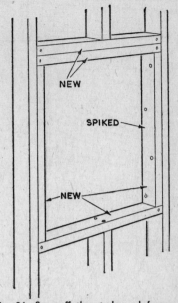

Fig. 36. Saw off the studs and frame the headers and trimmers.

level with a kitchen counter top and, if possible, situated near the kitchen range and sink for easy service of cooked food and removal of used dishes. If only one choice of location is practical, near the sink is best. It is not at all difficult to construct one of these openings in an existing wall between the kitchen and dining area, and it need not interfere with overhead kitchen cabinets, as the service height need only be enough to serve food through it conveniently. The opening can be quite high with the back of the kitchen wall cabinet exposed but actually hidden by a Venetian blind. The larger opening, of room-window height, will look better from the dining-area side and can be

treated architecturally in the same manner as the windows of the room, that is, casings and an apron can be framed around the opening to match the windows.

To make an opening, first mark out on the wall the dimensions, taking into consideration the removal of one stud for an opening approximately 32″ on stud centers. If a larger opening is desired, figure on removing two studs which will give you a width of approximately 48″ on stud centers. Then carefully remove enough of the wall on both sides of the partition to allow you to work comfortably when framing the opening—about 2″ on each side of the studs, and enough at the top and bottom to enable you to frame the headers. If you remove the

TRIM TO MATCH
OTHER WINDOWS

Fig. 37.

Fig. 38. Opening finished with scalloped
edges.

vall cleanly and more or less on a
straight line all around, patching will
ot be necessary as the casing or
rame of the finished opening will
over the plaster edges.

If it is a bearing partition, first
brace the proposed opening top and
bottom by nailing a 2x4 across the
studs in the same manner as for enlarging a window or door (Fig. 35).
Then saw off the studs and frame the
headers and trimmers (Fig. 36). For
the bottom or sill of the opening, use
″ stock, plywood or solid, wide
enough to butt the back edge of the
ork counter and overlap the apron
on the dining-area side. The lap
should be about the same as that
of the window stool. Use ¼″ plywood,
or ¾″ solid stock for the jambs at the
top and sides, and frame a casing to

Fig. 39. Opening finished with decorative
contour edges.

HANGING WALL SHELVE

Wall shelves for kitchens and othe rooms can easily be made withou taking up the usual floor space. The can be extremely decorative and hun in a variety of patterns to add to th general decor of a room. There is simple method of hanging shelves fo books, objects-of-art, etc., without th hangers showing when objects ar placed on the shelf.

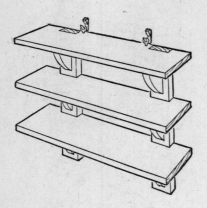

Fig. 40. Multiple hanging shelf.

To make a hanging shelf, be it si gle or multiple (Fig. 40), brackets ar necessary as a fulcrum against th wall. These brackets can be as decor ative as you desire, and should hav a bearing surface against the wall c about 6″ for single shelves. For mult ple shelves, the back pieces to whic a number of shelves are attached, ac in the same manner as a bracket fo a single shelf.

The hanging device is two or mor screw eyes—depending on the lengt of the shelf—screwed about ¼″ fror the back face of the shelf, and ove the back face of the shelf, and over th brackets (Fig. 41). Picture hangers c the type with needle-pointed nai driven at an angle into the wall, su, port the shelf or shelves. The hook c the hanger is bent out a bit to engag the screw eyes. Since this type of pic ture hanger is made in a variety c sizes to singly sustain weights up t 100 pounds, two of these hangers ar more than sufficient for any weight shelf would normally be expected t hold. Use the smallest hanger prac tical for whatever weight the shelf to support. Since the weight exerts downward pressure against the wal

match the other windows on the din-ing-area side (Fig. 37). Matching the window casings is not necessary, of course, as there are a number of decorative treatments possible to fin-ish the opening, such as scalloped edges (Fig. 38), decorative contour edges (Fig. 39), etc., cut out of ½″ or ¾″ stock.

On the kitchen side, a frame is also necessary and this depends on whether or not there is a wall cabinet overhead. If there is not a cabinet, a decorative frame in harmony with the kitchen trim will look good, and if a cabinet is over the opening, run the frame to butt against the bottom edge of the cabinet. The frame can be plain or have decorative edges. Install a Venetian blind to match the other blinds in the dining area. This closes off the opening when not in use, and hides the back of the kitchen wall cabinet.

the shelf brackets are merely braces, and the picture hangers sustain the weight with practically no outward strain. Shelves made in this manner should have their brackets screwed to the shelf with flat-head wood screws countersunk slightly deeper than flush and filled with water-mix wood putty or plastic wood. For both shelf and brackets ¾" plywood or solid stock should be used.

To attach the shelf, tilt the front upward and engage the screw eyes on the hooks. Corner shelves (Fig. 42), can be made in the same way, but with these the hooks of the hangers must be cut off enough so that the screw eyes can be slipped straight over the hooks without tilting the shelf—otherwise the shelf could not be hung in a corner.

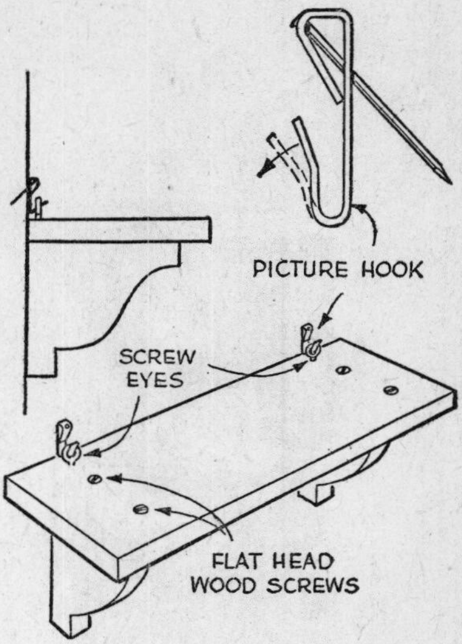

PICTURE HOOK

SCREW EYES

FLAT HEAD WOOD SCREWS

Fig. 41. The hanging device is two or more screw eyes, depending on the length of the shelf, screwed about ¼" from the back face of the shelf, and over the brackets.

A DUTCH DOOR

A Dutch door is simply one divided horizontally, each section being separtely hinged. Either section can be opened or closed, or the two sections can be bolted as one unit, making it a regular door. The advantage of a Dutch door is that it affords ventilation through the upper half, plus a barrier for small children and animals, and offers almost as much privacy as the conventional closed door. Dutch doors should swing inwardly (Fig. 43).

If you would like to have a Dutch door, you can easily make one out of your existing front or back door, or you can make a new one. The door most easily converted is one with a

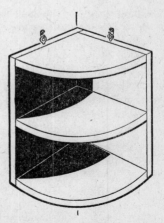

Fig. 42. Corner hanging shelves.

Fig. 43. A Dutch door is simply one divided horizontally, each section being separately hinged.

tom, or below the 36″ point, it is best to buy a new, inexpensive but well made door with a horizontal rail somewhere between these dimensions.

An existing hanging door is much easier to convert into a Dutch door than making a new one, because the door is already hinged at two points and is fitted to the opening. If your door has a third hinge at the center, so much the better, as you will then have to add only one hinge for the lower section of the door. If the door has only two hinges, two additional hinges will be necessary; a total of two for the upper and two for the lower sections.

Before removing the door, locate the additional hinges on the door and jamb. These should be equally spaced from the center line of the rail—3″ to the edge of the leaves which should be the same size as the existing hinges. Then remove the door and attach the hinge leaves to it and the jamb, mortising them into the jamb and door edge. Hang the door again to check if the new hinges are working properly. Again remove it and divide the rail between what is to be the upper and lower sections exactly in half, making certain that the sawing line is square with the sides of the door.

Now saw along this line squarely across the door (Fig. 44). The two halves should be weatherstripped where the edges come together. Get inswinging-casement type metal stripping and measure the clearance between the edges of the door necessary to apply this weatherstripping. Then

series of horizontal panels, usually five in number, or any door with a horizontal rail whose center line is about 37″ from the bottom. The door knob and lock are set about 3″ below this center line on most doors, and when converting, the knobs and lock are left in place, saving considerable work in remortising a new location and filling in the old mortise. If the horizontal rail which is to divide your door is more than 44″ from the bot-

Fig. 44. Divide the rail between what is to be the upper and lower sections exactly in half, making certain that the sawing line is square with the sides of the door, and saw along this line.

plane one edge enough to permit the application of the weatherstrip. Next, cut horizontal rabbets in both inner faces of the two sections, ¾"x13/16" (Fig. 45). These rabbets are for a ¾"x 1⅝" hardwood strip which acts as the horizontal stop for the sections. Glue (resorcinol resin glue) and screw this stop into the rabbet of the upper section. Attach the weatherstrips to both sections and then screw a drip molding (Fig. 46) to the outer face of the upper section so that the lip just clears the weatherstrip of the lower section.

Now hang the two sections and you have a Dutch door that is weathertight and hangs perfectly. All that is needed to complete the job is to attach a snap catch or sliding bolt on the inner stile face near the door

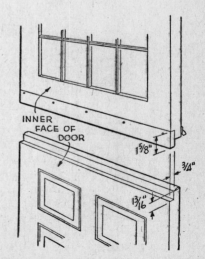

INNER FACE OF DOOR

1⅝"

¾"

13/16"

Fig. 45. Cut horizontal rabbets in both inner faces of the two sections, ¾"x13/16".

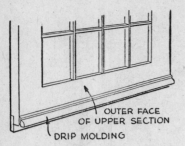

OUTER FACE
OF UPPER SECTION

DRIP MOLDING

Fig. 46. Attach weatherstrips to both sections and then screw a drip molding to the outer face of the upper section so that the lip just clears the weatherstrip of the lower section.

knob, to hold the two sections. Another snap catch or sliding bolt should be attached for the upper section to engage a strike in the door jamb, to hold the upper section closed if the lower one is open. A knob should also be attached to the upper

section for easy opening. Your existing lock in the door functions for both sections when together, or for the lower section when the upper one is open.

Batten Type

If you prefer to make a Dutch door from scratch, the batten type is the easiest, with the battens on the inside. A door of this type requires separate stiles and rails for each section, the body or panels thus formed being of ¾" tongued and grooved lumber. The stiles and rails should be 1⅛"-thick with a diagonal brace of the same thickness framed into both sections. Run one brace in one direction for the upper section, and the brace for the lower section in the opposite direction. While 1⅛"-thick stock will

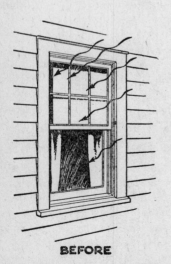

BEFORE

AFTER

Fig. 47. The modern method of having both air and protection from the sun and rain is to install louver-type awnings.

give you just enough thickness to mortise a lock, 1⅜" or 1⅝" stock is better. Be certain to leave that portion of the door where the lock is to be mortised, free of nails or screws when attaching the tongued and grooved lumber.

LOUVER-TYPE RIGID AWNINGS

The only way to prevent the sun from radiating heat through windows is to prevent the rays from reaching the glass. Either a large roof overhang or awnings to block the sun's rays is the answer. Conventional-type fabric awnings do the trick, but they also block off most of the air which would come through an open window. The modern method of having both air and protection from the sun and rain is to install louver-type awnings (Fig. 47). You can buy these at considerable expense, or make them yourself at a fraction of the retail price. Not only is this type of awning more efficient than the conventional fabric type, but it also adds a decorative note to the house exterior, particularly so if it is painted in gay colors harmonizing with the body color and trim.

The louver-type awning is also less obvious than the conventional type, giving just the right amount of decorative touch to the house. Basically, the idea is to make a frame with slats attached to the frame at an angle, the

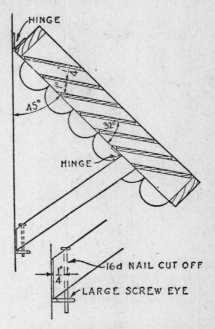

Fig. 48. Make the frames long enough so that when they are at 45° from the face of the house their bottom edges will be at about the horizontal center line of the window.

slats so angled that air and light can freely pass through the awning and yet block out direct sun's rays and rain. The frame is supported by two wood brackets which may be adjustable for various frame angles, if desired.

Use ¾"x2⅝" white-pine stock for the frame and ¼"x4½" Exterior Grade fir plywood, *sound on both sides* for the slats. The exterior-grade plywood is weatherproof and the veneer will not peel. Make the frames long enough so that when they are at a 45° angle from the face of the house, their bottom edges will be at about the horizontal center line of the win-

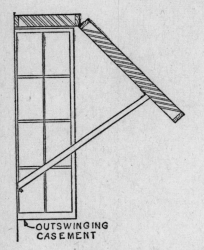

OUTSWINGING
CASEMENT

Fig. 49. For outswinging casements a supplementary frame with angled slats will have to be made to extend far enough out to permit the casement to clear the awning.

dow (Fig. 48). Moreover, make them wide enough to extend beyond the inner edge of the casing about 1" to 2" on both sides. The inside face of the two side pieces of the frame should be dadoed ¼"x¼" to receive the slats which are glued in with resorcinol resin glue which is waterproof and heatproof.

When cutting the slats, cut them with the veneer grain running the long way. The dadoes for the slats should have an angle of 32° upward from the bottom edge of the frame. No matter at what angle the frame is then positioned, air and light will pass almost straight through the slats, but the sun's rays and rain cannot— and rainwater will drain down and outward. The slats must be 1" apart, that is, 1" between the top of one slat to the bottom of the other, or

1⅛" on centers. Butt join the frame with resorcinol resin glue and two flat-head wood screws for each corner. For inswinging casement and double-hung-sash windows, the frame can be hinged at the head casing, about 3" to 4" above the window opening. For outswinging casements (Fig. 49). a supplementary frame with angled slats will have to be made to extend far enough out to permit the casement to clear the awning.

To arrive at this dimension accurately, open the casement as much as it is normally opened, and measure the clearance necessary. The awning, in this case, is hinged to the extension. Two wood brackets, ¾"x1⅛", are hinged about ¼ the length of the awning from the bottom, with tight-pin narrow butt hinges. These and the frame hinges must be chromium plated to resist rust. Cut the other ends of the brackets at an angle to fit flush against the casings. Then bore a hole about ¼" from the ends through the width of the brackets for a drive fit of a 16d nail. Cut the nail off so that it extends about 1" below the bracket. Use large and heavy screw eyes of a diameter to allow enough play for the nail so that you may remove it to another position if desired. Screw eyes at different positions on the casings allow the awning to be angled to suit. Actually, no angle adjustment should be necessary if the general dimensions and angles suggested have been followed.

An added decorative note can be achieved by facing the outside of the frame on three sides with ¼" exterior-grade plywood with the bottom

Fig. 50. Picture-type window.

Fig. 51. Picture-type window.

edges scalloped or contour-cut. This would require pieces 4¾″ wide, the scallops or contours cut out with a fine-tooth keyhole or coping saw. These facings can be either glued with resorcinol resin glue, or nailed on with brads—the glue being the more permanent method of attaching them.

A PICTURE-TYPE WINDOW

You can make a picture-type window (Figs. 50, 51 & 52) out of your present window opening by enlarging it if it is less than 48″ wide. While it is impossible for you to make the double-pane, clean-dry-air-sealed type, you can approximate these factory assembled windows. It requires,

Fig. 52. Picture-type window.

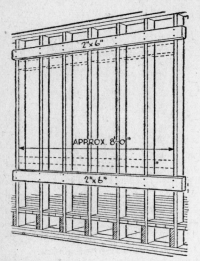

Fig. 53. The proposed opening must first be temporarily but well braced with 2x6's nailed across the studs at the top and bottom before removing any studs.

of course, the removal of the existing window frame and structural members framing the opening, and enlarging the opening to accommodate the larger panes of glass and sash. It will also require framing new trimmers and headers, top and bottom, with the top headers trussed to take care of the additional span.

If your windows are of the multiple type of two, three or four sashes separated by mullions, the span was taken care of when the house was originally built, since the mullions of these windows rarely support loads, and are usually there for sash-framing purposes only. This can be readily determined when you remove the window frames. If the mullion is an integral part of the window frame and does not extend from a header to the sill, it is not load bearing, and

the window opening has been trussed to take care of the span. All that is necessary then, is to change the frames to one enclosing a pair of large panes of glass.

A 48" pane of glass is about as wide and high as is practical for double-strength (DS) window glass. Wider and higher dimensions call for demi-plate glass. This is considerably cheaper than regular plate, being about the same thickness but not free from slight waviness. This waviness is practically unnoticeable and for general use demi-plate will serve for the more expensive plate glass.

If you plan to use double-strength window glass, which costs less than demi-plate, you can use up to and including a 48" width and height. Since window glass is sold in multiples of 2" both ways, and always comes absolutely square on all sides, plan your window sizes accordingly so that no glass cutting will be necessary. If you want a larger window than 48" glass will permit, use two panes 48" or less wide, separated by a 2x4 mullion—if the opening has been originally trussed.

If the opening is not trussed, it will have to be. If you double the 2x4 mullion, or use a 4x4 or steel pipe and frame it from a doubled header to sill or sole, it will support the wide span of the window opening. The proposed opening must first be temporarily but well braced with 2x6s nailed across the studs at the top and bottom before removing any studs (Fig. 53). Since non-bearing mullions are framed into the sill as part of the window frame, a load-bearing one

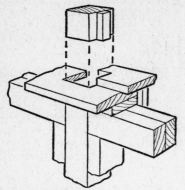

Fig. 54. Blocking nailed to the stud or post to support the sill, with the juncture of sill and post well caulked, will make the joint watertight.

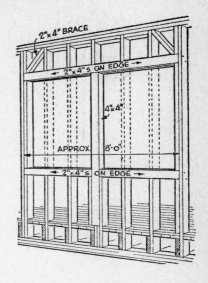

Fig. 55. If the solid 4x4 post is preferred, it should be surfaced on all four sides (S4S) and be clear ponderosa white pine.

offers a slight complication as the window sill would have to be cut around the supporting mullion. However, blocking nailed to the stud or post, to support the sill, with the juncture of sill and post well caulked with caulking compound, will make the joint watertight (Fig. 54).

Double-Glass Type

To achieve the double-glass of the commercial type, a secondary sash containing the inside pane must be made which, in effect, is similar to a regular storm-window installation—with one difference; the secondary sash is part of the picture window and need not be removed in warm weather. It must be so framed, however, that it can be removed, or preferably hinged so that it can be opened to permit cleaning of both panes of glass, and to remove any condensation which may occur. This is necessary because it is impossible for you to make the space between

the glass absolutely airtight and introduce clean dry air just before sealing the air space.

The reason for two panes of glass is that a large glass surface will be extremely cold in winter, and the two panes separated by an air space offer good insulation. They offer much better insulation than the commercial type of double-glass window, since the air space in your homemade one is greater.

If you plan to use doubled 2x4s to support the center of a wide span of 6 to 8 feet, No. 1 common dimension fir is good enough because you will have to face these 2x4s with ¾″ finish lumber—actually, jambs and casings. Should you prefer the solid 4x4 post, it should be surfaced on all four sides

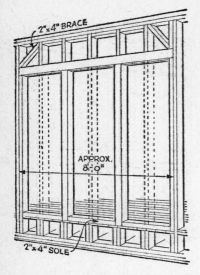

Fig. 56. If your window goes to the floor level, nail a 2x4 sole on the subfloor. The sill is then framed on the sole with ¾" stock as a facing from the floor to the sill.

(S4S) and be clear ponderosa white pine (Fig. 55). Then you will not need to face it and the sash could be permanently framed to it, reducing the overall thickness and increasing the illusion of one large window opening.

Another method of supporting a large span is to use a small diameter steel column with a cap and base, and boxing it in on all sides with ¾" stock as a framing device for the sash. A stock, 2" inside diameter, galvanized steel pipe threaded at both ends, with stock floor flanges screwed on, makes a good column with cap and base.

Height of Window

The height of your existing windows determines the glass size ver-

tically, unless you drop the sill lower than the existing sill. New headers must be framed in either case. Ceiling heights also determine how high you can make your picture-type window. You can, of course, run the window from the floor to its present height, bearing in mind that for DS window glass, 48" is the limit per pane of glass. A finished 2x4 must then be framed horizontally between the sides of the opening and mullion to support the additional glass. If your window goes to the floor level, nail a 2x4 sole on the subfloor. The sill is then framed on the sole with ¾" stock as a facing from the floor to the sill (Fig. 56).

Sills should have a slight downward bevel to shed water quickly. They need not have the pitch of a sill for windows that open, as the window sash is permanently framed in with caulking compound sealing all joints between the sash, sill and stops. The sill can be set flat on blocking on the header after you have planed a slight bevel outward from the point of sash contact. The sill should be 1⅛" stock wide enough to project about 1" beyond the face of the siding on the outside.

The Sash

For 48" glass, the sash should be 1⅝"x2⅝" (nominally 2"x3") stock. For glass 40" or less, the sash material can be 1⅝"x1⅝" (nominally 2"x 2"). A good wood for the sash is ponderosa white pine, S4S and clear.

To make the sash, cut the standard rabbet for window glass in the outside edges of the frame—¼"x½".

Add ⅛″ to the glass size for the inside dimensions of the rabbet edge of the sash when assembled. You do this to prevent any shrinkage of the sash frame from breaking the glass. Do not forget to deduct the ¼″ rabbet on both sides and top and bottom of the sash when calculating the overall dimensions of the sash. These dimensions are also the dimensions of the finished opening. If you planned, for instance, to use glass 38″x38″, and sash material 1⅝″x1⅝″, the outside dimensions of the sash would be 40⅞″x40⅞″, which would also be the dimensions of the *finished* opening to which the sash is framed:

Glass: 38″x38″ plus ⅛″ equals 38⅛″x38⅛″

Sash (1⅝″x1⅝″): inside dimensions ¼″ less on four sides—or ½″ less than 38⅛″x38⅛″ equals 37⅝″x37⅝″

Sash, outside dimensions: 1⅝″ added on four sides—or 3¼″ plus 37⅝″x37⅝″ equals 40⅞″ x40⅞″.

To frame the second or inner pane of glass, a secondary sash is needed. For 48″ glass the sash should be ¾″x1⅝″ stock (nominally 1″x2″). If the main sash is 1⅝″x1⅝″ for glass 40″ or less, the secondary sash can be ¾″x¾″ (nominally 1″x1″). Cut a rabbet in the inner face of the main sash to receive the secondary one flush. Cut a ¼″x⅜″ rabbet in the edge of the secondary sash for the glass (Fig. 57).

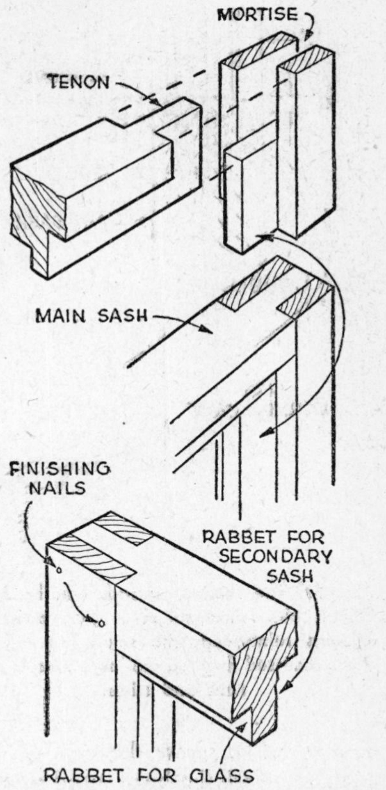

Fig. 57. Cut a rabbet in the inner face of the main cash to receive the secondary one flush, and cut a ¼x⅜" rabbet in the edge of the secondary sash for the glass.

The main sash should be put together with open mortises and tenons at the corners, the horizontal rails being tenoned to fit into the mortises of the vertical stiles. The tenon and mortise shoulders are cut so that the rabbets form a continuous recess around the sash. The secondary sash can be butt joined with resorcinol resin glue, and the corners reinforced with small flat corner irons recessed flush on the inner face to the rails and stiles (Fig. 58).

The secondary sash, as previously mentioned, should be either removable or hinged. If you prefer to make

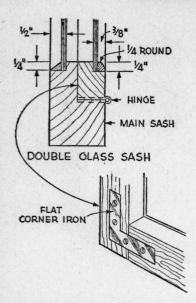

DOUBLE GLASS SASH

Fig. 58. The secondary sash can be butt joined with resorcinol resin glue, and the corners reinforced with small flat corner irons recessed flush on the inner face to the rails and stiles.

it removable, screw the sash to the main one with flat-head wood screws near the corners and one screw in the center of each rail and stile. For cleaning purposes and removal of condensation, when necessary, the job would be easier to perform if you hinged the secondary sash at the bottom to the main sash with narrow, tight-pin butt hinges. The sash would be held in place with screws near the corners and one in the center of each stile, and top rail. By doing it this way the sash could be swung in and downward, yet held in place by the hinges.

The glass for the main sash is glazed in the regular manner, using glazier's points and putty. The secondary glass is held with ¼" quarter-round molding, bradded.

To install the main sash, first coat all surfaces (edges of the sash, stop and jamb faces which contact the sash) with linseed oil, or white lead in linseed oil. Then liberally "butter" these surfaces with caulking compound and screw the sash to the stops with flat-head wood screws countersunk slightly deeper than flush and filled with putty (Fig. 59). Use plenty of screws evenly spaced— about 4" on centers—so that the sash bears evenly. Then remove the excess caulking compound which has squeezed out.

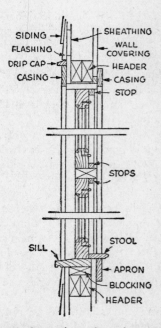

Fig. 59. Screw the sash to the stops with flat-head wood screws countersunk slightly deeper than flush and filled with putty.

The secondary sash can then be attached from the inside by one of the two methods suggested. A picture window should be framed like an outswinging casement, that is, about ¼" back from the outer edge of the frame.

When deciding on a picture window, do not forget to provide ventilation for your room as the picture window is sealed. If there are other conventional types of windows in the room they will provide the ventilation. Should your proposed picture window be the only one, you will have to provide movable windows at the sides or over the top of the window. The outswinging casement, hinged at the top, provides ideal ventilation over a picture window or, for that matter, at the sides, as it can be left open in average rainy weather —something you cannot do with other types of windows.

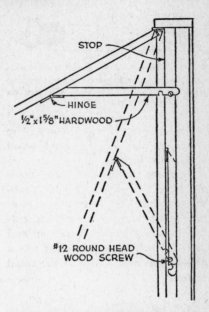

Fig. 60. Brackets to keep the window open at several points can be made of hardwood with a notch cut in the bottom edge to engage metal pins in the jamb, and hinged to the sash.

A MODERN-TYPE CASEMENT WINDOW

There is not much to converting the regular outswinging wood casement window to one that is hinged at the top. All that is necessary is to remove the hinges from the sides and place them at the top. With the inswinging type nothing is gained by changing the hinges. The top-hinged casement does not afford the same amount of air passage as the conventional type, but it does permit ventilation in rainy weather. Brackets are necessary to keep the window open at several points. These can be made of hardwood with a notch cut in the bottom edge to engage metal pins in the jamb, and hinged to the sash (Fig. 60). When the window is closed and latched, these brackets, one on each side of the sash, fold against the sash and out of the way. The brackets must be hinged about midway between the top and bottom rail, to clear the sill when the window is closed. Hardwood stock, ½"x1⅛", preferably maple or oak, is about right for the brackets which should be hinged to the sash with ½" tight-pin,

Fig. 61. The curved back with teeth makes the flooring saw the best for re-shingling work, although the backsaw will also do the job.

chromium-plated butt hinges. Use chromium-plated round-head wood screws for the pins.

To make the casement, use standard 1⅜"x1¾" sash stock which is rabbeted and molded, and cut open mortises and tenons for the corners, cutting the shoulders on the tenons and mortises to form a continuous recess around the sash. Glaze in the usual manner.

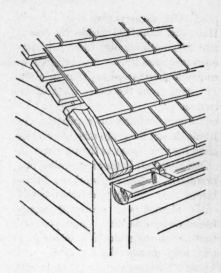

Fig. 62. By temporarily nailing a straight-edge strip to the eave, sawing the shingles is simplified.

RE-ROOFING OVER AN OLD ROOF

If you have a shingled roof which is in poor condition, that is, with the shingles badly warped and split, it is only a matter of time when leaks will occur and cause serious damage to the interior of your home. As mentioned previously, individual shingles can be easily removed and replaced when there are just a few scattered offenders, but when the entire roof requires repair, it is much cheaper to re-cover it. This is particularly true of a wood-shingled roof. Attempts to patch large areas, or many scattered areas, often cause additional and serious leaks by disturbing the old shingles.

Roofing materials for re-covering purposes, other than wood shingles and slate, are asbestos shingles and asphalt shingles. Asphalt roll roofing does not work too well when re-covering over old roofing unless it, too, is of the roll variety, as this material requires a perfectly flat surface for best results.

To re-cover an old wood-shingled roof, it is best to first cut back the shingles at the eaves and the rakes 3" so that when the new roof has been laid, all evidence of the old one is hidden. Cutting back the shingles at the eaves can best be done with a flooring saw (Fig. 61) which has a point with a curved back with teeth. However, a back saw also works well, and if you temporarily nail a straight-edge strip as a guide for the saw, cutting the shingles will not be difficult (Fig. 62). On the rake sides of the roof, a straightedge will also help to cut the shingles on an even straight line. This can best be done with a chisel which will split them easily.

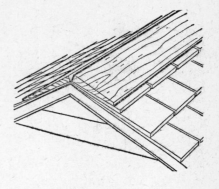

Next, remove the existing shingles or boards which form the old ridge or hip, and nail a furring strip (Fig. 63) —4"-wide beveled siding, thin edge facing down the roof, is fine—on each side of the ridge or hip. Nail down all loose shingles and, if they are warped or cupped, split them and nail down the corners. Rotted shingles must be replaced by new wood ones. The idea in back of all this preparatory work is to afford as flat and smooth a surface as possible for the new asbestos or asphalt shingles. Where you have cut back the shingles at the eaves and rakes, nail ¾"x3" boards, extending them beyond the rakes and eaves the same amount as the old wood shingles.

Valleys of the roof should be filled in with boards of a thickness to be flush with the existing shingles as a base for the new flashing. If the existing wood shingles are the thick-butt type, it is best to nail wedge-shaped wood strips (horsefeathers) ⅜"x4" along the butts of the shingles, the thick edge against the butts, to level out the roof surface. Then surface the roof with 15-pound asphalt-saturated felt (Fig. 64).

New base flashing around chimneys should be attached for the new

Fig. 64. Once the "horsefeathers," wedge-shaped wooden strips, are in place, overlapping rolls of asphalt-saturated felt are applied.

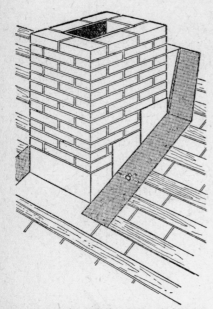

Fig. 65. New base flashing around chimneys should be attached for new shingles. For asphalt shingles, cut 8" strips of heavy roll roofing and butt them against the old base flashing on the sides of the chimney, extending the strips a few inches over the apron of the front metal base flashing.

Fig. 66. Strips of heavy roll roofing are coated with asphalt plastic cement and the shingles laid against the chimney faces and firmly embedded in the cement.

shingles. To do this for asphalt shingles, cut 8" strips of heavy roll roofing and butt them against the old base flashing on the chimney sides (Fig. 65), extending the strips a few inches over the apron of the front metal base flashing. Nail the outer edges of the strips to the existing shingles. When the new shingle courses have been laid near these strips, the strips are coated with asphalt plastic cement and the shingles laid against the chimney faces and firmly embedded in the cement (Fig. 66). Lift the apron of the front base flashing enough to slip the shingles at

this point under the flashing, and press the flashing back in place, imbedded in plastic cement.

Now cut strips of mineral-coated roll roofing about 8" wide. Coat about 3" of the strips with plastic cement and carefully lift the existing metal cap flashing where it laps the old metal base flashing. Slip the cemented strips under the cap flashing, bending the corners around the metal flashing front and back. Then press the cap flashing back into place and into the cement. Now coat about 4" of the tops of the shingles nearest the chimney with plastic cement and

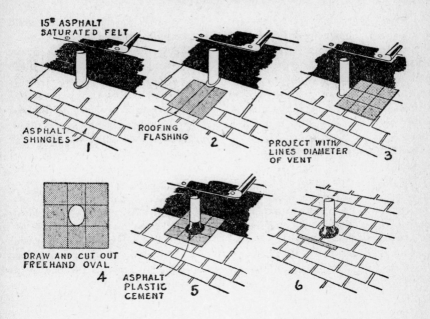

Fig. 67. Note carefully the steps necessary to replace metal flashings which have deteriorated. By applying new roll-roofing flashing in this manner, you are assured of maximum protection from the weather without marring the neat appearance of the shingled roof.

firmly embed the new flashing in the cement-coated shingles. The same general procedure applies to the "cricket" in back of the chimney.

If the existing metal flashing around vent pipes in the roof is in good condition, lift up the lower part of the flange and apply the shingles underneath it up to the pipe, cutting the shingles to fit around it. Replace the flange, bedding it in plastic cement. Apply generous quantities of plastic cement at the juncture of the metal sleeve and flange of the flashing. Then continue laying shingles around the pipe and up the roof.

Should the existing metal flashing be in poor condition, remove it and apply new roll-roofing flashing (Fig. 67). First, the shingle courses are laid up to and just around the pipe, the shingles being fitted around it. Then make the flashing by cutting a rectangle of heavy roll roofing large enough to extend 4″ below the pipe, 8″ above it, and 6″ on both sides. To locate the hole to be cut in this rectangle, first center it below the pipe and project the diameter by two lines marked on the roofing material. Then place the rectangle, in relation to its location, to the side of the pipe and project the diameter. This gives you a lined rectangle centered between the sides, and located 4″ from the bottom edge. Draw a freehand oval within the marked rectangle and cut it out. This oval will then fit snugly around the pipe when the flashing is fitted over the pipe and cemented down.

Form a flange by troweling plastic cement around the pipe and juncture of the flashing. It must be applied vigorously and thoroughly to make the cement adhere and to expel all air pockets in the cement. After the flashing is applied, the shingles are continued around the pipe. They are cut to fit snugly, and cemented where

they lap over the flange. Nails should not be used too near the pipe.

Valleys are reflashed with heavy roll roofing by first nailing down the outer edges of a strip about 9″ wide and then over this a strip about 18″ wide is cemented to the first. If these strips cannot be laid as one continuous piece, they must be lapped in cement about 9″.

Sloping Roof

Where a sloping roof abuts a vertical wall, cut a strip of roll roofing 8″ wide, butt one edge against the wall and nail it along all edges to the existing shingles. Then as the new shin-

BEFORE   AFTER

Fig. 68. The entire appearance of the house is impaired by unsightly broken and decayed siding. Both looks and value are enhanced by applying one of the many types of shingling material.

gles are laid, coat this strip with plastic cement and bed the shingles in the cement, butting them tightly against the wall. Nail the shingles only beyond the flashing strip. Now caulk the juncture of the shingles and the wall with plastic cement, forcing it well down between the joint.

Flashing around chimneys should be of non-corrodible metal if asbestos shingles are used. The new base flashing is made up of bent pieces of the same length as the wather exposure of the shingle plus 3″. The base flashing is slipped under the existing cap flashing, each piece lapping the other 3″. The asbestos shingles are then laid over the flange on the roof, and nailed beyond the flange edges. Methods of laying asbestos and asphalt shingles are described in Chapter 7.

RE-SIDING OVER OLD SIDING

As a general rule old siding materials may remain in place when you plan to apply new siding. Not only will considerable labor be saved in not removing the old material, but leaving it in place helps to further insulate the walls of your house. However, wood-shingled walls, if in very bad condition, are best removed if only for the reason that it is debatable which entails the most work—

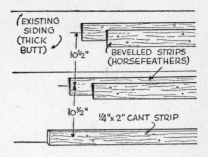

Fig. 69. "Horsefeathers" afford an even surface for applying new siding by leveling off old beveled siding.

carefully going over the entire surface and nailing down cupped shingles, or removing them entirely. Moreover, if a wood-shingled wall is in bad shape, practically every shingle is also badly warped (Fig. 68).

There is a variety of trade-name siding materials of the re-covering type, but they consist of two basic materials: asbestos-cement, and asphalt-impregnated felt. The latter offers a choice of shingles in a number of patterns; roll and panel imitation brick; and roll and panel imitation stone. The better quality imitation brick, when applied, is so close to the real thing that at a short distance it is impossible to tell the difference.

As in the case of roofing, the old siding must be well nailed down with decayed pieces removed and replaced with new, for both asbestos and asphalt siding are relatively thin, and any uneven or loose surface will either spoil the appearance of the new siding or damage it. From an

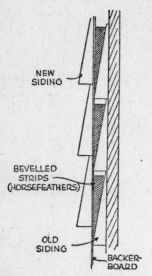

NEW SIDING

BEVELLED STRIPS (HORSEFEATHERS)

OLD SIDING

BACKER-BOARD

Fig. 70. How new siding is applied over old siding is shown in this cross-section. The shaded wedged shaped areas are the "horsefeathers" described in the preceding illustration.

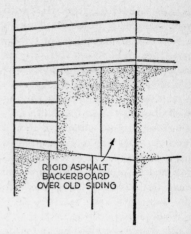

RIGID ASPHALT BACKERBOARD OVER OLD SIDING

Fig. 71. A rigid backerboard of asphalt can be used when the new siding is to be of that material also.

appearance standpoint only, it is important to have a firm, reasonably level surface on which to apply new siding material.

Old beveled siding, if it is the thick butt type, will have to be leveled off with wedge-shaped strips (horsefeathers), the thick end facing up and the strip placed along the siding at a point where it will level the slope (Fig. 69). Wood lath is almost as good as the beveled strips for leveling purposes. In the case of thick butt, wide siding, it may be necessary to nail two strips to achieve a level surface. This is particularly necessary if asbestos shingles are used (Fig. 70).

Asphalt Backerboard

If you are using asphalt shingles or imitation brick or stone, you can also use asphalt backerboard which is especially made for this purpose, and comes about ⅛" thick and in panels for an under surface for the siding material. This product affords a better, more rigid surface than the wood strip method. For the rigid asbestos siding shingles, the strips are adequate. If wood leveling strips are used, 15-pound asphalt-saturated felt must be applied over the strips before applying either asbestos or asphalt products. Run the felt vertically at the corners, using one width bent around the corners; then surface the wall with the felt run horizontally. Nail it just enough to hold it in place until the siding has been applied, and lap all edges at least 2". If asphalt backerboard is used, the felt is not necessary (Fig. 71).

For asphalt shingles, outside corners must have corner boards; one ¾"x3" and the other ¾"x4", nailed and butt joined for the shingles to butt against. Imitation brick and stone siding have special corner pieces which are nailed as a finish for outside corners. Metal corner beads, made for the purpose, can also be used for asphalt shingles instead of wood boards, the shingles being butted against the bead (Fig. 72).

Inside corners for asphalt-shingle application are either flashed with a strip of roll roofing about 12" wide with the shingles cut to fit snugly against each other and cemented to the flashing with plastic cement, or the shingles are warmed and bent around the corner without flashing. Around windows and doors, the shingles are brought up against the casings, and the juncture well cemented with plastic cement. A small staff molding is then nailed at the juncture to form a new finish, as the siding material over the existing one usually extends beyond the face of the casings. Flashing must be installed over doors and windows to make a watertight seal, and can be roll roofing, although metal flashing is best.

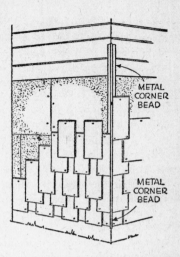

Fig. 72. These metal corner beads are made especially for use with asphalt shingles and are used so that shingles will form a good butt at corners.

lower edge of the prepared wall surface equal to ¼" less than the width of one course of the siding. Doing it this way will give you a projection of ¼" over the old siding when you line up the first strip (Fig. 73). As the work progresses, space chalk lines up the wall at intervals equal to the amount each course is exposed—this is to check for horizontal laying. Vertical chalk lines should also be snapped on each side of windows and doors to insure correct alignment of vertical "mortar joints."

To lay the first course, square a strip of siding through a vertical mortar joint and set the end even with a corner. Line up the top edge with the horizontal chalk line you have previously snapped, and nail the strip along the selvage edge

BRICK OR STONE ASPHALT SIDING

To apply imitation brick or stone siding, first snap a chalk line around the building at a distance above the enough to hold it in place. At the corner, nail the edge ½" back with the nails spaced 2" apart, and at the bottom of the strip 4" apart, which places two nails in each brick, evenly spaced. Then nail each vertical mortar joint with one nail in the center of the joint. Use non-corrodible nails with ¼" diameter checkered or smooth heads, and of a length to penetrate ¾" into the wall surface. Do not drive the nails too tightly, otherwise a "quilted" effect will result.

Succeeding Courses

The next and succeeding courses are lined up with chalk lines so that each succeeding course laps the one below it by the amount of the selvage.

Succeeding courses are nailed in the same manner as the first. Be careful to align vertical mortar joints as succeeding courses are laid. This can be done with a carpenter's level, using the plumb-level end, and also by using the vertical chalk lines which you have previously snapped. Where the ends of the strips butt, a 15-pound felt flashing strip 6" wide and as long as the width of the siding strip is centered behind each butted joint and cemented to the strips before their edges are nailed in place. Inside corners are flashed with 15-pound felt 12" wide, coated with plastic cement, and the strip ends fitted snugly against each other and edge nailed (Fig. 74).

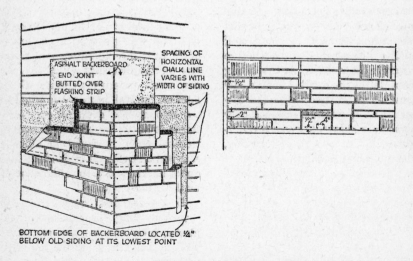

ASPHALT BACKERBOARD

END JOINT BUTTED OVER FLASHING STRIP

SPACING OF HORIZONTAL CHALK LINE VARIES WITH WIDTH OF SIDING

BOTTOM EDGE OF BACKERBOARD LOCATED ¼" BELOW OLD SIDING AT ITS LOWEST POINT

Fig. 73. Careful application of backerboard as a base for imitation brick or stone siding so that it extends ¼" below the old siding at its lowest point will assure a well-fitted covering from the very start. Note that the first course is begun at the corner.

Special outside corners are made for this type of siding and are applied over the siding with plastic cement and nailed 1″ back from each edge. Be careful when applying the cement at the corners so that it will not squeeze out at the sides when you nail the corner piece. Carry the siding up to the eaves and rakes, and embed the top course in plastic cement. The top edge of the top course must be protected from direct exposure to the weather. A frieze board slightly lapping the top edge will protect it (Fig. 75).

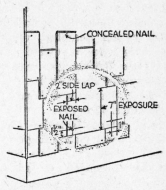

Fig. 74. The nailing method shown secures the shingles so that each course overlaps the one below it by the amount of the selvage.

ASPHALT-SHINGLE SIDING

Covering walls with asphalt shingles requires the same general procedure as that for brick or stone siding, except that each shingle is individually applied. There are quite a number of shingle patterns, but basically they are all laid with lapped joints in such a manner as to produce a particular pattern. Instruction sheets describing particular pattern laying are furnished with the specific material.

There are two methods of nailing: using three nails, one in the center at the upper edge and one at each corner, exposing two nails with one covered; and nailing with four nails, two covered and two exposed. Chalk lines are snapped to keep the shingles on a horizontal line, and vertical chalk lines should be snapped to align the shingles vertically.

ASBESTOS SIDING SHINGLES

These differ from roof shingles and cannot be used for roofing purposes. To apply asbestos siding shingles, snap a chalk line the width of the first course of shingles less ⅜″. This will give you a first course projection of ⅜″ below the existing siding to which you have nailed a cant strip. Start with two full length shingles at an outer corner, one edge lapping the other, top edges on the chalk line. Mark and cut adjoining vertical edges to form a lapped joint (Fig. 76). Cutting the shingles near their edges is best done with a small pistol-grip metal cutting saw, using the point to score the shingle. Run the saw point up and down the line a few times to score or groove the surface well. Then take a pair of flat-nose pliers and break off the edges on the waste side. Smooth the edges with a bastard double-cut flat file.

To cut a shingle along or near its center, score the shingle in the same manner as just described, using a wood straightedge to guide the saw. Then place the shingle, with the groove over the edge of a flat surface such as a board, and break the shingle (Figs. 77 & 78).

Cutting asbestos shingles is very much like cutting glass, using a scoring tool instead of a glass cutter. Holes can be punched in asbestos shingles by grinding a conical point on a nail set, making sure that the shingle is on a perfectly flat surface.

Secure one shingle at the corner temporarily with two nails partially driven, and then place a backer strip of felt, folded in half lengthwise, behind the shingle at the corner, and nail the shingle, making sure that the nail also pierces the backer strip. Place backer strips behind each pair of butted shingles, and nail the shingles and backer strips. Complete the first course around the house, lining the tops of the shingles with the previously snapped chalk line.

Second Course

To start the second course, snap a chalk line the width of a shingle less 1½″ which is the lap of the second and succeeding courses. Begin at the corner with a half shingle—which you must cut—applying backer strips as before. Then continue with full-length shingles. This method produces staggered joints as in brick laying.

Nails used for fastening asbestos shingles are of two types and, for residing use, 2″ long. For the concealed nails at the tops of the shingles, use needle-pointed galvanized flat heads. For the exposed nails, use bronze nails furnished for this purpose. Do not drive the nails too tightly, or you may break the shingles. Make certain,

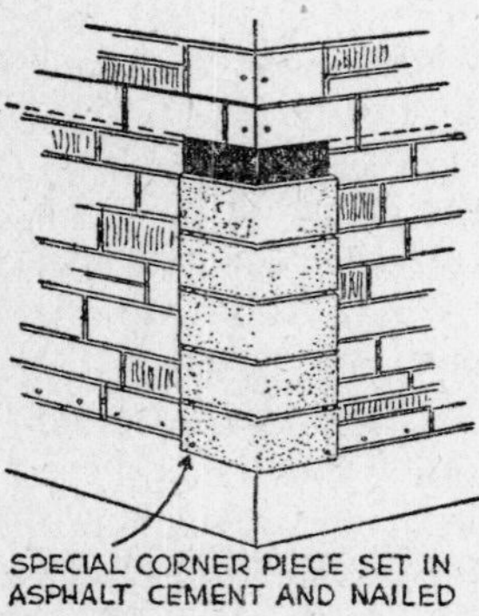

SPECIAL CORNER PIECE SET IN
ASPHALT CEMENT AND NAILED

Fig. 75. When attaching the special corner piece, take care that the cement used is not squeezed out at the sides when the nailing is done.

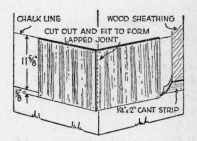

Fig. 76. Adjoining vertical edges on the two corner shingles are marked and cut to form a lapped joint.

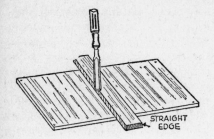

Fig. 77. To cut a shingle, use a straight-edge and some sharp instrument to score it at the point desired.

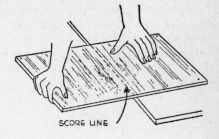

Fig. 78. Complete the cutting by breaking the shingle along the scored line over a board.

for both asphalt shingles and brick or stone siding, and asbestos shingles, that the surfaces to be covered and the shingles or siding are absolutely dry when applying.

Applying asphalt and asbestos siding materials to new walls calls for the same procedure as when re-siding, with the elimination of leveling methods. On new surfaces, 15-pound felt is applied over the sheathing before siding materials are used

A BAY WINDOW

Bay windows add charm to an otherwise uninteresting exterior wall face, and can enliven the interior as well. The bay window in a small house where space is at a premium can be used as a dining alcove, and brings added airiness and light to a room (Fig. 79). Bay windows are designed in different ways, extending beyond the face of the house as a square-cornered rectangle or with the sides at a 30° or 45° angle. The latter bay with the side angled is the more common and the 45° angle permits more of an extension for a given angle dimension.

Bay windows are built with an overhang framed by extending the joists of the floor, if the joists run at right angles to the wall, or with separate joists framed to trimmers if the floor joists run parallel to the wall. Some have a foundation of their own on which the sill rests. The least expensive to construct is one which is cantilevered, as you save the cost of the materials needed to build a foundation below frost line. However, cantilevering the bay window can be done only with a house of balloon-frame construction, as the platform construction of the western frame is such that to extend joists by first removing the studs, sole, subfloor and header at the first-floor line is next to impossible. A foundation for the bay in this case is necessary.

A 4-foot extension beyond the house is about the limit for cantilevered construction, and for the western platform frame you will have to build a foundation wall. How to build foundations is explained and illustrated in *The Wise Handbook of Masonry and Waterproofing.*

Removal of the siding and sheathing beyond the overall dimensions of the bay window is necessary to remove the old and to frame the new structural members for both the balloon and western frame. In the balloon frame the finish floor and subfloor within the area of the bay must also be removed to add new joists for the extension. When the floor joists run parallel to the foundation, a distance of four joists back from the wall must be uncovered. For joists running at right angles to the wall, at least 3 feet of flooring must be removed.

In the case of the latter, joists of the same size as the existing ones are

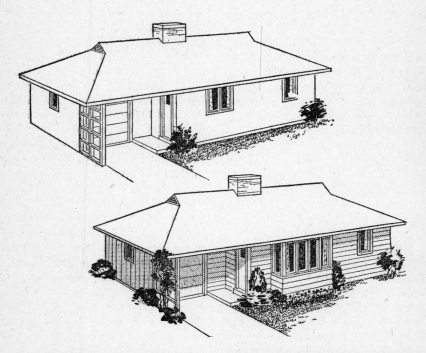

Fig. 79. A bay window adds additional space to the small home as well as beautifying it by adding variety and charm to its lines. All existing windows hold the possibility of being converted to a bay.

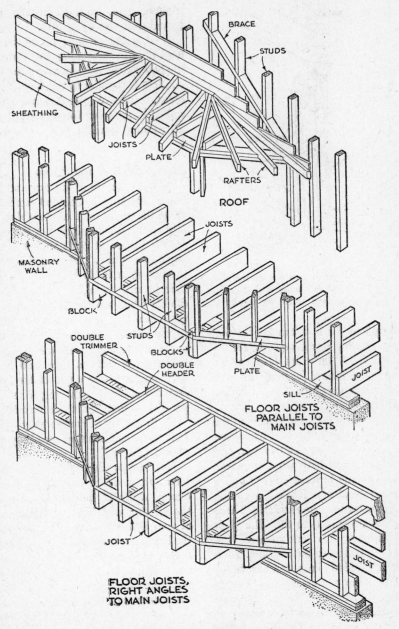

Fg. 80. Framing for the bay window.

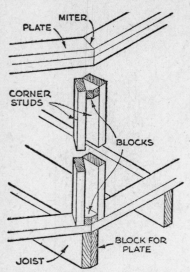

Fig. 81. It is necessary to double the stud at the juncture of the house and the bay. Wedges are used to fill the angle.

well spiked for a distance of 3 feet to the existing joists, and rest on the sill to which they are also spiked. They must extend beyond the wall for the distance of the bay at the new stud line.

If the floor joists run parallel to the foundation, the fourth joist back from the wall is doubled as a trimmer, and the three joists between the overall corners of the bay are cut out and a doubled header is framed from the sill to the trimmer on each side. These headers are spiked to the sill and to the trimmer. The cut ends of the joists are spiked to the headers. Then joists are added across the bay width on the same centers as the existing joists, and extended beyond the wall line to the extension dimensions of the bay, the joists being spiked to the

trimmer and, resting on the sill, spiked to it also (Fig. 80).

Next, a 2x4 sill is nailed on the extended joists, outlining the form of the bay. At the corners where the bay window is parallel to the face of the house, blocks of joist dimensions are spiked to the joists for support of the sill running parallel to the house.

Juncture of Bay and House

At the juncture of the bay and the house, the stud is doubled from the sill to the under edge of the ribbon or joist of the second floor, but the new stud is placed at right angles to the angle of the bay. The space between the two studs is blocked with wedges that fit snugly in the space. These double studs are the corner posts at the house line. Now frame two studs to the sill at the corners where the angle of the bay meets the parallel-to-the-house section. One stud is at right angles to the angle of the bay, and the other at right angles to the parallel section, the studs forming a "V." Brace these temporarily with 1x4s to the sill, making sure they are plumb (Fig. 81).

Now comes the problem of a doubled girder or header to span the overall width of the bay window at the existing wall face. As either side of your house where you are building the bay is made up of structural members which support overhead loads, these loads must be supported by temporary 2x4s at every point until the header is framed in place and can do its own supporting. These temporary 2x4s must be wedged tightly against all joists and supported by joists as near as possible to where the header is to be framed, allowing just enough room for you to work. If on the ribbon side, which supports the joists, a doubled header of joist dimensions, well spiked together, must support the studs just under where the ribbon is nailed. On the joist side of the house, the header must be framed just under the studs where the joist is nailed. After making sure that all points are well supported by the temporary 2x4s, saw off the studs between the bay opening and remove them from the sill. These should be sawed off about 2″ below where the top edge of the header will be.

Carefully measure the depth of the header and the thickness of two studs when doubled, and cut off the total of these dimensions from the tops of the *new* corner studs at the house line. Then frame one 2x4 plate between this stud and the corner stud forming the angle of the bay. Nail this plate on the tops of the two studs, with the end of the plate cut at the proper angle to fit snugly against the existing stud at the house line. This plate must overlap the bay stud to the center of the "V" and the end mitered. Do this on both sides of the bay and then fit a plate on top of the other two studs, forming the front face of the bay window. Now frame a second plate on top of the first, spiking it to the bottom one. This doubled plate, and sill below it, form the outline of the bay (Fig. 82).

Now place your doubled header on the plate next to the cut-off studs and mark each one a hairline lower

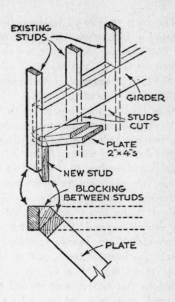

Fig. 82. The double plate of 2x4's extend out from the house studs and determine what the outline of the bay window will be.

than the *top* edge of the header. Saw each stud off again at this new line. Then force the header in under the studs, between the two existing corner studs against which the header should fit snugly. The header is now supported by the double plate which in turn is supported by the corner studs. Spike the header to the existing studs and plate, and spike the cut-off studs to the header. Your major operation has now been completed and the temporary stud bracing can be removed. Do not, however, remove the temporary diagonal braces from the bay corner posts, which as yet are only secured by the plate and sill.

The next step is to frame ceiling rafters for the bay window. These can be 2x4s resting on the plate and spiked to it and the header. They should be 16" on centers and extend to the outer edge of the plate.

Now replace the sheathing to the underside of the ceiling rafters, cutting out the bottom sheathing board to fit around the rafters. Then nail a ridge board against the sheathing, to which you nail roof rafters (2x4s). The roof of a bay window as described is the hip type. The rafters can extend beyond the plate for an open, closed or boxed cornice to match the cornice treatment of the main roof. Roof boards are then nailed to the rafters and should be tongued and grooved lumber not wider than 6".

Window Openings

Window openings are framed into the bay in the regular manner, that is, doubled headers of 2x4s are supported top and bottom by trimmers nailed to the corner posts, or near them, and cripples or short studs are nailed between the headers and sill, and between the headers and plate. The window frames of whatever type of window you prefer are then set in the openings, and horizontal sheathing is nailed to the studs. The underside of the joists for the bay are covered with tongued and grooved finished lumber. It is advisable to fill in the space between the bay joists with about 3" of vermiculite or mineral wool insulation to prevent cold drafts from penetrating through the floor.

The subfloor is now relaid and extended to cover the bay area. If the original subfloor was laid diagonally, it is continued to the joist edges of the bay. If it was laid straight, and the joists are at right angles to the foundation, continue the rough flooring. However, if the joists run parallel to the foundation, the new subfloor for the bay should be run diagonally so that when the finished floor is replaced and new flooring added, that portion of the bay will also be cross-laid.

Roof of Bay

The roof of the bay is covered with the same roofing material as the house, but flashing must first be applied at the juncture of the bay to the face of the house. This flashing can be metal preferably, or heavy roofing felt. The roof is then laid and the siding replaced on the face of the house. Siding material to match that of the house is applied to the bay.

Bay windows are usually equipped with a gutter and a downspout to prevent erosion of the soil around the bay.

The foregoing suggestions for building a bay window apply to a two-story house, but the procedure is the same for a one-story house, the roof of the bay in this instance being just below that of the main roof. If there is little distance between the ceiling line and roof rafters, the roof of the bay can be an extension of the main roof for that portion of the bay which is parallel to the house face. If this is done, the roof rafters of the bay are extensions of the main roof rafters and spiked to the latter, with the hip and side rafters framed in the same manner as for the bay of a two-story house.

Bay Window for Platform-frame House

Making a bay window for the western platform-frame house calls for the same procedure, the doubled header supporting the plate of the second floor, there being no difference on either side of the house. A foundation is necessary as previously explained. The new joists for the bay in this instance are framed to the header at the main foundation line, and can be of less depth than the main joists. A ledger strip is spiked to the header to support the new joists at this point, and the joists spiked to the header. The joists rest on a sill cemented and bolted to the bay foundation, in the same manner as regular foundation-sill construction, but for the bay extension, the platform system is not necessary.

After every point has been temporarily but thoroughly braced in preparation for the addition of the header, the studs are cut and removed as previously explained, including that portion of the first-floor subfloor sole between the opening. The original subfloor is left intact and a new subfloor added to the bay extension. It would, however, be well to take out an occasional subfloor board and install a new one extending from a joist of the main floor to the

sill of the bay, so that a form of interlocking of subfloor boards is achieved, tying the old subfloor in with the new one.

In many communities a building permit is required from the local government before any exterior major change can be made in a dwelling, so be absolutely certain of this before attempting any alteration such as described herein. One final word of caution — the temporary bracing which must sustain the overhead load until the doubled header or girder is installed, must be *more* than adequate. Thus if there is any doubt in your mind, double each temporary 2x4 support, spiking them together if necessary, or use 4x4s or 4x6s for the shoring. As loads vary in every house, no specific suggestion for size of shoring material can be given. If there is any doubt in your mind, consult with a builder or architect as to adequately dimensioned shoring material.

CONVERTING AN OPEN PORCH TO AN EXTRA ROOM

Many houses of yesterday have a porch of ample size. You may or may not have screened in this porch. Porches are one of the easiest spaces to convert to an extra room, as the structural framing is usually such that no additional reinforcement is necessary (Fig. 83). However, posts supporting a porch may not be designed to carry a living load and must be checked. Frequently, too, the sills and girders of such a porch, if open to the weather, have been damaged. This detail must also be examined.

A porch which does not support a room overhead can be jacked up with timber of sufficient dimensions to replace damaged sills or girders and, if it does support an overhead room, the sills and girders are of sufficient strength and usually well protected from the weather. If they are damaged, it is best to have a contractor

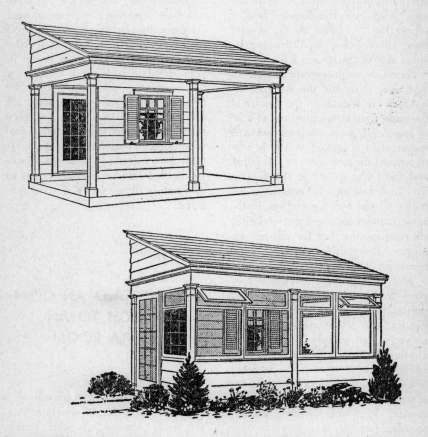

Fig. 83. Porches are one of the easiest spaces to convert to an extra room as the structural framing is usually such that no additional reinforcement is necessary.

experienced in this type of restoration do the job of replacing.

Porch floors are usually single and can be the subfloor of your new room. As they usually have a slight pitch to shed water, they should be leveled with wood shims on the floor joists and sills—unless you do not mind the slant to a finish floor. Additional joists may be necessary which, if the porch is low to the ground, will require your removing the porch floor to get at the house and porch sill or girders to add new joists. If this is not necessary, be sure to thoroughly nail down all loose floor boards and replace damaged or decayed ones.

Porch details differ, and framing studs for your particular porch will depend on how it is constructed. Usually all that is required is to nail a sill or shoe to the floor and frame the studs to this and the girder supporting the porch roof. If the roof is supported by square posts at the corners and intermediate points, these can remain, but if ornamental round posts exist, they should be removed after the header or girder supporting the roof has been temporarily shored with adequate material at post points. Then frame posts made up of three 2x4s in one of two ways, as for regular house construction.

Studs should be on 16" centers and wherever window openings occur, are doubled as trimmers to support headers at the top and bottom, with cripples spaced between. The entire face of the porch can be framed with homemade windows in any way to suit your taste and to serve the purpose of the new room.

Entrance Porches

Entrance porches can be left as they are, the entrance opening into the new roof. If they are long enough, a partition can be built to form an entrance hall with an additional door cut into the wall face of the house, giving access to the new room (Fig. 84). Another way of connecting an existing room to the newly made one is to construct a large opening between the room and enclosed porch. This requires, of course, the same procedure for installing a girder of sufficient dimensions to span the opening as for any similar type of renovation, only more so, as the girder must support the overhead load of the house which is considerable.

Treatment of the exterior face of the porch is identical with that of the regular wall face, that is, it must be sheathed, building paper applied, and siding material nailed to the sheathing. Instead of wood sheathing, asphalt-saturated fiberboard sheathing can be applied either vertically for ½"-thick board, or horizontally for 25/32" board. This offers good insulation and structural rigidity.

Building paper is not necessary with this type of sheathing. It is more economical than wood sheathing and structurally as rigid. This sheathing board is applied in solid panels nailed to the studding before window frames are installed, and the window openings cut out after the sheathing is partly up over the openings. End joints are staggered when applying the board horizontally.

Interior walls can be covered with one of the many varieties of wall boards, affording additional insulation, or you may prefer to insulate the new room with blanket or batt insulation before applying the interior wall surface.

Ceiling

The ceiling can be treated in a number of ways. Many porches have boarded ceilings of their own. Insulation ceiling tiles or regular fiberboard panels can be applied over the porch ceiling. If your porch roof is constructed with exposed roof rafters, the ceiling material can be applied to these with framing added to accommodate the ceiling-material dimensions. If you prefer a level ceiling rather than a slanting one, should the roof rafters be exposed, you will have to frame 2x4s or larger (depending on the span), as ceiling joists on which to attach the ceiling material.

Finished flooring should be nailed to the existing one, with heavy rag felt laid first as with a regular finish-floor job. If prefinished, thin hardwood flooring, linoleum or asphalt tile is intended, a ¼" fir plywood subfloor should be nailed over the existing one before the material is cemented.

ADDING A NEW ONE-STORY WING TO YOUR HOUSE

Have you contemplated for a long time adding a new wing (Fig. 85) to your house, and wondered just how to do it without adding the high

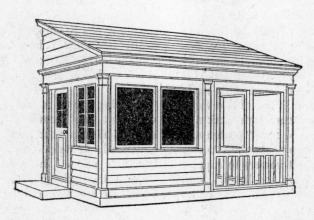

Fig. 84. Entrance porches can be left as they are, the entrance opening into the new room. If they are long enough, a partition can be built to form an entrance hall with an additional door cut into the wall face of the house.

cost of labor to the cost of building materials? If you have found the preceding chapters of interest and have carefully read about the various phases of building construction, you will be equipped with the know-how.

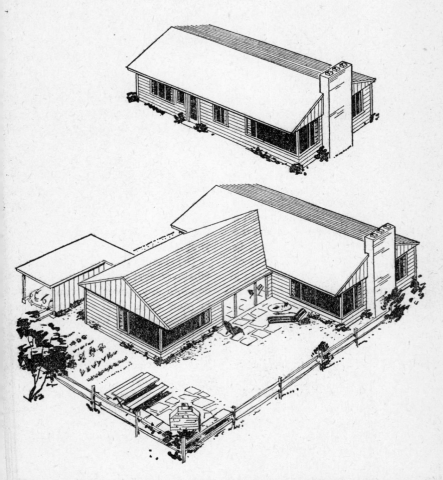

Fig. 85. A new wing can be added to your house without adding the high cost of labor to the cost of building materials. The wing should be of the same architectural character as that of your house.

Hints

A few hints may help you to choose the style of wing most suitable for your present home:

(a) Your new wing should be carefully planned from the viewpoint of practicability, and inner and outer appearance.

(b) The wing should be of the same general architectural character as that of your house, unless you plan to entirely renovate its outward appearance.

(c) Although you may change the appearance of your house, you will probably leave the roof structure as it is. Thus your new wing should have a roof design of the same general character to avoid the appearance of having been an afterthought.

(d) A shed-type roof is a perfectly good and legitimate roof, but does not look too well when combined with a gambrel, hip or gable roof, unless the wing is quite small. A shed roof, in combination with the above types of roof, has the appearance of lacking a roof by comparison. It is, however, the most economical to build within certain span limits. If the span is quite long, the shed-type roof becomes an expensive one to build because of the larger than usual roof and ceiling rafters required.

(e) If your budget is limited, do not make your room spans so wide that larger than usual ceiling joists and roof rafters will be necessary. The floor joists can be supported by girders on piers, but the ceiling joists must be self supporting, and roof rafters must, in a measure, carry additional roof weight and wind stresses.

(f) The purpose of your proposed wing is an important factor. If it is to contain a number of bedrooms with new bathroom facilities, the problem of sewerage connections and plumbing play an important role, as these must be connected to a main sewer. If the disposal problem is taken care of by a septic-tank installation, no particular difficulty arises as the septic tank and disposal field is probably large enough for the additional bathroom.

(g) Many building codes and restrictions require that sewer connections, plumbing and electrical wiring be installed by licensed plumbers and electricians. There is nothing you can do about this but to comply with these regulations, or to design your wing so that present bathroom facilities are accessible to the rooms contemplated. This design depends on the existing layout of the rooms of your house.

(h) Before you spend any money whatever, first check on the building codes, if any, governing construction in your area. Find out also about building permits which usually go with building codes. Violation of these codes and ignoring building permits lead you to nothing but trouble and wasted money.

(i) If you are not good at designing a wing, or making working drawings, it is more economical in the long run to have an architect do it for you.

Allowable Spans

The following table shows the allowable spans for floor joists sustaining a live load of 40 pounds per square foot (residence requirements), and a dead load of weight of joist and double flooring. It also shows the allowable spans for ceiling joists with a dead load of joist plus plaster, and the allowable spans for roof rafters with a live load of 30 pounds per square foot for an average pitch roof of average covering material—excluding slate.

Since Douglas Fir and Southern Pine are the most commonly used of the structural woods, with the highest modules of elasticity, the spans indicated are for these woods only. The modules of elasticity of common Douglas fir and southern pine are 1,600,000 pounds per square inch.

The spans shown are such that the deflection will not exceed 1/360 of the span, which is the standard practice of calculation. Moreover, thicker than nominal 2″ stock is omitted because the difference in the allowable span of a 2x6 joist on 12″ centers, and a 3x6 on 12″ centers is 1″ less than 2 feet, while the difference in cost is considerably out of proportion to the extra footage gained.

ALLOWABLE SPANS OF FLOOR JOISTS—
40 LBS. LIVE LOAD

	12″ o.c.	16″ o.c.
2x6 nominal	10′-5″	9′-7″
2x8 "	14′-2″	12′-11″
2x10 "	17′-11″	16′-3″
2x12 "	21′-7″	19′-7″

CEILING JOISTS (No Live Load)

2x4 nominal	11′-0″	10′-1″
2x6 "	16′-7″	15′-4″
2x8 "	21′-7″	20′-1″
2x10 "	26′-9″	25′-0″

ROOF RAFTERS—30 LBS. LIVE LOAD

2x4 nominal	7′-6″	6′-10″
2x6 "	11′-6″	10′-6″
2x8 "	15′-3″	13′-11″
2x10 "	19′-2″	17′-6″

The balloon-frame construction requires less material and is therefore less expensive than the western platform frame, and for a one-story structure may as well be employed. Use No. 1 common Douglas fir for all rough framing which includes sills, studs, joists, plates, soles and roof rafters. Southern pine is good for roof boards and sheathing—if you plan to use lumber for sheathing.

No. 2 common 1x4 square-edge southern pine is good for your subfloor, or you can use the 1x6 T&G for roof boarding, subflooring and sheathing. Asphalt saturated fiberboard sheathing is considerably cheaper than the T&G lumber for sheathing, gives better insulation, and is structurally as stiff. Either 25/32″ or ½″ thickness can be used, the latter being, of course, less expensive.

Design your house in modules of 2 feet, that is, design it so that you can use standard lumber which comes in lengths of units of 2 feet up to 24 feet long. This saves considerable waste in cutting, and as all lumber is sold by the board foot, you will have to estimate your lumber costs in that manner. The table in Chapter 3 gives you this information.

To estimate costs accurately, it is necessary that the length of each piece and the number of pieces required be noted to arrive at the cost of the total board feet of the lumber. The sizes of lumber should then be grouped, that is, so many pieces of 2x4s, 2x6s, etc., and their length specified when ordering for a minimum of cutting waste.

To estimate how many 1x6 T&G boards will be required to cover a roof or floor, or the side of a house, you must take the face measurement of the board which, in the case of 1x6 T&G is 5½", and divide the width of the roof in inches by 5½. The length of the roof determines the length of the lumber but, when ordering, this is not specified in the case of roof boarding and rough flooring, since random lengths are necessary for staggering joints. When estimating the cost of this lumber, however, the nominal size 1x6 and length is used to arrive at the number of board feet. Do not deduct openings, and add about 10 per cent to what you need for waste in cutting, etc.

Fiberboard Sheathing

To estimate the number of panels of fiberboard sheathing required, the square area of the face of the wing to be covered is calculated without deductions for window or door openings. As panel sizes vary with each manufacturer's product, these sizes cannot be given, but as an example: ½" thick sheathing panels usually come 4x8 feet, which contains an area of 32 square feet. These panels are sold at so much per square foot, which gives you the price per panel.

Dividing the square area to be covered by the square area of a panel will give you the number of panels required. Fractions of a panel left over are calculated as an additional panel needed. For instance: The area to be covered is 12 feet x 12 feet, or 144 square feet. A 4x8 foot panel is 32 square feet; thus 144 divided by 32 equals 4½ panels — or 5 panels needed with ½ panel as waste.

Wood singles are an excellent roof-covering material, but in many communities they are not allowed because of fire hazards, and the insurance rates for wood shingles are slightly higher than for other more fire resistant types. Asbestos shingles are fireproof, and asphalt shingles and asphalt-saturated roll roofings of various types are considered fire resistant and allowable practically everywhere.

Estimating the amount of roof covering required depends on the method of laying recommended by the individual manufacturer, and this information is freely given by consulting with the dealer stocking whatever roofing material you plan to use.

Siding materials, other than wood, such as asbestos siding shingles, asphalt siding shingles, and asphalt brick or stone-type siding are all excellent materials with varying degrees of permanency. Methods of estimating the amounts of these materials required can also be obtained from the dealers stocking a particular trade-name product, as they vary somewhat.

Foundation Wall

A foundation wall of adequate dimensions must be laid for the new wing, and must be well bonded to your existing foundation. The "how-to" is described and illustrated in *The Wise Handbook of Masonry and Waterproofing*. Small metal grills should be set in the foundation wall on each side for ventilating the space between joists and ground, if there is to be no basement.

Existing siding must be removed within the area of the new wing, and a little beyond it, but the sheathing should be left intact, partcularly so if you plan to have only a door connecting the wing with the existing structure. This idea is perhaps the best, because considerable removal and reframing of structural members is thus eliminated. All that would be required in this instance would be to cut a new doorway in the existing face of the house and frame it adequately.

Often, if an existing window is placed advantageously, this can be removed and enlarged into a doorway. If a large opening is planned, or an existing room is to be cut through into the new wing, adequate temporary shoring must be employed until the new opening span can be bridged with a girder of proper dimensions to sustain the overhead load of the house.

After the foundation is up and has "cured," lay a doubled 2x6 sill in stiff mortar and perfectly leveled on the foundation just far enough back from the outer face of the wall to allow for the thickness of sheathing material (Fig. 3, Pg. 117). The corners of the sill are staggered to form lapped joints. To level the sill, use small chips of stone, if necessary. The sill should be bolted to the foundation with bolts which you have previously set when building the foundation. When the mortar has hardened, the bolt nuts with a washer between nut and sill, are tightened.

If termites are present in your locality, first make a shield of copper extending 2" beyond the face of the foundation on both sides (Fig. 2, Pg. 116), and bend down the extensions to a 45° angle. Bed this shield in mortar and solder all joints so that a continuous strip of metal protects the sill along the foundation wall. Where the shield fits over bolts, apply heavy asphalt roofing cement liberally around the bolt. Then lay your sill in mortar on top of the shield.

Next, frame the floor joists (Fig. 14, Pg. 124), spiking them to the sill. The joists should run parallel to the existing house foundation wall because then you will not have to disturb the house sill construction. The first joist is spiked to the existing sill, studs and sheathing, and the joists are bridged every 6 to 8 feet of unsupported span with 1x2s for joists up to and including 2x10s, and with 2x2s for 12" joists (Fig. 20, Pg. 127).

Now frame your outside corner posts, made up of three 2x4s arranged so that an inside nailing surface is provided for a finished wall (Figs. 9 & 11, Pgs. 121-2). Spike them to the sill and brace them temporarily with diagonal braces of 1x4s nailed to the sill to hold them plumb. Doubled 2x4s spiked together are nailed to the existing sheathing and framing of the house where the wing joins the house wall.

Nail a 2x4 plate on top of the four posts, supported temporarily by a few 2x4 studs (Figs. 5 & 6, Pg. 118). Then frame your studs, 16" on centers, toenailing them to the sill, and spiking them to the joists. Nail them to the plate from the upper face of the plate. Brace these studs occasionally with temporary braces of 1x4s nailed to the joists, to keep the wall vertical and plumb. Now nail your second 2x4 plate to the top of the first one, making it a doubled 2x4. The corners of the plate, which are butt joined, are staggered to form lapped joints.

Brace the free corners with 1x4s let into the studs (Fig. 13, Pg. 123), sill and plate to fit flush with faces of these members. These braces should start from the fourth stud back from the corner at the sill, and run diagonally up to the plate. If a window opening interferes with this arrangement, double bracing from sill to post —the diagonal clearing the lower part of the window opening—is let into the studs, etc. Then a similar brace from post to plate is set to clear the upper part of the opening. On the other face of the corner, a diagonal brace is set from sill to plate in the regular manner or if a window opening interferes, then in the same manner as for the other window opening. Nail blocking between the studs about midway between the sill and plate (Fig. 19, Pg. 126).

Now frame your window openings with trimmers, headers and cripples between openings in the regular manner. Large window openings must be trussed as previously described (Figs. 1 & 7, Pgs. 115 & 119).

At this point you can switch to the western platform type of construction for your subfloor, if you wish (Pg. 123ff.). Nail the subfloor over the entire area of your wing, extending the flooring to the outer face of the studs, which means cutting

around them. Diagonal laying is not necessary and you will save a considerable amount of lumber by nailing the subfloor straight across the joists (Fig. 15, Pg. 124).

End joints in the floor boards must be staggered and rest on the joists. As you come to one of the temporary braces keeping the wall vertical, remove the brace from the joist and nail it back against a block nailed to the subfloor. These temporary braces should be kept in place until the ceiling joists and roof rafters are in place.

Put up all the partitions between rooms, nailing a sole to the subfloor (Figs. 38 & 39, Pg. 138), the studs topped by a 2x4 cap or plate. The studs are spaced 16″ on centers and braced with 2x4 blocking between studs. If there is a bearing partition which is to support the ceiling joist span, double the cap or plate. As with the outer-wall studs, temporarily brace the partitions to keep them vertical and plumb until the ceiling joists have been framed to them.

Now frame the ceiling joists, spiking them to the wall plates (Fig. 5, Pg. 118). Nail the partition plates to the joists. A hatchway should be framed into the ceiling joists where it is unobtrusive, so that access to the attic space is possible, should it be necessary. A closet if large enough is a good spot, or the hatchway can be located in a hall. Then frame your roof rafters to the design you are using (Figs. 5 & 6, Pg. 118). The roof rafters, notched to bear on the plates, are spiked to the plate and ceiling joists. Now remove the temporary bracing for walls and partitions.

For roofs with a ridge board — which can be 1" stock, but preferably 2" stock of the same depth as the roof rafters—nail a rafter to the plates on each side at the ends and center of the wing. Temporarily support them with 2x4s until you can get the ridge board in place and spiked to the rafters. Then frame the remaining rafters to the plate and ridge board. The rafter at the juncture of the wing and house is nailed to the sheathing and framing of the house. If the roof is of the hip variety, frame the hip rafters into the corners of the plates and ridge board (Fig. 16, Pg. 125), and then frame in your jack rafters.

Dormer Windows

If you plan to have dormer windows, frame them by one of the methods suggested in Chapter 7, depending on what type the dormer is to be. It must, of course, be framed at the same time as the roof and wall, being an integral part of both. Unless you plan to have a finished attic— requiring live-load sustaining attic floor joists instead of dead-load ceiling joists — the addition of dormer windows will only complicate your framing project, with added cost in materials. However, dormer windows in a roof make it possible for you to convert an attic space into living quarters at some future time, if the roof pitch allows enough ceiling height, in which case use joists of sufficient size to take care of future live loads.

If dormer windows are not used, provision should be made to ventilate the attic space. With a gable roof, this is easily solved by building a small louvered opening into the gable end of the wall. With a hip roof the problem becomes more difficult. If your roof has an appreciable overhang, small ventilators can be built either in the plancia, if the cornice is boxed, or in the frieze board if the cornice is open. Small openings should be left in back of the ventilators to allow air to pass into the roof, and heavy wire screening should be framed in back of these louvered ventilators.

Now nail on your roof boards which should be T&G lumber not more than 6" wide. Next comes the sheathing of your choice, either fiberboard or wood. The latter does not have to be applied diagonally, as you have braced the corners of your wing. Then set your door and window frames, with metal flashing over the head-casing drip caps when the outside casings are framed. Metal flashing must also be applied at the juncture of the roof and the main wall of the house. Methods of laying wood, asbestos, asphalt shingles and roll roofing are described in Chapter 7.

No mention has been made of electrical wiring installations, because *The Wise Home Electrical Handyman* is devoted exclusively to all phases of electrical wiring, appliances and repair. However, wiring, outlet receptacles, etc., must be installed during construction and before inside wall coverings can be applied.

CHAPTER 9

PAINTING AND FINISHING

FINISHES AND FINISHING

The success of many carpentry building projects depends largely on how well the piece is finished; and the success of any finishing operation depends on how well the wood surface has been prepared. A simply constructed piece of furniture can be made into a most attractive article by giving it a good finish. An elaborate piece of furniture, on the other hand, can be ruined if given a poor finish.

The first step in finishing is to remove any marks left on the wood during construction. The rough edges left by the saw should be sanded down with sandpaper until perfectly smooth. If they are very rough, touch

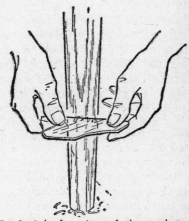

Fig. 2. A broken piece of glass makes an excellent scraper for smoothing off rough portions of wood.

them up with a plane or rasp, and then sand. Dents in the wood left by the head of a hammer can be eliminated by pricking slightly the wood with a sharp-pointed tool and then applying a few drops of water to the area. The water will make the wood fibers swell back to the original shape. After the area is dry, sand down the rough surface until it is smooth.

Wood surfaced at a mill may contain small rough spots. These must be removed before the wood is given a finish. The spots can be removed by sanding, planing, or scraping with a wood scraper or piece of broken glass. A piece of glass, by the way, makes an excellent scraper, especially for

Fig. 1. Dents in wood can be removed with a piece of wet blotting paper and a warm iron.

small spots difficult to remove with an ordinary wood scraper.

Joints between sections of wood that are not as tight as they should be can be filled with a wood filler. The seam should be first cleaned out and then packed with a wood filler such as plastic wood or spackle. As these fillers shrink slightly when dry, use a little more than is required. An excellent home-made filler is wood glue mixed with sawdust — use the same sort of sawdust, when possible, as the wood to be filled. After the filler is dry, shave down the excess with a razor blade and then sand. Similarly, cracks in end grain and other spots should also be filled.

Nail heads should be punched below the wood surface and the resulting hole filled with wood filler. Screw heads that have been countersunk can be treated in the same manner. But a more professional method is to glue a wood plug on top of the screw head. The wood plug is cut off flush with the wood surface after it is in place. Wood plugs made from different

Fig. 3. An electric sander is a great time-saver.

kinds of hardwood are available at some of the larger hardware stores and lumber yards.

Check all the joints on the piece to be sure they are solid. If they do not appear to be too strong, now is the time to do something about them. Additional nails or screws may be necessary. In some cases, metal angle irons or wood blocks may be required. In any event, do not begin finishing until you are certain that the project is good and solid.

SANDING

The next step in preparing the wood for a finish is to give all surfaces a thorough sanding. Start out with a No. 1½ grade paper followed by No. 0, No. 2/0 and finally a No. 4/0 paper.

All sanding should be done in the direction of the wood grain. If the sanding is done by hand, make a sanding block with a felt pad attached to the underside. This does a better, faster job than if the sandpaper is pushed by your hand alone. Sanding blocks can be purchased at paint and hardware stores. A good deal of time can be saved on large projects by using a power sander. Belt or oscillating sanders are excellent for this purpose. They can often be rented.

Most rotary sanders are not quite as good, as it is difficult to control the sander. Also a rotary sander works against as well as with the grain. Areas that cannot be reached with sandpaper can be smoothed out with steel wool.

SELECTING A FINISH

There are several ways in which a project can be finished. It can be finished with a paint suitable for furniture, such as an enamel. If the wood grain has an attractive appearance, a natural finish can be used or the wood can be bleached out to a lighter color and given one of the many attractive modern finishes.

The usual reason for painting a piece of furniture is that the wood is unattractive and ought, therefore, to be completely covered. Several coats of enamel properly applied will completely hide the defects in the wood and produce a finish with a high or semi-gloss. Much modern furniture is finished with enamel or lacquer. To match these pieces you would use a similar kind of finish.

If the wood in the project has an attractive wood grain, that is usually enough reason for wanting to preserve the natural finish. The wood may be darkened by staining before the finish is applied. The finish used to produce a natural effect is usually either varnish or shellac. Staining will also help to bring out the wood grain. A natural finish should only be used on woods that are naturally attractive.

Many homes are furnished with pieces done in the modern blonde effect. To match these, a blonde finish of one sort or another is required. Factory finished articles are almost impossible to match exactly as there are several methods used to obtain the same general appearance. But it is possible to come pretty close.

Of all the finishes, paint is the easiest to apply and usually requires the least work. It is also the most likely to turn out the way you expect. On the other hand, amateur builders who are willing to take the time can produce excellent results with other, more complicated types of finishes.

Where to Work

To obtain the best results, all finishing operations should be conducted in a room free from dust. If there is dust present, it is almost sure to stick on the freshly applied finish, usually spoiling your work.

Workshops are usually not suitable for finishing because of the amount of sawdust present. This is especially true where power saws and sanders have been used. Basements, too, are usually dusty. The best course is to select a room in the house which is not only free from dust but has good ventilation and where the temperature is about 70 degrees. This is important in getting the most out of a finish. Furniture and floors may be covered with dropcloths or old news-

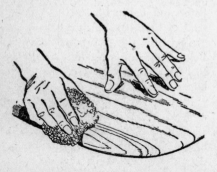

Fig. 4. Steel wool is better than sandpaper for smoothing off rounded edges.

papers during the finishing operation. Good illumination is most important, especially when you are working with any of the lighter finishes.

Separate as many parts of the piece as possible before finishing, and treat each as a separate unit. This, you will find, is easier and actually quicker than trying to finish the entire unit as a whole. Also, it will eliminate the possibility that doors and drawers will stick due to hardened paint or varnish in the seams or around the edges. On very fine work, it will be wiser to remove the hardware.

Small articles, such as chairs and the like, should be placed on a table for finishing. Nails driven into the end of each leg will raise the piece high enough to allow you to get at the under parts with ease. As a rule, it is better to do the small and hard-to-get-at portions first. Leave the large areas till last. By doing the inconspicuous

DIP ONLY HALF LENGTH OF BRISTLE INTO PAINT OR ENAMEL

Fig. 6. How to take paint on a brush.

portions first you also have an opportunity of seeing if the finish is going to come out as you expect.

ENAMELING

It is assumed that the wood has been sanded down until it is very smooth and that it is clean and dry. If the wood is plywood, the first step is to apply a special plywood primer. This is necessary because the grain in plywood, especially fir, is very pronounced and difficult to conceal unless many extra coats of paint are applied. Applying a special plywood primer wil save you both time and paint. After this primer is dry, an enamel undercoater is brushed on. This can be either an ordinary flat white paint or a special enamel undercoater.

If the finish is to be a color other than white, the undercoater can be tinted either by mixing some colors in oil into it or by adding a little of

TACKS

Fig. 5. For finishing, use tacks or small nails to lift the table or chair off the floor.

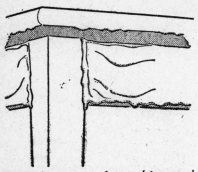

Fig. 7. Heavy coats of enamel improperly applied will run and sag around the edges.

the enamel you plan to use as the finish coat. Allow the undercoater to dry at least twenty-four hours and then give the surface a sanding with No. 2/0 sandpaper. Remove all traces of dust with a clean cloth dampened in turpentine. The surface is now ready for the enamel. Enamel is best applied with a special enamel brush having a chisel tip. Enamel, unlike paint, is flowed onto the surface and the action of the enamel removes the brush marks so that the surface dries out completely smooth. Once the finish has been applied, do not go back over it for additional brushing as this may leave marks which will not flow out. Be careful of accumulations of

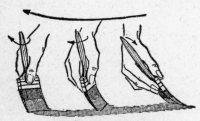

SHORT, LIGHT STROKES

Fig. 8. Enamel should be applied lightly with not too much paint on the brush.

enamel around edges. These must be removed at once before they dry.

In most cases, one coat of enamel will be sufficient. If it is not, allow it to dry thoroughly, give it a light sanding and dusting, and then apply a second coat.

TRANSPARENT AND SEMI-TRANSPARENT FINISHES

Many of the more expensive and better woods have very attractive natural coloring and grain, which you will naturally want to emphasize. There must, however, be some sort of protective coating over the wood. If there is not, the wood colors may soon fade and become dark due to dirt absorbed by the wood pores. Also, unprotected wood stains easily and discolors with water and other liquids. For some purposes, a finish as transparent as obtainable may be required. In other cases, the finish may be semi-transparent to darken the wood slightly. The most common kinds of transparent and seim-transparent finishes are varnish, shellac, anl lacquer.

If you wish to darken the wood slightly and emphasize the wood grain, then a stain is applied before the finish. A stain is unlike a paint, for while a paint is opaque and completely hides the wood, a stain is similar to a dye in that it merely colors the wood grain without hiding it. There are different kinds of stains. Each has certain characteristics which recommend it, so you must make your choice according to your own circumstances and your own tastes.

Water Stain

This is the least expensive kind of stain you can buy. It comes in powder form and is mixed with hot water for use. The main disadvantage of this stain is that the water leaves the wood surface very rough, and therefore the surface must be sanded smooth again after the stain is dry. The advantages of this stain, aside from its low cost, are that it is non-fading, and non-bleeding, and gives an even coloring. A water stain may be applied with either brush, spray gun, or cloth. Before the stain is applied, the wood should be sponged with water so that the grain rises, and then it must be sanded smooth. This eliminates some of the sanding necessary after the wood has been stained. When applied with a brush, the stain should be distributed freely. Allow the stain twenty-four hours to dry.

Oil Stains

These are sold ready-mixed at paint and hardware stores. They are applied with a brush or cloth. These stains do not penetrate very deeply into the wood and therefore are easy to control. If, when the stain is dry, it seems too dark, a light sanding will remove some if not all of the stain. Special shades can easily be mixed by thinning the stain with turpentine.

Non-Grain-Raising Stains

Most professional furniture builders prefer to use a non-grain-raising stain. These stains come in a wide range of colors which can be made into the desired shade. They have the permanency of water stains without causing the grain to rise. They can be applied either with a brush or with a spray gun.

Use of Stains

Before deciding to use a stain, there are several points to keep in mind. First, stains can only be used to darken wood — they will not make the wood lighter. The longer a stain is left on the wood surface before wiping it off, the deeper it will penetrate and the darker will be the final effect. If you wish to tint the wood only slightly, apply a thin coat of stain and wipe it off immediately. Remember that it is always possible to get a darker effect by applying another coat of stain once the first is dry. But

Fig. 9. Most of the stains you will use can be applied with a brush.

if the first coat dries out too dark, the only way to lighten up the wood is to sand out the stain. Also, the end grain of wood absorbs stain more readily and faster than the other areas, so use especially light coats on such places so they will not darken more than the rest of the wood, when you have finished the staining.

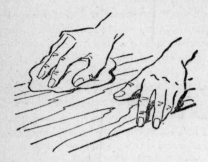

Fig. 10. Excess stain on the wood surface may be wiped off with a clean lintless cloth.

Bleaching

Just as stains are used to darken wod and bring out the grain, bleaching is used to make the wood lighter. Bleaching is done in most of the blonde finishes. The best sort of bleach to use on wood for furniture is a commercial type of bleach sold at the better paint and hardware stores.

When applying these bleaches, follow the instructions on the container. Drying time for bleaches will differ, but it is well to allow forty-eight hours or so. After the bleach is dry, the wood should be sanded lightly to remove traces of the bleaching solution as well as to smooth out the grain raised by the bleach. *Avoid inhaling any of the dust.* After the surface has been dusted, it should be

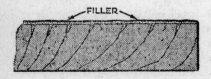

Fig. 11. The cross-section shows filler in the wood pores.

given a very thin coat of shellac to prevent the wood from becoming darkened by the oils in the filler.

FILLERS

Some woods, such as oak and chestnut, are called open-grained woods. The wood pores, or cells, in these woods are very large, and if a finish were to be applied directly to the wood, it would dry out rough and uneven due to the fact that some of it would sink down to fill the pores while the rest of the finish would be on the surface.

It is possible, of course, to sand this first coat smooth and then apply a second and third coat of finish, sanding each until at last you have built up a smooth surface for the final finish. It is much easier and faster, however, to fill these wod pores with a wood filler so that the surface is built up level before the first coat of finish is applied. Fillers may be stained or tinted, if desired, to produce additional coloring. Some woods which have a very close grain, such as cedar, cypress, and basswood, require no filler at all. Ash, beech, butternut, chestnut, elm, and hickory do require the application of a filler.

There are two types of fillers — paste and liquid. As a rule, the paste fillers are used on woods with open-grain while liquid fillers are used for the close-grain varieties.

Paste fillers can be purchased in neutral wood color and in several common wood colors. It is best to use a filler of the same color as the wood to be treated. If no such filler is available, a natural filler can be tinted with colors in oil.

Paste fillers must be thinned down somewhat before they are applied to the wood. Naphtha is usually used for this purpose. The amount of thinning required depends on the size of the wood pores. Fillers for use on oak and chestnut need not be thinned as much as fillers used on close-grain woods, such as walnut.

Application of Filler

The filler, when properly thinned, is applied rather freely to the wood with a brush. Do not cover too great an area with the filler because it will set in fifteen minutes or so and must be wiped off at this time. Brush the filler on, working in the direction of the wood grain.

After the filler has been brushed over the wood surface, it should be rubbed in a circular motion with a felt pad. This operation, known as "padding in," forces the filler into the wood pores.

It usually takes about fifteen minutes for the filler to set. As the filler begins to set, it becomes dull and starts to harden. This is the time to wipe off the excess filler on the wood surface. If the filler is allowed to set for too long, it will become so hard that the excess can only be removed by sanding. On the other hand, if it is wiped off before it has begun to set, there is a chance of pulling out the filler that has gone into the wood pores — and this defeats the purpose of the filler. It wil require a little practice on the part of the amateur before he is able to gauge exactly the

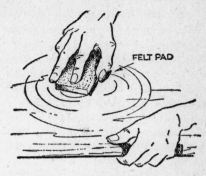

Fig. 12. Brush the thinned filler on in the direction of the grain.

right moment to remove the excess filler from the wood.

The process of removing the excess filler from the wood surface is called "towing off." This is done with a coarse piece of cotton or a piece of burlap. Wipe first across the grain with pressure and then with the grain. If some portions of the filler are too hard they can be softened up somewhat by adding a little naphtha. Coating the surface with a fresh coat of filler will also soften the hardened filler that has been already applied.

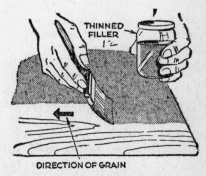

Fig. 13. Filler being padded in.

After the excess filler has been removed, dampen a piece of felt cloth in naphtha and wipe the surface very lightly. Allow the filler to dry hard and then sand the surface smooth with No. 2/0 sandpaper. After this operation, dampen a piece of lintless cloth in naphtha and wipe the surface down to remove any of the filler dust which may have been left by the sanding operation.

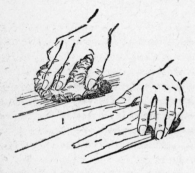

Fig. 14. This operation is known as towing off.

If, after the final sanding, you find that all the wood pores are not completely filled, another coat of filler should be applied.

Liquid Fillers

The most common type of liquid filler is shellac thinned down to a very light coat with denatured alcohol. One or two light coats are applied with a light sanding between coats to remove the shellac from the wood surface. Bleached shellac should be used for light colored finishes and orange shellac for darker finishes.

SEALING

This process is usually referred to as "washcoating." It consists of applying a thin coat of sealer to the wood before the finish is applied. This sealer serves many purposes. It provides a god bond between the finish coats and the wood and at the same time prevents the absorption of the first coat of finish by the wood. This usually eliminates the need for an additional coat of finish, for highly-absorbent woods will completely absorb the first coat of finish so that little or none of it remains on the surface.

The sealer also prevents the filler or stain from discoloring the finish. In very fine work, it is wise to use a sealer after the stain as well as after the filler. The sealer between stain and filler prevents any possibility of discoloration at this point. A sealer before the filler is applied is most important on bleached finishes because, if it is not applied before the filler, the oils in the filler will discolor the bleached wood.

Shellac makes an excellent sealer. Orange shellac is used for darker finishes and white shellac for light finishes. A 3½-pound cut is used for ordinary work. The shellac can be applied either by brush or with a spray gun. Another common kind of sealer is thin lacquer. This is best applied with a spray gun.

FINISHING PLYWOOD

Some of the projects outlined in this book call for the use of plywood, and by far the most common—as well as the least expensive—kind of plywood is made from fir. While this is an excellent material in many respects, it is a difficult one to finish because of the wild grain found in fir and the fact that the wood tends to fuzz, producing a rough surface. Before attempting to finish off this material, a special primer and sealer should be applied. This is applied in a heavy coat and allowed to dry thoroughly. If the wood is to be stained, the sealer can be tinted with stain before it is applied or a stain may be applied after the sealer is dry. Another finishing problem connected with plywood is the treatment of the edges, which expose the various layers of veneer. These can be filled out smooth with filler and then painted, but a somewhat more satisfactory solution is to cover them with strips of half-round molding of the same diameter as the thickness of the plywood.

FINISHES OR TOP COATS

The most common materials used for the final finish or top coat are varnish, shellac, lacquer, wax, and oil.

Varnish

Varnish is a very old finish, and over a period of years many different types of varnish have been developed for special uses. For most woodworking purposes, only a few of the many kinds are of any interest.

Spar Varnish: Also called marine varnish, this type is very hard and very tough when dry. It is used mostly for exterior work, but it is also useful for interior work, especially in the kitchen, where it will be subject to moisture. It dries in twelve to twenty-four hours.

Rubbing and Polishing: This group of varnishes is designed for use on furniture. These varnishes contain less oil than do some of the others and this prevents gumming of the abrasives used to sand out any irregularities.

Polishing Varnish: This is used as a top coat over rubbing-and-polishing varnish. It can be polished out to a high gloss.

Table Top Varnish: This dries out to a very tough surface which is very resistant to scratching and staining from moisture and alcohol.

Varnish Stain: This is a varnish tinted with stain. It is used, where appearance is not too important, in place of a regular stain followed by varnish. As it combines two operations in one, it is a time-saver.

Flat Varnish: This type of varnish dries out to a dull gloss and is useful for most general work.

Application of Varnish

To get good results with varnish it is necessary to fulfill certain rather

Fig. 15. Before varnishing, remove traces of dust from the surface with a lintless cloth dampened in varnish.

exacting conditions. First, the wood surface must be sanded out until it is perfectly smooth. It must also be clean and dry. Before the varnish is applied, dampen a piece of lintless cloth in a little varnish and wipe the surface with this. The small amount of varnish in the cloth will pick up dust which would not otherwise be caught with a dry cloth. It is best not to try to varnish in the same room where you have been working with wood because the sawdust in the air may fall on the freshly varnished surface and spoil it. It is better to do the varnishing in a room as free from dust as you can possibly get it.

Varnishing should not be done during wet weather or when the humidity is very high. For best results select a warm dry day and be sure that the room in which you work is not damp.

VARNISH

Fig. 16. Cold varnish can be brought to the proper temperature by placing the container in a pan of hot water.

Varnish applied in a damp basement will not dry properly. The temperature of the air has a good deal to do with how well varnish dries out. For best results, the temperature should be between 70 and 80 degrees.

This means that during the winter months varnish must be applied indoors in a heated room. If the varnish container has been stored in a cold room, place it in a pan containing warm water until the varnish has reached a good working temperature.

Because varnish can so easily be ruined by dust or dirt, it is best not to put the brush directly into the varnish container. Pour a quantity of varnish —the amount you expect will be required for the job at hand — into a clean container, and use this for brushing. When the job is finished, do not pour this varnish back into the original container. Instead, cover it and use it for some other job where the appearance of the varnish is of no particular importance to you.

The best kind of brush to use for varnishing is a varnish brush with a chisel point. These brushes should be used only for varnish—never for paint. The reason for this is that once a brush has been used for paint or enamel, no matter how well it is cleaned some of the paint or enamel will remain at the base of the bristles, and when the brush is next used for varnish, this paint will discolor the varnish. Keep varnish brushes just for varnishing and have a good selection of them in different sizes for both large and small jobs.

The application of varnish by brush is divided into three operations. The first step is called "cutting in." In this operation the brush is dipped about one-third the length of the bristles into the container. The varnish is then applied to the surface with smooth strokes. The next step is "cross brushing"—the brush is drawn across the wood grain. Start from either side and work the brush half-way across. The final step is "tipping off." Here the brush is drawn with the wood grain so that the tips of the bristles just touch the surface. Excess varnish around the edges of the piece or in the molding should be removed immediately before it has set. Make a careful inspection of the piece to be sure that there are no areas which have been missed.

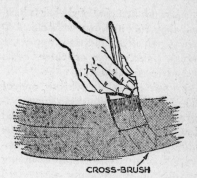

CROSS-BRUSH

Fig. 17. Cross-brushing.

Give the first coat of varnish about twenty-four hours to dry and then give it a light sanding to cut the gloss. Use No. 6/0 paper for this operation. Dust the surface and then apply the second coat. The number of coats required is a matter of personal taste. Two coats will produce a very adequate finish for most jobs. For very fine work, three or even four coats can be applied. For the final step in obtaining an attractive finish with varnish, the surface should be polished down. This operation is covered later in this chapter.

Shellac

Shellac may be used for the final finish in place of varnish. As is the case when using a shellac sealer, use white or bleached shellac for finishing light woods and orange shellac for the darker woods. When used as a finish, a standard 4-lb. cut of shellac must be thinned down. Use ¾ quart of de-

natured alcohol to each quart of shellac. Shellac spoils if kept too long, so be sure to purchase fresh, pure shellac and do not get more than you can use over a period of six months. Also, shellac should not be stored in a metal container. Store it either in a special lead-lined container or in a glass container. Take the same precautions when applying shellac as outlined above for varnish. Shellac sets and dries rather rapidly, so you must work fairly fast to get it on properly. On the other hand, since it dries rapidly, there is less chance of its picking up dust.

Fig. 18. Shellac should be stored in a lead-lined or glass container.

After the first coat of shellac is hard and dry, rub it down with No. 2/0 sandpaper, dust, and then apply the second coat. Two or three coats should be enough.

French Polishing: This is one of oldest methods of finishing fine furniture. White shellac should be thinned down to a 1-lb. cut. This is done by adding two quarts of denatured alcohol to each quart of shellac, assuming the shellac is originally a standard 4-lb. cut. The shellac is applied to the surface with a piece of soft lintless cloth rolled into a ball. The cloth is dipped into the shellac and then rubbed over the wood in straight strokes. Use very light pressure. Allow the surface to dry and then sand lightly with No. 6/0 sandpaper. Dust and then apply a second coat of shellac in the same way as the first. Additional coats are applied until a light glow begins to appear on the finish. At this stage, add several drops of boiled linseed oil to the shellac and apply this mixture to the surface with the cloth using a circular motion. Add additional drops of oil to each coat until the deep finish you want has been satisfactorily obtained.

Dip and Rub Finish: This is another type of shellac finish. It is somewhat easier and faster to apply than the French polishing method. Fill one saucer with pure turpentine and another saucer with white shellac from a 4-lb. cut. Roll a piece of lintless cloth into a pad and dip it first into the turpentine and then into the shellac. Rub the pad over the surface with a circular motion. Apply four or five coats in the same fashion. When the final coat is dry, rub the surface down with a cloth dipped in linseed oil.

Lacquer

Roughly speaking, lacquer can be divided into two groups — brushing lacquer and spraying lacquer. Lacquer dries through the absorption by the air of the solvent or thinner in it. As this solvent has a fast rate of evaporation, lacquers dry very rapidly. The brushing lacquers dry more slowly than spraying lacquers. Spraying lacquers dry so rapidly that they cannot be applied by brush — they must be used only with a spray gun. The solvent used with lacquer for thinning or other purposes, such as cleaning brushes, is lacquer thinner. Thinners suitable for paints and varnish should not be used with lacquer. While paints and varnish can be applied over lacquer, lacquer should never be applied over paint or varnish because the solvent in the lacquer will soften up all of these base coats.

There are several special types of spraying lacquer which can be used for various finishing operations:

Clear Gloss Lacquer: This is a clear lacquer which dries to a high gloss in four hours or so. When dry, the surface may be rubbed and polished.

Clear Flat: This is the same as clear gloss except that it dries out flat.

Rubbing and Polishing Lacquer: This is a very high grade of lacquer suitable for rubbing and polishing.

Shellac-Mixing Lacquer: This is a special type of lacquer which mixes with shellac to provide better surfaces for sanding.

Water White Lacquer: This is a perfectly clear lacquer used on blonde finishes.

Application of Lacquer

Brushing Lacquer: While brushing lacquer dries much more slowly than spraying lacquer, it does dry fast. To apply it properly you must work with a good deal of speed. The lacquer should be flowed on and brushed out as little as possible. As speed is important, use as large a brush as is effective and let the brush carry as much lacquer as possible without dripping. Apply the lacquer in one direction only. If a second coat is required, it must be applied with even more speed or the solvent in the second coat will soften up the first coat.

Spraying Lacquer: By far the best method of applying lacquer is to use a spray gun, but this calls for a very high-class piece of equipment — not the ordinary kind found in many homes. (See SPRAY GUNS, below.)

RUBBING AND POLISHING

To produce a really fine finish of varnish, shellac, or lacquer, the final coat should be rubbed and then polished. On very fine work, all coats are rubbed down before the succeeding coat is applied.

Rubbing is the first operation. It removes any rough spots, brush marks, or bits of dust or dirt from the finish. The rubbing is done with a felt pad. The abrasive used for the operation is FFF grade powdered pumice stone mixed into a paste with water or light oil. Rubbing is faster with a water paste than with an oil paste.

Rubbing should be done in the direction of wood grain. From time to time, clean the surface of the work and examine it to be sure that the rubbing action is uniform. When the entire surface is flat and free from any flaws, remove all traces of the rubbing abrasive. Areas which cannot be rubbed easily with the felt, such as legs of tables or chair and trim, can be rubbed with a cloth that has been saturated with the abrasive paste.

Polishing is a continuation of the rubbing operation, except that an even finer abrasive, such as rotten-stone, is used to remove any of the marks left by the coarser pumice stone. Instead of polishing, a high sheen can also be produced by buffing. This is done with a buffing wheel attached to an electric drill. The buffing wheel should be several inches thick and the buffing compound should be applied either to the surface of the work or to the wheel itself. The final buffing is accomplished with the use of a dry and clean wheel.

SPECIAL TECHNIQUES

Special effects can be achieved during the finishing operation by the use of various techniques to produce special results.

Shading

In some work it is desirable to have contrasting shades. The best time to achieve this is during the application of the stain with a spray gun. All that is required is to spray some areas lightly and others more heavily. More control over the degree of shading can be achieved by first spraying on a very light coat of stain and, before this is dry, spraying again with the same mixture where you wish to have the darker areas. In some cases, an article will have been made from several kinds of wood, all of different shades or colors. In this case, if you

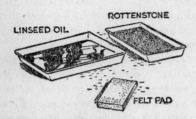

Fig. 19. Equipment required for polishing.

wish to have a uniform finish, it will be necessary to bring the various pieces to a uniform color. Shading is best accomplished with a non-grain-raising stain applied with a spray gun. If the staining must be done with a brush or cloth, then a wiping stain can be used.

Highlighting

This is very useful when trying to match period pieces such as Colonial American. Highlighting can be produced by first giving the wood a coat of stain so that the color is uniform. After the stain is dry, the areas you wish to make lighter are sanded with very fine sandpaper or steel wool. The technique of highlighting calls for a good deal of practice and skill, for if too much of the color is removed during the sanding operation, it is usually necessary to remove all the

stain and start out anew. Trying to patch up the spots with more stains is all but impossible.

Glazing and Antiquing

Another method used for finishing period pieces and for achieving interesting shades is through the use of a glaze. Glazing liquid can be purchased in various shades at paint and hardware stores. In some cases, paint or even stain is used in place of the liquid glaze. The wood is first given a base coat of enamel, paint, or sealer. The exact shade of glaze to use will depend on the color used for the base coat. If the base coat is light, then a rather light glaze will be sufficient to produce the desired amount of shading. As darker base colors are used, darker glazes must be also used to produce the right amount of contrast.

The glaze is applied over the entire surface with a brush. Before it has a chance to harden, it is wiped off with a piece of clean cheesecloth. The wiping should begin in the center of the surface and should be done with a circular motion. The amount of glaze left on the surface depnds on the amount of pressure used in wiping.

More and more glaze is allowed to remain as the wiping gets closer to the edges of the surface. The final effect should be a gradual blending, starting with little or no glaze at the center and with a greater and greater intensity of glaze as the edges are reached. If the glaze appears to be too heavy in some places, or if it becomes too stiff for easy wiping, dampen the cloth with a little turpentine. Interesting effects can be achieved by using your fingers or a brush instead of a cloth. On large surfaces it is best to add a little linseed oil to the glaze to slow up the drying so that the work can be accomplished unhurriedly.

Getting the proper technique with glaze will require a little practice. Your first attempts may not be all satisfactory. If so, it is a simple matter to remove all the glaze with some turpentine and start again.

The glaze in molding, carvings, and the like can be blended out for the desired effect with a brush.

Stencils

Many pieces of furniture, both modern and period, can be improved considerably by stenciling designs on them in contrasting colors. Ready-made stencils are available at paint and art supply stores, but it is a simple matter to make your own. Draw out the design and then transfer it to stencil paper. The design is then cut out with a very sharp knife or a razor blade. The cuts must be very sharp or the final transfer will have enough edges. After the stencil has been cut out, it should be coated with shellac or lacquer to stiffen the paper. The stencil is then placed on the work and held securely with masking tape. If you are going to use a spray gun, mask a sufficiently large area around the stencil to protect it from the spray.

Paint can be applied either with a spray gun or with a stencil brush. A spray gun will produce better results than applying the paint by hand, but care must be taken not to allow the paint to become too thick. And don't hold the gun in such a fashion that some of the paint gets under the edges of the stencil and spoils the design. If the paint is to be applied with a brush, then a special stencil brush should be used.

Ordinary paint is too thin for good stenciling. Colors in oil are far superior. As they come from the tube too thick for application with the stencil brush, they must be thinned down to the proper consistency with turpentine.

Fig. 20. Buffing can be done with a buffing wheel attached to a small electric drill.

After the paint is dry and the stencil has been removed, the design can be protected against wear with a thin coat of clear varnish.

Decalcomanias

Another method of transferring designs is the use of decalcomanias, or "decals," as they are popularly known. There are two kinds of decals available for use. One is the water type, which is soaked in water for a short period before it is applied to the surface to be decorated. The paper is then removed, leaving the design. This type is suitable for most work.

The other type is the varnish decal. It leaves no overlap at the edges as does the water decal, and, therefore, it more closely resembles the effect of freehand painting.

SPECIAL FINISHES

Over the years, special finishes have been developed to meet certain requirements or to stimulate certain effects. Various kinds of so-called "modern finishes" are especially popular today. As different methods are employed by professionals in obtaining these finishes, duplication is difficult unless you happen to know the exact technique used on the original. On the other hand, it is possible for the amateur working with a home-constructed article to finish it so that its appearance is profesional.

Wax Finish

This is a relatively easy technique to use and one that will provide a long-wearing, durable finish. The wood should be sanded smooth, stained if desired, filled, and then given two coats of thin shellac or one coat of varnish or lacquer. After the final coat is dry, sand lightly with steel wool and then apply a rather heavy, but even, coat of good paste wax.

Allow the wax to dry for about one hour and then rub the wax with a piece of felt. Rub it in the direction of the wood grain. Allow the wax to dry for a day or so and then apply a second coat somewhat more lightly

than the first. Several additional coats should be applied in the same manner, allowing a day for drying between each coat. The success of this finish depends on the quality of the wax used and the thoroughness with which the rubbing is done.

Linseed Oil Finish

This finish produces excellent results, especially on walnut. The final finish is extremely resistant to heat and scratches. When wear begins to show in certain areas, it is a simple matter to patch them up with additional coats of oil. There are several methods used in producing this finish. A simple method is to mix two-thirds boiled linseed oil to one-third turpentine. This solution may be tinted with a stain, but it should be remembered that the linseed oil alone will darken the wood somewhat, and this usually gives enough color.

Warm the linseed oil solution in a double boiler. Don't place it over an open flame as the solution is a highly inflammable one. The oil mixture is applied to the wood with a brush or clean cloth and rubbed into the surface. Put on a heavy coat.

Allow the oil to remain on the wood for several hours and then wipe off the excess with a clean cloth. The piece should then be rubbed down with a piece of felt wrapped around a block of wood. Allow the oil to dry for several days, and then apply a second coat of linseed oil in the same manner. This process is repeated until the wood will no longer absorb oil. Additional rubbings at frequent intervals over a period of many weeks will improve the appearance of the finish. Rubbing several times a year will maintain it.

Another method of applying this finish calls for the application of linseed oil without the turpentine. The oil is applied with a cloth or brush and then rubbed into the wood by hand until the wood will no longer absorb oil. Frequent hard rubbings by hand over a period of months is necessary to produce the final effect. But many people consider it well worth the trouble.

An oil finish is often used on knotty-pine paneling and on other pine articles where a natural finish is desired. The mixture used here is one that consists of one part linseed oil to two parts turpentine.

Limed Oak

This type of finish is used extensively in modern furniture. The wood must first be bleached out with a commercial bleaching agent. After this, the wood may be tinted with stain or left as it is. Seal it with a wash coat of water-white lacquer and then fill with a white filler (made by adding zinc white color to natural filler). The top coat of the finish must be water-white lacquer.

Pickled Pine

This finish can be used on a wide variety of woods. Dark woods must first be bleached out to a light color. This is not required on the lighter woods. In the case of pine, a gray stain is applied to the wood. This is followed by a thin wash coat of white shellac. A light filler is then applied

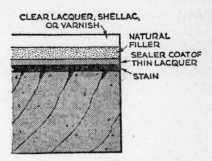

Fig. 21. The cross-section shows the average number of steps in finishing.

or a light wiping stain. Finally a thin coat of white shellac is applied.

Honey-Tone

This finish is particularly effective on light-colored woods like maple and birch. If dark woods are to be used, they must first be bleached out. A toner of one part white lacquer and four parts clear lacquer is applied directly to the wood. This produces a thin and transparent coating. Several applications of the toner are made. The final coating consists of two coats of water-white lacquer.

Bone White

The base needed for this finish is a coat of bone-white enamel, which comes ready-mixed. After this dries a glaze or brown wiping stain is applied and then wiped away, but with traces left in the corners, on edges, and so on. When the glaze or stain is dry, apply a top coat of clear or water-white lacquer.

Heather Mahogany

In this case the effect desired is created by using a white filler in the wood. Remove the excess filler by wiping across the grain and then apply a top coat of water-white lacquer.

Blonde Finishes

There are a wide variety of finishes that fall under the general classification of "blonde finishes." The blonde effect can be obtained with light-colored woods by the application of a tinted coat of flat varnish or of a blonde sealer. Either will produce a blonde effect without covering the wood grain. The top coat must produce a transparent covering. In the case of dark woods, it is necessary to bleach them to a lighter shade.

Cedar Finish

This is a type of paint which produces the aromatic odor of cedar. It is used for coating the inside of closets and chests.

Crackle Finish

This is an extremely popular type of finish and falls in the "novelty" group. After the wood has been sanded, a coat of lacquer is applied.

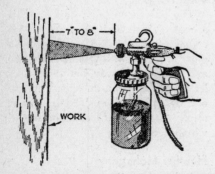

Fig. 22. Hold the spray gun perpendicular to your work and about 8" away.

When this is dry, a coat of crackle enamel is applied. As this enamel dries out, it shrinks and cracks into small sections.

BRUSHES AND SPRAY GUNS

Brushes

To produce fine results when finishing furniture and other articles, it is essential to have a good selection of high-quality brushes. The number and size of brushes to buy for a finishing job depend on your needs. The brushes range in size from the very fine type necessary for getting into small corners to the fairly large ones used in applying fast-drying finishes, such as for brushing lacquers on large surfaces. Before using a new brush, work it back and forth on the palm of your hand to remove any loose bristles that might otherwise come out on the finish. After use, thoroughly clean the brushes in the proper solvent and wrap them in wax paper with all the bristles straight, so the brush will be ready for the next project.

Brushes used with paints and enamel should be cleaned with turpentine, naphtha, benzine, or linseed oil. Shellac brushes are cleaned with denatured alcohol. For lacquer brushes, use lacquer thinner.

Spray Guns

While not absolutely essential, a spray gun is a great convenience and time-saver in applying professional-looking finishes. It is also necessary for applying lacquers other than brushing lacquer because of their fast-drying properties. If you should decide to get a spray gun, get a good one and be sure that it is suitable for use with lacquer. Some kinds of spray guns cannot operate properly with fast-drying materials.

Much of the trouble encountered with spray guns is due to improper adjustment and inadequate cleaning. Either of these can ruin a finish. Be sure you understand the proper adjustment of the gun as well as the mixing of the paint. Be sure, too, that the gun is properly cleaned after use.

The spray gun must always be held perpendicular to the work. Pointing the gun up or down will result in an uneven coating. The gun should be held about eight inches from the work. In any event, do not hold the gun more than ten inches or less than six inches away from the work. As the gun is moved across the surface to be finished, try to keep it an even distance away. Move the gun across the work with an even, free sweep of the arm. The trigger of the gun should be pulled before the gun hits the edge of the work and not released

Fig. 23. The triggering of the gun should start at the beginning of the stroke to insure getting a clean edge.

until after the gun has passed the other edge. This gives you an even coat of finish along the entire surface.

It is best to spray the small and difficult-to-reach areas first, before you do the large sections. If you do the large sections first, you will have trouble preventing additional spray from getting on these pieces when you begin working on the small pieces. Outside corners can be sprayed head on. For inside corners, do the two adjacent sides independently, trying, as much as possible, to prevent overlapping of the areas sprayed.

INDEX